DEDICATION

In memory of my mother, Fannie L. Houck, who always encouraged me to "write it down."

To my husband, Greg, and my children, Krista and Jonathan, the best taste-testers in the world!

ACKNOWLEDGMENTS

To my family and friends: Thanks for your outstanding support, prayers, recipes, and ideas. Special thanks to Rhonda Curry for inspiring many vegan recipes, to Julia Darrow for a multitude of taste tests and recipe consults, and to Christy Gremillion for helpful peer review. Thanks to Inge Houck and Sherry Lacey for loaning their bread machines.

To God: Thanks for health, inspiration, and sustaining grace.

To my critique group: Barbara Bryden, Lydia Harris, Agnes Lawless, Jackie McFadden, Lorinda Newton, and Marjorie Stewart. Thanks for your encouragement, prayers, and practical help.

To Marian Forschler, Carrol Grady, Barbara Roberts, Maylan and Shelley Schurch, and others in the Adventist Writers Association: Thanks for inspiring me to persevere.

To the Northwest Christian Writers Association: Thanks for taste-testing and equipping me to be a better writer.

Thanks to Pat Fritz and Jeannette Johnson and all the others involved in the production of this book.

Thanks to wonderful recipe testers: Linda Ball, Susan Bebee, Fred and Dorothy Berger, Jean Boller, Mickey Bowers, Barbara Bryden, Darlene Bryner, Sherri Burch, Elizabeth Coleman, Julia Darrow, Lola Deckard, Kathryn Dennis, Lucia Dexter, Linelle Eckhout, Heidi Erickson, Lea Funderburg, Michelle Gaither, Christy Gremillion, Gloria Hall, Suzie Honeywell, Inge Houck, Pauline Houck, Mary Huber, Leif King, Sierra Koerting, Alline Ladish, Mike Lee, Jackie McFadden, Enid Newton, Lorinda Newton, Deena Nixon, Gina Olds, Heidi Parrish, Uma Pattabhiraman, Jennifer Phillips, Marlene Pyrhorocki, Cindy Reseck, Greg Reseck, Lillian Reseck, Hilda Riston, Laura Ritzenthaler, Mary Rollins, Barb Rogers, Shelley Schurch, Trish Scott, Teri Stanley, Ruth Stephens, Chris Swamy, Dana VanHook, Alvin Wolcott, Tina Weber, Gail Welborn, Violet Wentland, and anyone else I forgot to mention.

CONTENTS

- Fix-it-fast formula
- Meatless meals in minutes
- Fast-food alternatives
- Nutritional preparedness
- Office survival kit suggestions

11. The Eight Traits of Great Cooks / 103

12. More Mary, Less Martha / 105

- A different paradigm
- Perspective
- Planning
- Preparation
- Cooks need the Sabbath rest too

13. Sharing Delicious Dividends / 108

- Spontaneous hospitality
- Planned hospitality
- Hospitality to go
- Have food, will travel
- Tips for caregivers
- Dealing with dietary differences
- Team cuisine
- Holiday hospitality
- Reproducible Food Preference Questionnaire

14. Keys to Conducting a First-rate Cooking Class / 119

CHAPTER 1

CLIMBING OUT OF FOOD RUTS

Phyllis closed the front door behind her. Frank looked up from his newspaper. "How'd your appointment go?"

"The doctor told me that I need to try a more healthful diet; he said to try a vegetarian diet."

"What? So now we're going to spend our retirement years eating strange food?"

"It's worth a try. I'll do anything to feel better," Phyllis said.

Are you stuck in an unhealthy eating rut? Like Phyllis, are you wondering how to stop spinning your wheels and get on track nutritionally?

It's time for a tune-up! Here's how to PROCEED. Use this acronym as your map to guide you on the road to better health:

P: Prioritize
R: Revise
O: Organize
C: Capitalize
E: Energize
E: Emphasize
D: Devise

Prioritize

Climbing out of a food rut is much like climbing a mountain. At the bottom the task of climbing the mountain looks insurmountable, but the view from the top is worth the effort. Set your sights high. Begin by deciding you want to climb out of the rut and up the peaks of good health. Ask God to be your trail guide. He created you and wants you to be healthy: "I pray that you may enjoy good health and that all may go well with you" (3 John 2).

Prevention, by attention to the Creator's laws of health, is the best route to follow: "There is sickness everywhere, and most of it might be prevented by attention to the laws of health" (Ellen G. White, *The Ministry of Healing,* p. 146).

Why wait for a heart attack or some other life-threatening illness before making your health a priority? Decide now to become nutritionally proactive, and choose an achievable and measurable nutrition goal. Maybe you'll focus on eating more vegetables, meatless meals, drinking eight glasses of water, or finding ways to satisfy your sweet tooth without refined sugar. Write down your goal and refer to it often. Use positive language, such as "I choose to eat at least one whole grain each meal," rather than "I will never eat white flour again."

Make health-promoting activities a priority. At the beginning of each week, ask yourself, "What is the most important thing I can do to achieve a healthier life?" Schedule it. You may need to say no to some things in order to say yes to healthier living: take a walk instead of watch TV. Avoid excessive time at the computer. Find ways to simplify your life.

Revise

On the path to health it's never too late to turn around. But the deeper the rut, the more effort it takes. To illustrate: fold your hands. Which thumb is on top? Fold your hands again. This time, clasp them the opposite way with the other thumb on top. How does that feel? Folding your hands differently takes a conscious effort and feels awkward. Change takes effort, too. New habits feel awkward at first, but with repetition they soon feel natural.

Good health begins with your mind. Thoughts repeated form actions, actions repeated form habits, and good habits repeated develop a healthier body. Revise your thinking based on God's Word: "Do not conform any longer to the pattern of this world, but be transformed by the renewing of your mind" (Romans 12:2). Otherwise, you may be blown off the path by the winds of food fads, or kept off by inertia.

Revise your food supply, if necessary. Stock your kitchen with an abundance of nutritious convenience foods. (That's not an oxymoron, as you'll discover in this book.) Try not to keep nutritionally depleted foods around. The absence of junk foods makes nutritious choices more attractive. But dried beans and uncooked grains in the cupboard do nothing to quiet a growling stomach! See "Kitchen Provisions" (Chapter 5) for a wealth of ideas for a well-stocked kitchen.

Organize

Organize your time to fit your new priorities and mind-set. Give yourself every advantage for healthier food choices. That's what this book is all about: creating healthy, homemade convenience foods.

Organize your recipes, and use the speedy menu-planning system outlined in "Make-Ahead Cooking" (Chapter 3). Organize your kitchen for efficiency, including a timesaving slow cooker ("Fix and Forget," Chapter 9).

Capitalize on Learning

Do you know people whose health values are ones that you want to learn? Ask them to mentor you. They might say yes! If the names of some good cooks don't come to mind readily, pray about this.

Ask God for insight and wisdom: "If any of you lacks wisdom, he should ask God, who gives generously to all without finding fault, and it will be given to him" (James 1:5). The Master Chef will surprise you with encouragement, instruction, and creative ideas for your journey.

Enhance your cooking skills by reading this cookbook. Try new recipes with an open mind. Most of the time, you'll be pleasantly surprised. Use a rating system for recipes to help you decide which ones are "keepers."

Scout out tasty and healthful recipes everywhere you go. At potlucks ask until you find out who made that great-tasting dish, then request the recipe. Be prepared with blank, self-addressed postcards so at home the cook can jot down the recipe and mail it to you.

Ask friends to recommend cookbooks that match your needs. Borrow cookbooks from the public library so you can "try before you buy." Browse through vegetarian cookbooks at bookstores, natural food stores, and Adventist Book Centers (call 1-800-765-6955 for the location nearest to you).

Explore the Internet for a wide variety of vegetarian recipes. Subscribe to magazines: *Vibrant Life, Veggie Life,* or *Cooking Light.* Sign up for a vegetarian cooking class. Offer to help the instructor; it's a great way to learn.

Energize

Regular physical exercise is the single-most-important health habit you can establish. When you feel more energetic and optimistic, it's easier to succeed at climbing out of food ruts. If you're not exercising regularly, this is the place to start.

Adequate hydration, a must for any mountain climber, often dramatically improves energy and endurance. Drink at least eight glasses of pure water daily. Coffee, tea, and soda can't substitute because they contain caffeine, sugar, or sugar substitutes. Water is the only beverage with the clear advantage.

Do you want to feel better and think more clearly? Try what the biblical Daniel did (Daniel 1:8-20). Move away from the rich and refined "king's food." Instead, choose more "peasant foods," such as fruits, vegetables, whole grains, beans, and nuts. Trying it for 10 days could convince you of the vegetarian advantage, just as it convinced King Nebuchadnezzar.

Emphasize

Proceed with caution: In kindness to your taste buds and your body, make dietary changes gradually. Climb slowly, step by step. For example, serve new recipes as side dishes. Or have other foods on hand to fill up on. And to ease the transition, have something familiar on the table (one of the best ways to avert a mutiny): if the recipe doesn't pass your family's taste test, they will know they won't starve. If family members resist dietary changes, you may need to slow the pace (or be more innovative).

Don't exceed the feed limit: Try new foods often, but avoid repeating them too soon. Success is exciting, but excess is boring. If you discover how wonderful fresh basil tastes, don't put it in everything. Your family might wonder if, next time, they'll find it in their granola!

Perseverance: Don't give up. Remember, you're aiming for permanent lifestyle habits, not temporary quick fixes. Climbing out of a lifelong rut requires commitment, perseverance, and a determination to get up again when you fall down. Keep your eyes on the goal.

Devise a Plan

Track your progress: A worthwhile journey such as this one is worth recording. Jot notes on your calendar or in a journal. Keep a chart of your goals, and track your progress. A year from now, you'll be amazed at how far you've traveled.

Evaluate weekly: If your goal is measurable, you should know by the end of the week (or day) if you've met it. Review your chart weekly. Were you successful at taking one step—even a baby step—to climb out of your rut? Or did old habits cling to your feet like mud, causing you to slip back? Keep your focus on where you're going, spending just enough time studying the mud to learn from your mistakes and avoid future pitfalls.

Devise a reward system: A reward dangling in front of you can make the long haul easier. A short-term reward can close the gap between knowledge and action. For example, if you're dragging your feet at starting an exercise program, try rewarding yourself after exercising once. The reward doesn't have to be expensive or indulgent, just something that's motivating for you. It could be taking the luxury of soaking in the bathtub or hot tub, reading a favorite magazine from cover to cover, buying a new book, or . . . Next, reward yourself after five times. Keep increasing the time interval between rewards until you're hooked on the healthy habit. Remember, it usually takes 21 days to develop a new habit.

Devise a support system: Find supportive friends to journey with you. Their encouragement and accountability make the trip seem faster and easier. Put your trust in God. Paraphrasing Psalm 37:24, When you stumble, you won't fall, because the Lord holds you with His hand.

Inquire about a vegetarian support group: If you struggle with weight issues, join a Christian weight-loss program. You'll learn from the successes and mistakes of others and be guided in making healthy changes as you climb the mountain of healthy habits.

CHAPTER 2

THE BEST FAST FOOD COMES FROM YOUR OWN KITCHEN

Slumped behind the steering wheel, Carolyn thought, *I'm finally out of the office. Now what?* At the light she pulled her calendar from her purse. *That's right! Pick up the boys from gymnastics, stop by the vet's for the dog, and off to choir practice at 7:00. That leaves me 45 minutes to fix dinner, eat, and get out the door again.* She sighed and punched the gas pedal.

At the next stoplight Carolyn grabbed her cellular phone and dialed. "Hi, Randy. I'm so glad you haven't left yet. Could you pick up some fast food on the way home?" Carolyn paused, then plunged ahead in frustration. "Something's got to change. What can we do to get out of this rut? We have to find a better way!"

Carolyn found a better way, but it was Randy's sudden hospitalization for a lifestyle-related illness that motivated their change in priorities. "That scared us," she recalled later. "Randy and I seriously considered our options, and decided to take a more active role in preserving our health and sanity."

Carving time out of her weekend schedule, Carolyn now plans and stocks the refrigerator, freezer, and pantry with ready-to-eat, nutritious choices. Chili beans simmer in the slow cooker; and while she mixes several casseroles, brown rice cooks in the rice cooker. In between she makes up some versatile corn bread and Mexican-seasoning mixes.

Carolyn later told a friend, "I'm so glad I discovered investment cooking. I can easily get supper on the table in 30 minutes or less each night. Dinnertime has changed from pandemonium to peace! We eat better and we feel better. Randy loves the change. Plus, I'm less stressed, and have more control of my life. Planning makes such a difference for our family."

What's for Dinner?

The daily dilemma: "What's for dinner?" It's 5:30 p.m. Are you going to win the race against the clock and hungry stomachs? What will you do for dinner tonight?

Eat (a) out; (b) take-out; (c) out of a can or box.

If these are your usual survival tactics, you may be surprised: *the best fast food comes from your own kitchen!* You can enjoy healthy homemade meals without spending hours in the kitchen.

Carolyn discovered a better, easier way to eat right, and so can you. Carolyn's new investment-cooking approach, like money in the bank, pays high dividends—quick, easy, and nutritious foods—especially when you're too bushed or pushed to cook. Mere minutes invested in meal planning and cooking ahead saves hours at mealtime.

The Steps of Investment Cooking

Here are the three simple steps of investment cooking.

1. *Plan:* Invest time in planning. Lack of planning, according to the experts, is the real cause of kitchen chaos. Consider this evidence (*USA Weekend* [November 7-9, 1997]):

   - Seven out of 10 meal preparers don't think about what they will cook until it's almost time to eat.
   - Four out of 10 adults complain that when they're ready to eat dinner, they're too tired to cook.
   - Nine out of 10 Americans say it's impossible to cook a meal in 30 minutes or less.
   - One out of 5 adults say eating nutritiously takes too much time.
   - Forty-four cents of every food dollar is spent on food prepared outside the home.

Without a plan, meals disintegrate into a scramble to find anything edible, and nutrition becomes haphazard. A menu puts you in charge, moving you out of crisis-management mode. In "Make-Ahead Cooking" (Chapter 3) you'll learn about flexible menu planning and how to choose a system that works for you.

2. *Purchase:* Invest time in purchasing quality, nutritious ingredients. "Supermarketing" (Chapter 6) is devoted to streamlining the chore that so many cooks hate. Learn about the kitchen-provisions strategy, which focuses on keeping a well-stocked kitchen and making good choices easy.

3. *Prepare:* Invest in measuring, mixing, and making ahead. Invest 15 minutes to get a jump start on dinner. Invest several hours, and you can produce a week's worth of entrées; invest a whole day, and you can produce a month's worth of main dishes. This cookbook shows you how to have tasty and healthy ready-to-cook-and-serve meals on hand. You'll learn how to combine the nutritional and taste benefits of home cooking with the timesaving advantages of convenience foods.

Timesaving Strategies

Investment cooking consists of four timesaving strategies:

1. *Fix and Freeze:* Invest in time-and-motion economy with make-ahead entrées such as Pecan Patties (p. 245), Calzones (p. 335), and Lasagna (p. 320). Cook once—eat twice. When you prepare a casserole, double or quadruple it. With a tad more time, you can make 48 patties instead of 12. Deposit them in your freezer; withdraw them at your convenience. These ready-to-heat dishes pay delicious dividends with nutritious, expeditious meals.

2. *Fix a Mix:* Invest in making mixes such as Brown Gravy (p. 249), Whole-Grain Muffins (p. 175), or Creamy Herb Dressing (p. 367). Make-it-your-way mixes allow you to adjust for allergies and food preferences. For the ultimate in convenience, pour soup mix into the slow cooker, add the liquid ingredients, and at dinnertime, you've got it made.

3. *Fix and Forget:* Invest in a slow cooker and create no-fuss

meals such as Black Beans With Cilantro and Lime (p. 297). This is the easiest of all the investment-cooking concepts. Before work, start dinner in the slow cooker. Enjoy the welcome, tantalizing aroma of home-cooked food when you walk in the door. Another option: Start breakfast in the slow cooker before going to bed.

4. *Fix it Fast:* Invest in healthy store-bought convenience foods. You'll amaze yourself with marvelous meatless meals in minutes, such as Tofu Cutlets (p. 95), Speedy Stir-fry Vegetables (p. 263), and Sloppy Joes (p. 340).

Advantages of Investment Cooking

Investment cooking helps you win the race against the clock when mealtime nears. In a rush? Heat and eat a frozen entrée. Add salad and a vegetable, and you have a nutritious home-cooked meal in 20 minutes. Feel like cooking? Do so! While the entrée heats, you have time to prepare a special salad, side dish, or dessert.

When you have tasty and healthy ready-to-cook-and-serve meals on hand, you'll gain these delicious dividends:

- Spend less time in the kitchen cooking and cleaning up
- Spend less money on meals away from home
- Be more in control of your time and nutrition
- Eat more healthy, nutritious food
- Make meals with a minimum of last-minute fuss
- Enjoy delicious home-cooked meals with more flavor and satisfaction
- Have food on hand for company, Sabbath meals, or the unexpected

Once you try investment cooking, you'll find yourself serving hot, healthy, homemade meals more often. This proactive approach to cooking is what you've been looking for—delicious, nutritious and expeditious! Read on to discover surprisingly simple shortcuts for streamlining time in the kitchen without shortchanging nutrition or taste.

CHAPTER 3

MAKE-AHEAD COOKING

In our grab-and-go society, convenience food is in; complicated cuisine is out. For the harried and hungry, a cache of prepared entrées is like a stash of emergency cash. Investment cooking can help you experience the convenience of delicious, nutritious, and expeditious homemade foods. Make-Ahead cooking—either sprints or marathons—depends on the time invested.

Sprint Cooking

Sprint cooking requires only a short cooking-ahead investment of time.

Once-a-week cooking. Cooking in weekly intervals works best for some. Much in our lives revolves around a weekly cycle, so planning and cooking one week at a time fits right in. In an afternoon or evening, you can prepare four or five tasty, home-cooked entrées ready for the freezer or refrigerator. Graham Kerr recommends turning "your kitchen into a Fresh-Food Fun Factory once a week for 2 to 4 hours" (*Graham Kerr's Swiftly Seasoned* [New York: G. P. Putnam's Sons, 1996], p. 8).

Jump-start cooking. Some prefer to plan from day-to-day. They spend 15 minutes the night before assembling a casserole, or in the morning starting soup in the slow cooker. Ronda Barfield uses this method in her book *15-Minute Cooking* (St. Charles, Mo.: Lilac Pub., 1996).

Marathon Cooking

Optimize your kitchen time with a cookathon: a large block of time devoted to making food ahead.

Once-a-month cooking. Other cooks prefer marathon cooking—

preparing 30 entrées in one day. This approach requires a larger initial investment of planning, shopping, chopping, and cooking. "It's one horrendous day," says Mimi Wilson, coauthor of *Once-a-Month Cooking* (Marilyn Wilson, Mimi Wilson, and Mary Beth Lagerborg [New York: Broadman and Holman Pub., 1999, revised]), but the dividends last a whole month. *Dinner's in the Freezer,* by Jill Bond, calls it Mega Cooking: preparing food for 45 to 60 days at one time. Cooking on this larger scale requires organization, tested recipes, and adequate freezer space.

Once-a-year cooking. The oldest of all marathon cooking techniques, once-a-year cooking—canning, freezing, dehydrating, preserving seasonal produce—concentrates on stocking up and making ahead. Yes, canning peaches or applesauce requires slaving over a hot stove for a day. But all winter long you enjoy the fruits of your labor. A special satisfaction comes from seeing an array of canning jars on the counter, each one filled with luscious fruit, and hearing the seal pop as you open a jar.

Make It Ahead

By cooking ahead, you can stock your freezer with a variety of healthy vegetarian entrées. Make-Ahead foods often taste better because the flavors blend while chilling.

Your cooking frequency may vary, but remember this investment-cooking motto: "Make it ahead whenever possible." Try experimenting with frequency to discover a realistic cook-in-advance schedule that works best for you. Whatever your approach, the critical component is planning ("Meal-planning Primer," Chapter 4). Keep these investment methods in mind: concentration and diversification.

Concentration

Concentrate on one investment by making large quantities of a particular entrée or food at once. Quantity cooking multiplies the savings in kitchen and shopping time and saves money. It enables you to take advantage of grocery store specials or use up that large container of canned tomatoes.

This approach uses time-and-motion economy, minimizing the setup, preparation, and cleanup. While the ingredients and measuring utensils are out, it takes practically no additional time to double or quadruple a recipe. For example, quadruple a chili recipe and make 40 servings. Or make four dozen pecan patties or two pans of lasagna. Or focus on making staple foods such as granola and seasoning mixes.

Cook once, eat twice. If you don't have time for a cookathon, simply double the recipe you make for dinner, and freeze one batch for later use.

Beverly, a friend who struggles with multiple chronic diseases, uses this concept to cook ahead when she is feeling up to it. She can never predict her energy level. "Cooking is out of the question on my bad days, when I'm doing well to have enough strength to eat," she says. "I need food on hand for my low-energy days."

When her body refuses to cooperate for extended periods of time, her husband sometimes does the cooking, but mostly they have canned or boxed dinners (Chapter 10, "Fix It Fast"). Some of her friends hire someone to cook for them when their energy level is low. But Bev says she doesn't have that option. She makes some recipes, such as granola, on three consecutive days:

Day 1: Mix the dry ingredients together.

Day 2: Mix in the liquid ingredients.

Day 3: Bake the granola.

After each step she places the mixing bowl in the refrigerator. When she doubles or triples the recipe, she marks down what she has done and places it on top of the plastic wrap covering the mixing bowl.

Double-duty chopping. When you need part of an onion for a recipe, chop all of it and refrigerate or freeze the rest. The next time you need chopped onion, you'll be glad you did.

What do you do when you find onions that are starting to

sprout in the large bag of onions? Food processor (or chopping knife) to the rescue. Spread the chopped onions on a baking sheet and freeze. When they're frozen, transfer them to freezer containers. This simple process salvages the onions from ruin, and produces recipe-ready onions (plus you get the crying done all at once). The convenience of frozen onions will convince you of the benefits of investment chopping.

Or cut up a whole cantaloupe at one time, making the extra portion ready to eat at a moment's notice.

Dealing with abundance. Focused investment cooking works well when dealing with an abundance of one food item. Several times a year my mother would devote a day to "big city" (Seattle) shopping. One of her usual stops included a small tofu manufacturing business in the international district. She brought along her large plastic container and requested, "Fill it up." She came home with 12 pounds of just-made tofu. For the next week her cooking focused on tofu, so it could be enjoyed in its prime freshness.

You also may freeze picked-at-its-peak produce such as blueberries or corn. During the long winter months it's the next best thing to fresh.

Planned-overs. My mother used the expression "planned-overs" to describe intentional leftovers. In this age of political correctness, perhaps we could call it "encore presentations" or "recycling." Whatever the term, this investment-cooking concept makes sense. Here's how it works: Make a big batch of one food, such as refried beans, and prepare it in a variety of ways. Start by freezing some in two-cup portions for quick thawing when needed. Then assemble a quantity of bean burritos to freeze ahead for lunches. If beans still remain, make bean enchiladas.

Make tacos one evening, purposely making extra seasoned vegetarian burger. Use the planned-overs as the base for sloppy joes or add to chili, or freeze for a future meal. Cook a large amount of brown rice for stir-fry, cabbage rolls, and to freeze ahead. When cooking or baking potatoes, cook twice as many for another meal. My father, a former Army cook, frequently followed this planned-over philosophy, which he summarized as "Take a pot and make a lot."

Guidelines for Multiplying Recipes

If you want to double or quadruple a recipe, keep these guidelines in mind:

- Try a single recipe first. Don't mass-produce a new recipe that your family may not like.
- Adjust the seasoning. Less is best. You can always add more.
- Write the larger quantities in the margin of the recipe. Otherwise it's easy to get mixed up. Trust me; I learned the hard way.

Diversification

Diversify your assets, and make a variety of dishes. Jessica, a stay-at-home mother of three preschoolers, wanted to serve healthier food to her family. "But making meals from scratch every day takes up so much time," she complained. "I can't spend all day in the kitchen!"

She attended a class that featured menu planning and make-ahead cooking techniques. What she learned revolutionized her life. "After experimenting, I discovered weekly cooking sessions work best for me. I love this make-ahead method because it gives me more quality time with my children. I've done it for more than a year now and can't imagine going back to cooking every day."

Jessica plans main dish menus for the entire year and writes them on a calendar. Each Thursday she shops for the following week. She cleans out the refrigerator on Saturday evening. Early Sunday morning, with the children still asleep, Jessica and her physician husband begin cooking. She gets the ingredients organized while he chops the onions, celery, and other vegetables and places the appropriate amounts by each recipe card on the counter.

After the children wake up, their father takes them out for breakfast and playtime. The children, ages 2, 3, and 5, look forward to this "date with Daddy." Depending on the southern California weather, they may go to a park or an indoor play area. This gives Jessica three to four hours of uninterrupted time to prepare eight or more main dishes. "This way I'm done cooking before it gets hot outside." Jessica grinned. "And I reheat the casseroles in the microwave, so my kitchen stays cool the rest of the week."

After the casseroles are cooked and partially cooled, she transfers them to zip-top bags and labels them. Jessica spreads the bags out in a single layer in the refrigerator to finish cooling. When chilled, she stacks the bags on top of each other in a designated section of the refrigerator for use throughout the week.

At mealtime, while the main dish reheats, she prepares a vegetable and a salad. "It's a cinch to prepare my husband's lunch, too. I include a serving of casserole for him to microwave at work," Jessica said. "By planning and working ahead, I enjoy convenience without compromising nutrition."

Make-Ahead entrées expand the number of fast routes available during dinner rush hour. This kitchen expressway bypasses red lights (highly processed food) and stop-and-go traffic (drive-through restaurants). We can operate on cruise control, adding the finishing touches to the meal while the entrée heats. We arrive at our destination in record time with less stress; we can shift gears and spend time with fellow travelers. After minimal cleanup we can speed out of the kitchen.

CHAPTER 4

MEAL-PLANNING PRIMER

Diane's stomach growled as she opened the kitchen cupboard door. She surveyed the shelves, hoping to find something satisfying for dinner. Unmarried, Diane, had just arrived home from her job at the library. She loved to cook, but when she was famished, the enjoyment disappeared.

She spotted the spaghetti. *That's what I'll fix. No, I can't—I don't have spaghetti sauce. Maybe I have the ingredients for sauce. Let's see, what do I need?* She walked across the kitchen, grabbed her recipe box, and sat down at the table. She thumbed through it but couldn't find the recipe.

I know . . . stir-fry. I'll use the frozen vegetables out of the freezer. Diane sighed. *Oh, the brown rice takes 45 minutes to cook. I need something faster.* Her stomach grumbled about the delay. *What about microwaving a potato? No, I did that last night, and the night before.*

"I haven't a thing to eat!" *Here I am, talking to myself.* A wry grin spread over her face. *I sound just like Mother, who'd announce while staring at a crowded closet, "I haven't a thing to wear." Dad always teased her about that.*

Guess if Dad saw me now, he'd tease me, too. It's a shame to have all this good food in my cupboard—dry beans and whole grains—and not eat any of it because I didn't think ahead.

Diane pulled a can of lentil soup out of the cupboard. *I'll have to settle for this. Not exactly what I had in mind, but at least my stomach will quiet down.*

While she ate, she planned food for the rest of the week, including a make-ahead casserole and two slow cooker meals: vegetable stew and baked beans. She also wrote instant brown rice on her grocery list. *Then I can enjoy some quick, healthy meals. And Dad won't tease me . . . except about being single!*

Minutes Invested in Meal Planning Save Hours at Mealtime

While on a long interstate highway trip, why wait until the gas gauge points to empty before looking for a gas station? That's what many people do with their bodies. They speed through the day until low blood sugar forces them to slow down long enough to refuel. Then they tank their tummies with the fastest fill-up they can find, usually a low "octane," with a multitude of additives.

Meal planning—mapping out healthy choices—ensures finding premium fuel at each pit stop. It optimizes our performance. Meal planning need not be considered as old-fashioned as a Studebaker or as time-consuming as making bread. It takes time to save time. Mere minutes invested in meal planning save hours at mealtime. Ninety percent of the challenge is deciding what to serve. Everything else hinges on planning. The choice is ours: spend 10 minutes planning six meals for the week or 10 minutes (or more) picking up fast food for one meal.

Invest in your health by making time to plan menus. Plotting meals on paper is a vital component of proactive planning and one of the distinguishing traits of great cooks (Chapter 11). Quality food depends on proper planning. Purchasing and food preparation revolve around the menu—just as for a restaurant.

Menus Made Easy

For the most flexibility and reusability, plan menus using 3" x 5" cards, Rolodex cards, or the computer. Word processors, spreadsheets, and recipe software offer a wide range of easy-to-customize possibilities. Try copying the reproducible menu planners at the end of this chapter. Some cooks prefer a calendar, notepad, or loose-leaf notebook.

Some people like to use cycle menus, usually 14, 21, or 28 days in length. Cycle menus are usually repeated for three months, then changed with the season. Others, like Jessica in Chapter 3, like to plan a year in advance. Most people I know prefer to deal with meal planning on a weekly basis, since it is a more manageable block of time. If you plan further in advance than a week, the menu should be reviewed and fine-tuned weekly.

Adapt menu planning to fit your time constraints and temperament. If you love details (and have the time), plan a sophisticated menu, complete with garnishes and serving dishes. If you find it hard to sit still long enough to formulate a menu, try the speedy menu planning strategy outlined below.

Experiment with a variety of menu-planning approaches until you find what works best for you. Then use it regularly, keeping these principles in mind as you develop your menu:

- User-friendly: Keep it easy to read and simple enough for other family members to decipher.
- Flexible: Use the menu as a flexible guide. Circumstances inevitably change.
- Reusable: Since you are investing valuable time in this project, make it easy to use again.
- Economical: Capitalize on seasonal foods and sales, and keep them affordable.

Speedy Menu Planning, Game 1

So you want to invest in a healthier lifestyle but don't have time to devote to menu planning. Try this survival tip: Set the timer for five minutes and play "beat the timer."

1. Start by quickly choosing three main dishes, such as a one-dish meal, a bean dish, and a soup. Write them down (Table 1).
2. Next, add two to four foods to complete the meal. Include side dishes, vegetables, salads, breads, and fruits, as appropriate, plus an occasional dessert. You don't need to fill in every space on the chart.
3. Make a list of ingredients you need to purchase.

Table 1: "Speedy Meal Plan" Example

Main Dish	Side Dish	Vegetable	Salad	Bread	Fruit	Dessert
Tofu Stir-fry	Brown Rice				Kiwi	Date Bars
Chili		Carrot Sticks	Green Salad	Corn Bread	Frozen Grapes	
Lentil-Barley Soup			Fresh Veggies and Dip	Multigrain Bread	Cantaloupe	

When the timer rings, you'll be amazed at how much you've accomplished. Now you have a game plan for three meals. That doesn't sound like much, but if you extend it by preparing extra amounts ("planned-overs") to use for four other lunches or dinners, that takes care of seven meals. Half of the 14 lunches and dinners for the week are planned.

While this menu is not complete, it does represent a significant stride in thinking ahead, and you deserve an A for effort.

Charisse, a full-time teacher, relies on planned-overs in her menu planning. On the weekend she likes to serve a pasta dish, such as stuffed shells. While she's at it, she prepares extra to serve for Monday dinner. She also prepares a large pot of soup, such as garden vegetable soup, for reheating on Tuesday.

She involves her husband and daughter, Emily, in the planning process. With their input, she has compiled a list of 20 entrées. Each week she asks her family to choose ones that they would like. Those entrées become the basis of her menu. She plans three dinners each week that Emily, age 11, can fix by herself. "It's wonderful to walk in the door at 5:30 and see the table set, candles lit, and food ready to eat," Charisse raved.

Speedy Menu Planning, Game 2

Now set the timer for another five minutes.

1. Plan two breakfasts (cold cereal doesn't count). See Table 2.
2. Plan two lunches (besides peanut butter sandwiches). See Table 3.

Policy on receipt may appear in two sections.

Return Policy

With a sales receipt or Barnes & Noble.com packing slip, a full refund in the original form of payment will be issued from any Barnes & Noble Booksellers store for returns of undamaged NOOKs, new and unread books, and unopened and undamaged music CDs, DVDs, and audio books made within 14 days of purchase from a Barnes & Noble Booksellers store or Barnes & Noble.com with the below exceptions:

A store credit for the purchase price will be issued (i) for purchases made by check less than 7 days prior to the date of return, (ii) when a gift receipt is presented within 60 days of purchase, (iii) for textbooks, or (iv) for products purchased at Barnes & Noble College bookstores that are listed for sale in the Barnes & Noble Booksellers inventory management system.

Opened music CDs/DVDs/audio books may not be returned, and can be exchanged only for the same title and only if defective.

NOOKs purchased from other retailers or sellers are returnable only to the retailer or seller from which they are purchased, pursuant to such retailer's or seller's return policy. Magazines, newspapers, eBooks, digital downloads, and used books are not returnable or exchangeable. Defective NOOKs may be exchanged at the store in accordance with the applicable warranty.

Returns or exchanges will not be permitted (i) after 14 days or without receipt or (ii) for product not carried by Barnes & Noble or Barnes & Noble.com.

Policy on receipt may appear in two sections.

Barnes & Noble Booksellers #2213
95 N. Moorland Road Unit C-1
Brookfield, WI 53005
262-796-8550

STR:2213 REG:007 TRN:0766 CSHR:Lissa H

Vegetarian: Tasty Recipes for Every Day
9780760782996   T1
                    (1 @ 7.98)   7.98
Easy Vegetarian (Better Homes & Gardens)
9781435126312   T1
                    (1 @ 8.98)   8.98
Calvin and Hobbes
9781449407094   T1
                    (1 @ 6.98)   6.98

Subtotal   23.94
Sales Tax T1 (5.100%)   1.22
TOTAL   25.16
VISA DEBIT   25.16
Card#: XXXXXXXXXXXXX1007

A MEMBER WOULD HAVE SAVED   2.40

Thanks for shopping at
Barnes & Noble

01/28/2012 08:55PM   101.278

With a sales receipt or Barnes & Noble.com packing slip, a full refund in the original form of payment will be issued from any Barnes & Noble Booksellers store for returns of undamaged NOOKs, new and unread books, and unopened and undamaged music CDs, DVDs, and audio books made within 14 days of purchase from a Barnes & Noble Booksellers store or Barnes & Noble.com with the below exceptions:

A store credit for the purchase price will be issued (i) for purchases made by check less than 7 days prior to the date of return, (ii) when a gift receipt is presented within 60 days of purchase, (iii) for textbooks, or (iv) for products purchased at Barnes & Noble College bookstores that are listed for sale in the Barnes & Noble Booksellers inventory management system.

Opened music CDs/DVDs/audio books may not be returned, and can be exchanged only for the same title and only if defective. NOOKs purchased from other retailers or sellers are returnable only to the retailer or seller from which they are purchased, pursuant to such retailer's or seller's return policy. Magazines, newspapers, eBooks, digital downloads, and used books are not returnable or exchangeable. Defective NOOKs may be exchanged at the store in accordance with the applicable warranty.

Returns or exchanges will not be permitted (i) after 14 days or without

YOU MAY ALSO LIKE...

The Accidental Vegetarian: Delicious...
   by Simon Rimmer

Simply Delicious Vegetarian
   by Carla Bardi

Something Under the Bed Is Drooling: A...
   by Bill Watterson

Yukon Ho!: A Calvin and Hobbes Collection
   by Bill Watterson

Weirdos From Another Planet!: A Calvin...
   by Bill Watterson

3. Add ingredients to your grocery list as needed.

Table 2: Breakfast Menus Samples

Main Dish	Side Dish	Vegetable	Salad	Bread	Fruit	Other
Microwave Oatmeal and Milk				Whole-wheat Toast	Orange Juice Banana	Cashews
Whole-grain Waffles	Blueberry Sauce				Grapefruit	Peanut Butter

Table 3: Sample Lunch Menus

Main Dish	Side Dish	Vegetable	Salad	Bread	Fruit	Other
Avocado Sandwich	Crackers	Cucumber Slices			Apple	Fig Bars
Bean Burrito	Tortilla Chips and Salsa				Fruit Salad	Oatmeal Cookie

Do a quick inventory to make sure your kitchen is stocked with staples and "instant" foods for quick, last-minute meals such as couscous, canned beans, and tofu (Chapter 5, "Kitchen Provisions.") Add the missing items to your shopping list.

You are finished! Did you beat the timer?

Speedy menu planning provides a jump start for several meals. The time invested yields much greater dividends than wasting time foraging through the kitchen, guessing what to fix. Once you discover the ease of speedy menu planning, you'll want to plan the rest of the meals. You can continue to play "beat the timer," or you can use the following steps:

Meal-planning Steps

1. Start with the main meal of the day, dinner, for most people. Plan five or six main dishes for the week, allowing for leftovers and meals away from home. Choose a variety of entrée types (Table 4).

Table 4: Entrée Types

Beans	Grains	One-Dish Meals	Soups
Casseroles	Leftovers	Pasta	Tofu
Cheese and Eggs	Meat Substitutes	Patties	Vegetables
Ethnic	Nut Dishes	Salads	Wheat Meat

Retta, a working mother, designates a specific type of entrée for each day of the week.

Sunday: Leftovers

Monday: Pasta/Italian

Tuesday: "Meat" and Potatoes

Wednesday: Mexican

Thursday: Casseroles/Miscellaneous

Friday: Soup and Sandwich

Sabbath: Special

Then she compiles a list of entrées for each category for reference when making her menus. This streamlines the decision-making process, enabling her to create a month of entrée menus in five minutes.

2. Devise easy menus (soup, slow cooker, one-dish meals) for the days you know you'll need to "dine and dash," as my brother Tim calls it.

3. Add appropriate side dishes to accompany the entrées: starches, vegetables, salads, and breads. Keep them simple. Don't expect to put something in every column. Figure three to five items per meal.

4. Plan lunches next. If you eat leftovers from dinner, your lunch menus can be quite simple. Add a variety of soups, salads, and sandwiches. Lunches at work or school usually require a little more planning but are well worth the effort.

5. Plan breakfasts. The most important meal of the day often gets neglected. Some forethought can banish cold cereal

monotony and create something worth waking up for.

6. Compare your menu with the Vegetarian Food Guide Pyramid ("Mathematics of a Good Diet") and adjust as needed.

7. Consult the recipes, and make a shopping list. Purchase the needed ingredients.

8. Post the menu in a prominent place, such as the refrigerator or family-message center. You may also want to make a copy to keep in your personal planner for easy reference. Include reminders on your menu or calendar, such as "take casserole out of the freezer" or "start soup in slow cooker."

The Mathematics of a Good Diet

When planning your menu, use this chart to "check your math."

Vegetarian Food Guide Pyramid

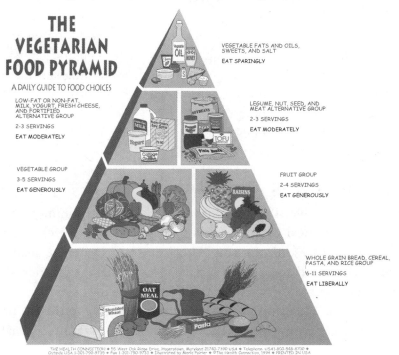

THE VEGETARIAN FOOD PYRAMID
A DAILY GUIDE TO FOOD CHOICES

VEGETABLE FATS AND OILS, SWEETS, AND SALT
EAT SPARINGLY

LOW-FAT OR NON-FAT, MILK, YOGURT, FRESH CHEESE, AND FORTIFIED ALTERNATIVE GROUP
2-3 SERVINGS
EAT MODERATELY

LEGUME, NUT, SEED, AND MEAT ALTERNATIVE GROUP
2-3 SERVINGS
EAT MODERATELY

VEGETABLE GROUP
3-5 SERVINGS
EAT GENEROUSLY

FRUIT GROUP
2-4 SERVINGS
EAT GENEROUSLY

WHOLE GRAIN BREAD, CEREAL, PASTA, AND RICE GROUP
6-11 SERVINGS
EAT LIBERALLY

THE HEALTH CONNECTION ♦ 55 West Oak Ridge Drive, Hagerstown, Maryland 21740-7390 USA ♦ Telephone, USA1-800-548-8700 ♦
Outside USA 1-301-790-9735 ♦ Fax 1-301-790-9733 ♦ Illustrated by Merle Poirier ♦ ©The Health Connection, 1994 ♦ PRINTED IN USA

The Art of Meal Planning

To get an A in the art of meal planning, incorporate the following factors to delight the senses:

Color: Choose a pleasing variety of complementary colors. One of my favorite color combinations is black beans on a bed of fluffy brown rice, topped with green onions, diced tomatoes, and a dollop of low-fat sour cream or yogurt. A few years ago, I demonstrated this dish at a cooking class. For the next couple of weeks the only grocery store in town couldn't keep black beans in stock.

Here's a meal my children enjoy eating, one color at a time:

Pecan patties with brown gravy (brown)
Baked potatoes (white)
Steamed baby carrots (orange)
Tossed salad (green)

To make it more convenient to add a variety of colors to your meals, I've compiled a list of vegetables grouped by colors (Table 5).

Shape: Vary the shapes for visual appeal. For example, serve a square of Lentil Loaf with whole red potatoes and long green beans.

Texture: Select contrasting textures: soft, crisp and chewy, firm. Include something raw every meal. With something soft like potato soup, serve a platter of crisp fresh vegetables. With chewy Wheat Meat, serve mashed potatoes.

Flavor: Pair a strongly flavored food with mild foods. Serve chili with cornbread or rice, and a salad.

The Science of Meal Planning

Variety. Diversify your nutritional assets by planning a variety of foods from meal to meal, day to day, week to week, month to month, and season to season. This is the best insurance against deficiencies. Avoid too much variety at any one meal, since this encourages overeating and can cause indigestion.

Quality. Focus meals around quality natural foods with minimal processing. Simply prepared foods retain maximum nutritional value and bring vitality to the body. Make attractive, appetizing, and tasty meals a priority (Chapter 11, "The Eight Traits of Great Cooks").

Suitability. Adapt meals to the season and climate. Lighter, less sweet foods are preferable for hot weather. Adjust the types and amounts of food to best match the type of work you do. A physically demanding job requires more food. Persons with sedentary jobs may do better with two meals a day. (If you can, arrange to eat your most substantial meals earlier in the day.) Personalize the diet to match individual needs and preferences (Reproducible Food Preference Questionnaire, Chapter 13).

Regularity. When possible, schedule each meal at a specific time. Space meals five to six hours apart to allow the stomach adequate time to complete digestion and rest before introducing the next meal. Avoid snacking. It often interferes with digestion and competes with good nutrition.

The ABCs of Meal Planning

Assign a weekly time for menu planning.

Build meals on whole grains, legumes, fruits, vegetables, and nuts.

Choose to use sparingly concentrated foods such as meat substitutes, cheese and cheese alternatives, oils, margarine, butter, and sugar.

Now you're ready to get cooking, eat better, and feel better.

Table 5: Vegetables Grouped by Color

Green Vegetables	Orange Vegetables	Yellow Vegetables
Artichokes	Carrots	Acorn squash
Arugula	Orange bell pepper	Corn
Asparagus	Sweet potatoes	Yellow bell pepper
Beet greens	Winter squash	Yellow snap beans
Broccoli		Yellow summer squash
Broccoli raab	**Red Vegetables**	Yellow tomatoes
Brussels sprouts	Beets	
Cabbage	Red cabbage	**Other Vegetables**
Chicory	Radicchio	Eggplant
Celery	Radishes	Purple kale
Cucumbers	Red bell pepper	Purple wax beans
Escarole	Red onions	Mushrooms
Fennel	Tomatoes	
Collard greens		
Dandelion greens	**White Vegetables**	
Green beans	Cauliflower	
Green bell pepper	Belgian endive	
Kale	Jerusalem artichokes	
Lettuce	Leeks	
Mustard greens	Onions	
Okra	Parsnips	
Peas	Potatoes	
Scallions	Rutabagas	
Sorrel	Sprouts	
Spinach	Turnips	
Swiss chard		
Turnip greens		
Watercress		
Zucchini		

Menu Planner

	Breakfast	Lunch	Dinner	Reminders
S				
M				
T				
W				
T				
F				
S				

SPEEDY MEAL PLANNER

Main Dish	Side Dish	Vegetable	Salad	Bread	Fruit	Other

CHAPTER 5

KITCHEN PROVISIONS

Chris leaned over and kissed her husband's feverish forehead. "Is there something I can fix for you to eat?"

Dan hesitated. "Maybe some soup. Noodle would be good."

"Coming right up," Chris replied, heading toward the kitchen. She opened the cupboard door. *Noodles. What else do I need?* She reached for the chicken-style seasoning and placed it on the counter. *Now, parsley.* Chris looked in the refrigerator. *Fresh parsley. Good. I have everything. What a relief. With Rachel and Dan sick at the same time, I'd hate to go to the store right now.*

Soon noodles simmered on the stove. Chris poured the steaming soup into a mug and placed it on a small plate with two crackers, next to a blue-and-white cloth napkin. She carried the tray to the bedroom. "Here you are, dear. I hope this hits the spot."

Dan sipped the soup. "Mmm, tastes good, even if I can't smell it. Thanks for pampering me with homemade comfort food and tender loving fare."

By keeping the kitchen supplied with a variety of staple foods and ingredients, cooks can easily accommodate changing circumstances. Two family members suddenly get sick. The boss asks us to work late. Auntie Marilyn, with multiple food allergies, stops by at mealtime. When we are forced to abandon our original plans, we turn to ingredients on hand for preparing a different meal. With our pantries, freezers, and refrigerators stocked with staples, we can prepare last-minute meals without advance planning.

The Kitchen Provisions Strategy

I call this the kitchen provisions strategy. Here's how it works. We stock our kitchen with an abundance of items necessary for making the foods we most frequently prepare. Then we shop to restock our kitchen provisions rather than buying just the necessary ingredients for specific recipes. "In the house of the wise are stores of choice food and oil, but a foolish man devours all he has" (Proverbs 21:20). "Go to the ant, you sluggard; consider its ways and be wise! It has no commander, no overseer or ruler, yet it stores its provisions in summer and gathers its food at harvest" (Proverbs 6:6-8).

Avoiding Panic in the Pantry

Adequate kitchen provisions avert panic in the pantry and make the difference between enjoying home-cooked meals and resorting to "assembly-line" food. Sometimes we crave satisfying *real* food, like a thick slice of homemade bread slathered with strawberry jam. So we decide to squeeze in time to make bread only to discover we're out of yeast.

Then comes the agonizing process: Is it worth wasting prime time to make a quick trip to the store? Do we settle for store-bought bread? Do we borrow yeast from the neighbor? Can we make something else that will satisfy the craving? The frustration uses precious time and drains mental energy.

While we can't always have every ingredient on hand, the goal is to maintain a kitchen stocked well enough to accommodate changing needs, such as unexpected company, food for a sick neighbor, or getting snowed in for a week. If we don't have time to shop one week, we can rely on what we have on hand. We don't need to worry if we run out of flour in the middle of making muffins. We simply get more flour out of our kitchen "store."

Accessible Assets

Kitchen provisions are a short-term investment that keeps our assets accessible. Investing time and money to stock the pantry, refrigerator, and freezer with an ample supply of food pays high dividends, and yields healthy "stocks." While it doesn't replace menu planning, abundant kitchen provisions create additional healthy options by:

- Making good choices more convenient
- Creating a springboard for spontaneity
- Enabling impromptu meals and instant hospitality
- Streamlining mealtime preparation
- Avoiding last-minute trips to the grocery store
- Decreasing food costs
- Supplying food during personal disasters (losing a job, running out of money before payday)
- Providing food reserves during natural disasters

Well-stocked larders sound like part of Grandma's house. They belong in modern homes, too. But if our cupboards look like Old Mother Hubbard's, where do we start? *Before* exhausting our supplies, buy two cans of beans and store one. Instead of the bare minimum, purchase extra each time. Buy two bags of rolled oats and squirrel one away.

Tracking Inventory

The key to a successful kitchen provisions strategy is tracking inventory. Develop an early warning system. As soon as an item starts getting low, put it on your shopping list. Train family members to do the same.

Consider how grocery-shopping trends have changed in recent years. Why is buying food in large quantities at warehouse stores such a popular strategy? It frequently saves money (but not always) *and* time—two commodities we're usually short on. Buying in larger quantities is a step toward stocking up.

Other Kitchen-stocking Strategies

There are many other approaches to kitchen-stocking strategies. For example, Amy Dacyczyn, in *The Tightwad Gazette II* (Villard Books, 1995), uses "the pantry principle" as a frugal practice for saving money and time. She stockpiles her pantry with food purchased at rock-bottom prices. If she runs out of an item, she waits until she can buy it at the lowest possible price and relies on her full pantry for other options. She does short-range menu planning, deciding what to prepare for the following day's dinner while washing the dinner dishes. By thinking ahead, she can start beans cooking or thaw an entrée in the refrigerator.

Jay P. Curry describes his approach to kitchen provisions in an article entitled "Sensible Stocking and Storing" (*Mother Earth News:* August/September 1997). His pantry storage system enabled his family to live for 11 months without outside supplies. Working together as a family, they wrote favorite menus on 3" x 5" cards, remembering the KISS principle (keep it simple and short). Then they used the cards to plan seven breakfast, lunch, and dinner menus, repeating the process until they had the desired number of menus on which to base their storage.

Making the Best of Basics: Family Preparedness Handbook, by James Talmage Stevens (Seattle: Gold Leaf Press, 1997), a comprehensive book on in-home storage, outlines step-by-step preparedness strategies. It contains charts for determining quantities of food to store for up to a year, and details how to store and use grains and sprouts.

Kitchen Provisions Decisions

It's up to you to decide which approach fits your situation best. Here are five factors to consider when evaluating kitchen provisions:

1. What is my *ambition?* To aim for the best nutrition with available resources?

2. What is my *mission?* To be prepared with a supply of healthy provisions?

3. What is my *decision* about the desired amount of provisions? Two weeks? Two months?

4. What is my *opposition?* Lack of space? Limited knowledge or finances?

5. What *acquisitions* will I need? Pantry items? Storage containers?

Stocking the Pantry

Once you've answered these questions, you're ready to begin with the first step, stocking the pantry. Use the chart at the end of this chapter as a starting point. Begin by filling the pantry with whole grains, including flours, cereals, breads, crackers, and pastas. Include convenience grains, such as instant brown rice and whole-wheat couscous.

Add dried beans of all kinds. For convenience, include canned beans, vegetarian baked beans, meatless chili, and refried beans. Precooked bean flakes and bean flours are also available.

Include dried fruits, such as raisins, apricots, and prunes. Their long shelf life and sweetness make them a popular provision. Keep trail mix on hand to satisfy a sweet tooth. Our family loves dried pears, so we dehydrate some every summer. Whenever we find an extra low price on bananas, we buy a large quantity and dehydrate them. On one occasion we bought a shopping cartful of bananas at nine cents a pound. John, a friend in our church, takes long strips of dried bananas on every backpacking trip. The guys tease him about his "lizard skins."

Herbs, spices, and dried vegetables, such as dried onions and celery, come in handy for everyday cooking and making mixes. Be sure to maintain a larger supply of your favorite seasonings. Canned tomatoes, corn, and other vegetables are valuable pantry additions.

Meat substitutes made from soy and wheat protein add variety to the diet. Look for textured soy protein (TSP) chunks or granules in dry form or canned products such as Fri-Chik and Chai Pow Yu.

Other staples to keep on hand: oil, nuts, peanut butter, and sweeteners such as honey, molasses, or Sucanat. Keeping powdered or shelf-stable milk (dairy or nondairy) on hand eliminates trips to the store "just for milk." Just being in the store makes it possible to leave with at least one bag of groceries, spending more than we had planned.

I like to buy shelf-stable silken tofu by the case, since I use it frequently. With its long shelf life, I don't need to worry about it going bad in the refrigerator. (Yes, it happens to veteran tofu users too.)

Firm tofu is the most versatile for most of my cooking purposes, but I keep extra firm and soft on hand as well.

Homemade and purchased tofu seasonings come in handy for quick meals. A tofu pudding mix is also available. Mixes of all kinds make meal preparation easier. Look for (or make) soup mixes, seasoning mixes, and entrée mixes.

Stocking the Refrigerator

Stock up on produce and perishables weekly or twice a month, including pre-washed salad mixes and other ready-to-eat vegetables. Peeled baby carrots, for example, are ready to munch, cook, or grate in the food processor. Although their per-pound price is about twice the cost of large carrots, many families find the added convenience worth the extra money.

After purchasing produce, invest time in making it convenient. Wash grapes, snip into small clusters, and keep them in a bowl in the refrigerator. Cut the entire cantaloupe into cubes and refrigerate. (Using soap and water, wash the outside of the cantaloupe before cutting it to prevent possible salmonella contamination.)

Do your nutritious intentions spoil in the back of the refrigerator? Do you find slimy tofu, stinky broccoli, and moldy beans? Keep track of leftovers by storing them in clear containers in a designated area. Post an inventory on the refrigerator. Remember: "Out of sight, out of mind" and "When in doubt, throw it out."

Stocking the Freezer

Frozen foods generally have a shorter shelf life than dried or canned, but they make valuable contributions to the variety in our diets. The main problem, though uncommon, is when the power fails (Chapter 7, "Fix and Freeze," p. 63).

Keep a supply of sandwich fillings and ready-to-heat-and-eat casseroles and bean dishes in the freezer. Cooked brown rice and other grains, chili, and refried beans are particularly versatile.

Stock up on a variety of whole-grain breads at the bread outlet.

Double bag them and store in the freezer for up to two months.

Storage Solutions

I like to use rectangular 12-cup capacity Rubbermaid containers for canisters. Sized to fit in kitchen cupboards, they work well for flour and oats. I also use one for storing whole-grain cornmeal in the extra refrigerator in the garage. See the chart in the appendix for storage guidelines for various foods.

Use round turntables in cupboards and the refrigerator to make foods and spices more accessible.

A gallon of cooking oil won't fit in my small kitchen, so I fill a plastic flip-top squirt bottle with oil, and store the gallon jug in the garage. The small pour spout makes it easier to control the amount of oil dispensed, so I use less.

Use the same principle for olive oil. Store small amounts at room temperature and keep the extra in the refrigerator.

Fill plastic honey bear containers with honey, molasses, and liquid lecithin. Store the containers with baking supplies for easy measuring. Keep another one in the refrigerator for pure maple syrup.

Store natural peanut butter upside down to better distribute the oil. Soften the peanut butter in microwave for easier stirring. After it's mixed well, transfer the peanut butter from warehouse size containers to smaller containers. Keep one container out at a time and store the rest in a cool place.

Have you noticed that peanut butter often disappears quicker from a large jar than from a small jar? I call this "abundance mentality." With a large container full of peanut butter, we tend to scoop out a more generous amount because of the visual abundance.

Herbs and spices are best kept for only six months. Of course, they can be kept longer, but the flavor deteriorates with time. Purchasing herbs and spices by the ounce enables you to buy the quantity you will likely use.

Whole-grain kernels have the longest shelf life, five years or more, but require milling before they can be used as flour. Milling grains into flour, meal, or flakes exposes the nutrients to the damaging effects of light, oxygen, and moisture. Careful storage (preferably refrigerator or freezer) delays the deterioration of the vulnerable nutrients, and prevents rancidity. White flour has a long shelf life because the germ has been removed, leaving no oils to become rancid. The bran portion is removed, taking away the fiber.

The advantage of whole-grain flours and meals, such as whole wheat and cornmeal, is that they retain the germ, the power plant of a seed. The germ nurtures the sprouting seed with beneficial oils, vitamin E, B vitamins, and minerals. The germ nourishes us with the same nutrients.

Storing Bulk Foods

I buy many items in bulk from a food co-op, so I end up with food in hard-to-store plastic bags. For items that I use in smaller quantities, such as nutritional yeast, I fill a rectangular two-cup plastic container, label it, and stack it with similar containers in my kitchen cupboard. (The rest of the product is stored in a covered pantry in the garage.) The result is neatly stacked containers in my cupboard. Although I have to stack a row of containers behind the front row, it is easy to remove one item to pull out what is behind. Every container is labeled, so it's easy to see at a glance what I have.

Other items, such as wheat germ, require refrigeration or freezing, so I use the same principle to store foods in the freezer or refrigerator. Neatly stacked square containers store kitchen provisions more efficiently.

Sample Kitchen Provisions List

Pantry
Baking powder
Baking soda
Bean flakes (dried)
Cereals
Cornstarch or arrowroot
Egg-replacement powder
Flour (unbleached)
Fruits (dried)
Grains
Honey
Juices
Milk (shelf-stable)
Milk powder
Mixes
Oats
Oil/olive oil
Pasta
Peanut butter
Powdered egg whites
Powdered milk
Seasonings
Sprouting seeds and supplies
Sun-dried tomatoes
Sweeteners
Tofu (shelf-stable)
TVP

Canned
Beans
Fruits
Meat substitutes
Olives
Salsa
Soups
Spaghetti sauce
Tomato paste and sauce
Tomatoes
Vegetables

Refrigerator
Ketchup
Lemon juice
Margarine
Mayonnaise
Pickles
Salad dressing
Whole-wheat flour

Produce Bin
Garlic
Onions
Potatoes

Other
Comfort foods
Pleasure foods

Freezer
Beans (cooked or soaked)
Casseroles
Fruits
Grains (raw and cooked)
Juice concentrates
Vegetables
Yeast

Seasonings
Basil
Bay leaves
Beef-style seasoning
Braggs Liquid Aminos
Cardamom
Chicken-style seasoning
Chili powder
Cinnamon
Coriander
Cumin
Curry powder
Dill
Dried onions
Garlic powder
Italian seasoning
Marjoram
Nutmeg
Onion power
Oregano
Paprika
Rosemary
Sage
Salt
Thyme
Turmeric
Vanilla
Vege-Sal
Vegetable seasoning

CHAPTER 6

SUPERMARKETING

Pam, a dental office receptionist, prefers to shop at one grocery store. Knowing the store's floor plan well, she prides herself in quickly finding every item on her shopping list without backtracking through the aisles. Pam organizes her shopping list according to the store's layout, and if the store rearranges the merchandise, she changes the order of her list on the computer. Since she knows the store manager and many of the stockers and clerks by name, they often tell Pam about unadvertised specials and new products. By frequenting the same store, Pam finds it easier to track trends for sales, markdowns, and store traffic. She likes to shop at the same time each week and begins with her favorite spot: the closeout bin.

Pam's father, Mike, a retired military officer, approaches shopping differently. Prompted by the hunt for a bargain, he tracks prices in his daily planner to find the best deals at a variety of stores. He studies the weekly supermarket advertisements to locate sales and methodically plans his "hunting" strategy. He keeps grocery bags in the car for easy reuse and even remembers to take them in. He willingly endures inconvenience, such as driving 15 miles out of his way, to get the lowest possible price on a case of canned black beans. Other strategies Mike uses to keep costs down include monthly orders from a local food co-op, and frequent stops at bread and grocery outlets to look for discounted items.

Time Versus Money

Some of us are one-stop shoppers, like Pam. Others are bargain hoppers, like Mike. While we tend to choose predominately one shopping style, we may fluctuate between the two, based on our time, energy, and finances.

Exchanging our money for food is like a balance beam act. It requires skill and concentration. Time and financial constraints tug at us, threatening our balance. Sometimes our energy levels plunge, and we tumble off the beam. Fortunately, an ample supply of kitchen provisions, the thick mat underneath, cushions our fall.

When we have more time than money, we are likely to follow the steps of bargain hoppers like Mike. Investing time in scouting for bargains rewards us with more food for less money. In order to maintain our balance, we do things ourselves, such as cooking dry beans, making bread, and grating cheese.

When we have more money than time we may seek balance by purchasing as much healthy convenience food as possible. We are more likely to buy canned beans, bread, and grated cheese. Shopping a full-service grocery store, like Pam, plus the warehouse club, provides the speediest solution.

When we're short on time *and* money however, the balance beam becomes narrower, making it harder to maintain our equilibrium. Organization, resourcefulness, and a sense of humor help us develop creative solutions to prevent falling off.

Streamlining Grocery Shopping

Time invested in developing a streamlined supermarket strategy—I like to call it supermarketing—multiplies the savings of time and money. Supermarketing streamlines grocery shopping because it:

- Speeds shopping time
- Reduces decisions made at the store
- Decreases number of shopping trips
- Assists in maintaining ample kitchen provisions
- Limits impulse buys

Supermarketing is essential to the kitchen-provisions strategy as it equips us for preparing nutritious meals in a hurry and prepares us for the unexpected. The sense of control and peace of mind liberate our minds to be more creative and relaxed. (However, we need to guard against becoming obsessed with making kitchen provisions our source of security.)

Plan to restock your kitchen provisions on a regular basis. Your approach to shopping, menu planning, and storing kitchen provisions will impact the frequency. Find what works best for you. A retired couple may stock up every two months, while a family of seven may stock up twice a month.

Supermarketing involves these five steps:

1. Plan menus.
2. Inventory kitchen provisions.
3. Write out an organized list.
4. Shop to restock kitchen provisions.
5. Buy perishables weekly or every other week.

Organized Grocery List

An organized grocery list, the middle step, is the secret to streamlining grocery-shopping time. Of the many ways to achieve an organized list, a systematic one works best. Kathy, my neighbor, writes her grocery list on the back of an envelope, grouping foods by categories. By keeping a mental inventory of her kitchen provisions, she shops to restock for a family of two. For example, she tries to keep on hand: three cans of tomatoes, four cans of tomato sauce, two cans of tomato paste, four cans of soup, two kinds of frozen vegetables, plus rice and beans. She purchases the number needed to maintain the desired inventory.

I like to keep large self-sticking notes on the side of the refrigerator, one for each primary place I shop, such as Trader Joe's, Costco, and the food co-op. I also maintain a separate list for perishables and produce. When I notice I am getting low on an item, I add it to the appropriate list. On shopping day I grab the lists and stick them on my daily planner. For easy reference at the store, I often stick the list on the handle of the shopping cart.

For items to be purchased at a grocery store, I use a preprinted, organized grocery list ("Master Grocery List," p. 59). The list can be reduced at a copy center to fit inside a daily planner. A preprinted list reminds me to stock up on items that I forgot to write down. Using a pencil, I lightly check the items needed and asterisk the priority items in case I don't have the time or money to purchase everything on my list. Then I erase the marks after the items have been purchased, making the list reusable. Or you can laminate the list, use a water-soluble pen, then wash it off.

If you wish to compile your own master grocery list, start by recording every item you buy for one month. Then add the staple items you regularly use.

For less clutter, some prefer to use a list with only printed categories. They write in what they plan to buy under the appropriate category. Others keep their grocery list on a clipboard inside the kitchen cupboard. It's not the system that matters but being systematic and organized. Choose the method you can use efficiently for supermarketing.

Some additional supermarketing strategies include tracking usage, prices, and sales.

Tracking Usage

When stocking up, it's helpful to have an idea of how much you use. The simplest method is to write the purchase date on the container of dishwasher detergent when you open it. This helps you see how long it lasts, which makes it easier to know how much to buy at a time. Some families make a game to see how long they can make a product last.

Another way to track usage is with a simple log written on a calendar, 3" x 5" cards, or typed on the word processor. For example:

Ripe olives: 11/24: 12 cans
Used last can 2/6 (10 weeks)
Slightly more than 1 per week

Tracking Prices

A system for tracking prices can give you much greater control over your food budget and help save money at the shopping game. *The Tightwad Gazette* recommends a price book, a small loose-leaf notebook with an alphabetically arranged separate page for each food. I've adapted the idea for my daily planner. To avoid using a multitude of pages, I group items by category. For each food listed, I include the store, price, unit of measure, and price comparison (price per pound or can). See the end of the chapter for a sample price-tracking log. Here's an example of what it looks like when filled out:

Table 6: Price Tracking Example

Store	Item	Unit	Price	Price Comparison
FM	Rolled oats—bulk	1 lb.	$ 0.49	$0.49 lb.
FM	Rolled oats—bulk—sale	1 lb.	$ 0.39	$0.39 lb.
FM	Rolled oats—store brand	42 oz.	$ 2.19	$0.83 lb.
PC	Rolled oats—5-minute brand	9 lb.	$ 5.49	$0.61 lb.
Co-op	Rolled oats	50 lb.	$13.90	$0.27 lb.
Co-op	Rolled oats	25 lb.	$ 7.90	$0.32 lb.
Co-op	Rolled oats	5 lb.	$ 2.20	$0.44 lb.

Tracking Sales

The simplest way to track sales is to study advertisements for several months. Jot notes on a calendar, or record them on a price-tracking form. Then look for trends.

Example 1:

Ripe olives on sale @ $.79 the week before Thanksgiving

On sale again just before Christmas

Example 2:

February is Canned Foods Month—look for sales.

March is National Frozen Food Month—look for sales.

Buying Bulk Foods

Bulk foods, available at natural food stores, some supermarkets, and food co-ops, offer healthy foods for lower prices. Here's a list of advantages:

- Less expensive
- Minimizes production and advertising costs
- Less packaging
- Reduces the number of containers to recycle or throw out
- Larger quantities available
- Allows consumers to purchase large quantities for stocking up
- Smaller quantities available
- Provides a low-risk way of trying new foods
- Greater variety of whole-food choices
- Broadens the nutritious possibilities available

The disadvantages of buying bulk foods:

- No directions for using the products. Some stores provide copies of directions and/or recipes. If you have questions, ask the sales staff. Many natural foods cookbooks include recipes.
- No nutritional analysis. For nutritional information, refer to books at natural food stores and libraries. *Bowes and Church's Food Values of Portions Commonly Used* (Jean A. T. Pennington [Philadelphia: Lippencott-Raven Publishers, 1997]) is a readily available reference. Check the Internet for other sources.
- No information about freshness of products. Look for stores with a high turnover of bulk foods. Don't purchase whole-grain flours if they smell rancid. Check for signs of infestation. Insects love whole foods (they're smart).
- No storage containers provided. Reuse. For example, clear plastic nut containers (from warehouse stores) hold nearly nine cups (three and a half pounds) of beans. Large frosting buckets with lids can often be obtained at grocery store

bakeries, often inexpensively or free. New containers are available through food co-ops and home storage suppliers.

Here are some pointers to make the best of the different food sources.

Supermarkets

Supermarkets excel in offering a wide variety of merchandise. They have a lot of competition and offer frequent sales. Every week they feature different loss leaders, items priced at exceptionally low prices intended to draw customers into the store.

For my husband, Greg, a southern California transplant to the Pacific "Northwet," daily orange juice at breakfast is as essential as sunshine. When frozen orange juice is on sale as a loss leader, I buy a whole case (unless there is a limit), enough to last until the next sale in about two months. If I run out between sales, I purchase orange juice at the warehouse club but pay more.

Supermarkets offer coupon redemption. Coupons offer money-saving potential, especially when paired with a sale if you have them with you at the store (not in a drawer at home). Attach coupons you expect to use to your shopping list. Keep other coupons in your purse, daily planner, or car.

The more natural foods I eat, the fewer coupons I use, since most coupons are for highly processed foods. If I do find a coupon for a low-sugar, whole-grain cereal, for example, I try to gather additional coupons (from friends or the recycling bin) for stocking up when the item goes on sale.

Most grocery stores display unit pricing on the shelves, making it easier to compare prices. Sometimes the unit price is based on a different unit than I have on my price-tracking form. I carry a calculator along when shopping so I can easily compare prices.

Warehouse Clubs

The best rule for shopping at warehouse clubs: know prices. Don't assume the prices are lowest. Decide if the quantity is cost-effective for your situation. Our family prefers low-fat tortilla chips, sold only in four-pound packages. Often they would get stale before we could eat them all. But they offer less fat and better value than the higher fat variety, especially since we discovered some solutions. Freeze them for longer shelf life, split the case with a neighbor, or make a big batch of salsa and invite friends over.

Restaurant Supply Stores

Restaurant supply stores provide another option for buying large quantities, such as 20 pounds of frozen blueberries or 25 pounds of black beans, items frequently not stocked at a warehouse store.

These stores are also good places to purchase heavy-duty rubber spatulas, wire whisks, and other equipment made for institutional food services.

Natural Food Stores

You'll find a great variety of nutritious options at natural food stores. Do yourself a "flavor"—don't be reluctant to make a separate trip to a specialty store. If you find a well-stocked store, you'll greatly expand your healthy horizons. Natural foods don't always cost more, and often the bulk foods cost less. Other items do cost more, but I would rather spend more money on healthy choices than pay less for food with little nutritional value.

Example: $1.79 for whole-grain hot dog buns versus $.69 for white hot dog buns.

Fortunately, more grocery stores are adding natural food sections, which makes one-stop shopping easier for people wanting healthy options.

Food Co-ops

Food co-ops usually offer the best prices on natural foods because of group buying. Some highly structured co-ops have a coordinator who charges a 2 percent markup for the work of ordering, receiving, and sorting the order. Other co-ops require all members to share the responsibilities, and some are loosely organized.

Many co-ops give the option of ordering smaller amounts, such as a five-pound bag of rolled oats. The price per pound is slightly higher on the smaller packages (Table 6: Price Tracking chart, p. 54), but it is a nice feature if you don't want 50 pounds of oats or a lifetime supply of alfalfa seeds.

Food co-ops can be harder to find, as they often operate out of homes. (Co-ops located in commercial buildings usually function more like natural food stores.) Most suppliers that distribute natural foods to co-ops are regional. Ask around. The following suppliers specialize in vegetarian foods:

> Azure Standard (delivers primarily to the Pacific Northwest;
>   UPS shipments also)
> 79709 Dufur Valley Road
> Dufur, OR 97021
> 541-467-2230; fax: 541-467-2210; www.azurefarm.com

> Country Life Natural Foods (delivers primarily to the Midwest;
>   UPS shipments also)
> P.O. Box 489
> Pullman, MI 49450-0489
> 616-236-5011; fax: 616-236-8357; e-mail: clnf@i2k.com

Outlet Stores

Many cities have bread outlets that sell day-old bread at discounted prices. Check under Bakers in the Yellow Pages for those in your area, or check the Internet. At bread outlets, I stock up on whole-wheat breads such as hot dog and burger buns, sourdough, and inexpensive breads for bread crumbs and croutons.

Other outlet stores vary by region and may be more difficult to locate in the phone directory. My best advice for locating one is to ask a frugal friend. In the Seattle area we have Grocery Outlet stores, which carry discontinued and closeout foods. The merchandise because of its one-of-a-kind nature, is always different. Look in the

Yellow Pages under Liquidators for other possibilities.

Mail-order Sources

Mail-order sources provide the convenience of in-home shopping. Many companies also offer Internet ordering. Mail-order eliminates driving and searching for hard-to-find items such as Instant Clear Jel and diastatic malt. See the resources section in the appendix for mail-order sources that carry healthy foods.

Table 7: Master Grocery List

Produce: Vegetables	Refrigerated	Frozen
Avocados	Egg roll wrappers	Juices
Bell peppers	Tofu	Apple juice
Broccoli		Orange juice
Cabbage		
Carrots		
Cauliflower		**Fruits**
Celery		Blueberries
Corn	**Dairy Case**	Strawberries
Cucumbers	Cheese	
Eggplant	Cottage cheese	
Garlic	Cream cheese	
Green onions	Egg product	**Vegetables**
Herbs	Eggs	Green beans
Lettuce	Margarine	Mixed vegetables
Onions	Sour cream	Spinach
Potatoes	Yogurt	Stir-fry vegetables
Radishes		
Spinach		
Squash	**Breads/Spreads**	
Sweet potatoes	Bread	**Natural Foods/Bulk**
Tomatoes	French bread	Baking powder
	Hamburger buns	Beef-style seasoning

Produce: Fruits	Hot dog buns	Braggs Liquid Aminos
Apples	Pocket bread	Pocket bread
Bananas	Sourdough bread	Chicken-style seasoning
Berries		Cornmeal (stone-ground)
Grapefruit		Date pieces
Grapes		Flours
Kiwi	Honey	
Lemons	Jam	Grains
Limes	Peanut butter	
Mangoes		
Melons	Crackers	Lecithin
Oranges		Pasta
Papayas		Rice milk
Peaches		Soy flour
Pears		Soy milk
Plums		Sweetener
		Whole-wheat pastry flour
Baking/Seasonings	**Breakfast**	**Canned**
Baking soda	Dry cereal	Beans
Herbs/ spices		
		Fruits
Oil		
Olive oil	Hot cereal	
	Quick oats	
Nuts	Rolled oats	Soups
	Five-grain rolled cereal	
Raisins	Seven-grain cereal	
Sugar		
Unbleached all-purpose flour	Maple syrup	Vegetables
Unbleached white flour	Pancake mix	Diced tomatoes
Vanilla	Wheat germ	Stewed tomatoes

Whole-wheat flour		Tomato paste
Yeast		Tomato sauce
Ethnic	**Pasta/Rice/Beans**	
Corn tortillas	Pasta	
Flour tortillas		**Condiments**
Refried beans	Spaghetti sauce	Ketchup
Salsa		Olives
Soy sauce	Brown rice	Pickles
	Instant brown rice	
	Dried beans	
Beverages	**Nonfood**	**Specialty/Other**
Herb tea	Dishwasher detergent	Clear Jel
Lemon juice	Hand dishwashing liquid	Instant Clear Jel
Lime juice		Pectin
Juices		
	Napkins	
	Plastic bags	
	Plastic wrap	
Water	Toilet paper	

Table 8: Price-tracking Log

Date	Store	Item	Size	Price	Price Comparison

CHAPTER 7

FIX AND FREEZE

Karen drove her van into the garage and turned off the ignition. Zachary and Andrew bounded out. Unbuckling the baby from the car seat, she carried him into the house.

Zachary dashed into the kitchen and opened the refrigerator door. "I'm starving. Can I eat something?"

"Hi, Mom," Jessica called from the family room. "I'm hungry too. What's for dinner?"

Before Karen could answer, Lindsey interrupted, "My teacher says I need two dozen cookies for the bake sale tomorrow. I forgot to give you the note yesterday."

"One thing at a time," Karen replied as she turned on the oven. "Zachary, how about some baby carrots and dill dip—after you wash your hands. Jessica, will you please get the nut balls out of the freezer? And show Lindsey where the frozen cookie dough is. She can slice the cookies while I prepare supper."

"Yes, Mom." Jessica started for the garage. "How much should I get out?"

"One container of nut balls and two rolls of cookies." Karen placed a pot of water on the stove for cooking the spaghetti. Then she opened a jar of spaghetti sauce.

Baby John giggled. Karen glanced up to see Andrew tickling John's face with a feather. "Andrew, thanks for entertaining the baby."

"Here are the nut balls."

"And the cookie dough," Lindsey added.

"Jessica, please put the nut balls in the baking dish, and pour the sauce over them. Then put them in the oven. I'm going to get Lindsey started on the cookies."

Frozen Assets

When we invest time to fix and freeze healthy homemade foods (frozen assets), we secure a net gain of time and profit in many ways:

F: Fresh, flavorful, favorite foods

R: Rapid, ready-made recipes to relish

O: Outstanding options that overcome obstacles

Z: Zesty, quick to zap in the microwave

E: Easy, economical, and enjoyable

N: Notably natural nourishment

These dividends make fix-and-freeze foods a "hot" choice for weeknight dinners, weekend guests, entertaining, or anytime we want to "chill out."

Review the strategies outlined in Chapter 3, "Make-Ahead Cooking" (p. 23), and decide how to develop your freezer "portfolio." Choose the fix-and-freeze investment most likely to bring the greatest return on your time and money, then choose the appropriate investment package.

Investment Packages

Proper packaging protects frozen investments by locking out air and sealing in freshness and flavor. Air is the biggest enemy of frozen-food quality and the cause of freezer burn. Although seemingly contradictory at first, keep these two principles of packaging in mind:

1. Remove as much air as possible.

2. Leave space for expansion during freezing (headspace).

With these two investment guidelines in mind, let's look at several ways to achieve airtight packaging: freezer bags, freezer containers, and freezer wraps.

Resealable Freezer Bags

Resealable freezer bags, the most popular choice for freezing, offer many advantages. They are affordable, compact, and resealable.

Resealable bags make the most of freezer space by allowing you to freeze a variety of foods and stack them flat, like books. Overfilled bags will not stack as well. When you use a one-quart bag, fill it with no more than four cups of food, leaving one to two inches of headspace at the top.

Freezer bags also allow the food to freeze faster because the food is in a thinner layer, about an inch. Then you can break off the amount of chopped onions needed, rather than trying to thaw a solid block.

Resealable bags range in capacity from two cups (great for small portions) to two gallons, which hold 13" x 9" x 2" casserole dishes or large loaves of bread.

Although they cost more, use the thicker bags designed specifically for freezing. Thinner bags, such as sandwich bags, are more susceptible to odor transfer, leakage, and freezer burn. Case in point: A friend decided to try investment chopping for the first time. She chopped 10 pounds of onions and froze them in small bags. A few days later she asked, "Why does my freezer smell like onions?"

"What did you freeze the onions in?"

"Sandwich bags," she replied. A thicker bag could have prevented this problem.

Resealable freezer bags make it easier to remove excess air, prolonging food quality and preventing freezer burn. This can be done in three ways:

1. Lay the filled bag on the counter, expelling the air from the bag with your hands before sealing.
2. Seal the filled bag, leaving about a half inch unzipped on one end. Insert a drinking straw, and suck out the air before sealing.
3. In a large bowl of water, submerge the filled bag almost to the top. The water pressure on the outside of the bag forces the air out. Seal the bag and dry it off.

Although many people consider freezer bags to be disposable, they can be washed and reused. Before reusing resealable freezer bags, examine them for cracks and holes. Guard against potential leaks by using new bags when freezing foods high in liquid content.

Freezer Containers

Freezer containers offer another economical method of freezing food. They are usually square, made of rigid plastic, and most commonly hold two to four cups. Although they cost more than freezer bags, they offer reusability and can be washed in the dishwasher (unlike freezer bags). They stack easily and allow proper air circulation. They require more space to store, but most of them nest for compact storage. Freezer containers are thicker than freezer bags, less likely to leak, and better suited for liquid foods such as soup. Because the food freezes in a solid block, it takes longer to thaw, a plus when the power goes off.

The lids manufactured by different companies are not interchangeable, resulting in a matching game. Over time, freezer container lids may warp, split, and get lost, adding a greater level of difficulty to the matching game.

When filling freezer containers, leave a half inch headspace in pint containers, and one inch in quart containers to allow for expansion. Check the lid to make sure it seals tightly. Most freezer containers are not intended for the microwave. Thaw the food enough to release it from the container, and transfer it to a microwave-safe or oven-safe dish.

Heavy-duty microwave reheatable containers cost more, but offer freezer-to-microwave convenience. Tupperware has a line of durable containers intended for microwave reheating. Lightweight microwave-safe containers, one of the newest and least expensive container options, are considered reusable and disposable, making them perfect for lunches.

Freezer Wraps

Freezer paper provides flexible packaging for larger, odd-shaped foods. Look for a wrap designed for freezing to provide the moisture-proof, vapor-proof, airtight protection needed to preserve food quality. Freezer tape works best to secure freezer paper. Heavy-duty aluminum foil can also be used if the food is wrapped first with heavy-duty plastic wrap. This prevents chemical reactions from occurring when food comes in contact with aluminum.

Investment Options

Some cooks like to freeze entrées in baking dishes. This requires a larger inventory of baking dishes and takes more freezer space, but the convenience outweighs the disadvantages, especially for short-term use. Inexpensive extra baking dishes can be purchased at garage sales and secondhand stores. Look for square and rectangular ones, which use freezer space more efficiently, and also round ones, which heat more evenly in the microwave.

Another option, freeze and transfer, uses the baking dish as a freezer mold. It involves more steps but frees up baking dishes and requires less freezer space:

1. Freeze the casserole in the baking dish until the contents are solid.

2. Loosen the casserole with a knife or by running cold water on the bottom of the dish. Remove the frozen casserole, and place the contents in a freezer bag, or wrap in plastic wrap and again in foil.

3. Label and refreeze.

4. To reheat, remove contents from the bag and place in the original baking dish.

Small Investments

Packaging food in smaller portions allows faster freezing and reheating. It also provides greater versatility for the number of servings if you want 12 servings, not 8 or 16.

Having frozen entrées on hand combats cooking inertia, a common ailment of singles and seniors who find it hard to cook for themselves. Start by preparing a favorite main-dish recipe. For example, if a casserole makes eight servings, divide it into four portions of two servings each. Place three portions in separate freezer containers. Label and date, and freeze for future meals. Repeat this once a week for four weeks, and theoretically you could have 24 entrées stashed in the freezer. But don't just freeze them, eat them. Keep adding to and rotating your inventory.

Producing Quality Investments

Tips for producing quality fix-and-freeze foods:

- Choose high-quality foods for freezing.
- Freeze as soon as possible after preparation.
- Undercook entrées—about three-quarters of the usual time is a basic guideline.
- Turn the freezer down to the lowest setting the day before filling the freezer with a large quantity of investment cooking. After the food is frozen, about 24 hours later, turn the setting back to zero degrees Fahrenheit.
- Thoroughly wash hands with soap for 20 seconds before handling food.
- Wash the work area and utensils with soap and hot water.

Cold Facts

Many people hesitate to freeze foods because of a fear of the unknown: "What will happen if I freeze this?" Relax. No explosions or toxic chemical reactions will occur. Overcome freezer phobia by remembering that the majority of foods are "feasible freezables." If you're not sure how well a food freezes, freeze a small test batch first.

But the cold fact is that freezing produces unacceptable qualities in some foods, such as lettuce (Table 9: "How Freezing Affects Foods," p. 74). Ice crystals puncture the cell walls of watery vegetables, resulting in limp vegetables after thawing. While no longer

suited for eating raw, vegetables such as onions, celery, and bell peppers work well for cooking. Foods not listed on the table generally,
freeze well. Consult a food preservation guide for more information.

Sometimes freezing produces a desirable change in texture.
Frozen tofu (refrigerated, not shelf-stable) develops a spongy, chewy
consistency, which retains its shape better and soaks up marinades
more readily.

Other changes occurring during freezing can be remedied with
simple solutions or substitutions. For example, soup and gravy thickened with wheat flour, cornstarch, or potato flour separate and cur-
dle when frozen.

Solution: Thicken after freezing. Or whisk until smooth while
heating. Substitution: Use Clear Jel or Mochiko rice flour to thicken.

Protecting Investments

Protect your frozen assets by monitoring the freezer temperature
regularly. Place a freezer thermometer inside the freezer where you
can see it every time you open the door. For the highest food quality, maintain the freezer temperature at 0° F or colder. Higher tem-
peratures cause the quality of the food to deteriorate more rapidly.

For the greatest efficiency, keep the freezer at least 75 percent
full, but don't overfill. Allow space for air circulation (and leave
room for stocking up on a special buy). Replace a declining freezer
inventory with empty containers filled with water. Better yet, fix
and freeze more homemade convenience foods.

Investment Identification

Label all packages with the contents and date. This simple step
protects your frozen assets from becoming UFOs (unidentified
frozen objects). If you skip labeling, the UFOs bewilder you. Is it
spaghetti sauce, tomato paste, or tomato soup?

For labeling, you need only two items: a fine-point permanent
marker and masking tape. Attach a strip of masking tape to the
freezer container, and write the contents and date. To make it more

convenient, include pertinent reheating information such as the time and temperature.

You can write directly on resealable bags in the area designed for labeling. If reusing the bag, stick a strip of masking tape over the label and write on top.

For best results, label bags and containers while the food is warm. Tape resists sticking after moisture condenses on the outside of the container.

Cooling Trends

Protect your investments from the risk of food poisoning. Minimize the time food spends in the prime bacterial growth zone by not allowing food to sit at room temperature for more than two hours. Take extra care with high-protein foods, the most susceptible, especially those containing eggs, cheese, and milk. Place unbaked entrées, such as lasagna, directly into the freezer after wrapping. Prebaked casseroles, such as lentil loaf, or precooked foods, such as gluten, require quick cooling. Try these methods to speed cooling:

- Place foods, such as chili, two inches deep or less in shallow pans. Stir to speed cooling.
- Divide large quantities of food into smaller portions.
- Use small shallow containers (less than two inches deep) or resealable freezer bags.
- Use an ice-water bath. Place shallow pans of food into larger containers filled with ice water. Add ice periodically, and stir the food for even chilling.
- Cool in the refrigerator in shallow pans. A partial covering allows the food to cool faster.
- Space containers in the freezer to allow the cold air to circulate freely around them, and if possible avoid stacking until frozen.

Warming Trends

Extreme cold slows bacterial growth, but bacteria survive. When frozen foods thaw, bacteria revive in the warm environment. Bacteria thrive and multiply rapidly between 45 and 140° F. Avoid this danger zone by not defrosting entrées at room temperature. Thaw them in the refrigerator instead. Breads, muffins, and cookies (foods usually stored at room temperature) may be safely thawed outside the refrigerator. Thawing time varies according to the type and density of the food and the method used. To safely defrost foods, use one of these methods:

- Thaw frozen foods in the refrigerator overnight. Thinking ahead to do this is the most time- and energy-efficient method, but not always possible.
- Immerse sealed container or bag in cold water no longer than two hours.
- Defrost in microwave for several minutes until the food can be removed from freezer packaging. Place in a microwave-safe dish, and microwave, using the defrost setting until thawed.

No rigid rules apply to cooking frigid foods. Heating times vary. Precooking before freezing decreases reheating time of most foods. Entrées may be cooked when completely thawed, partially thawed, or frozen, depending on what works best for the situation. The principle is obvious: the colder the food, the longer the cooking time. For example, to heat a frozen casserole, place it in a cold oven and turn the oven on. Plan on the casserole taking one and one-half times the usual baking time (45 minutes instead of 30 minutes).

Investment Tips

- FIFO: first in, first out. Rotate your investments.
- Designate an ice cube tray for freezing small amounts of leftovers, such as tomato paste. Transfer to a freezer container when frozen. Use tomato paste cubes when you need small amounts. Each cube contains about one table-

spoon and defrosts quickly. Freeze foods to be used in small amounts, such as onions, in a resealable freezer bag that is lightly filled and laid flat to freeze. Once the food is frozen, small amounts can be easily snapped off for use.

■ Slice bread before freezing for faster thawing. Take out slices as needed.

■ Insert wax paper between tortillas to make it possible to use a partial package. Package foods in meal-sized containers. For example, small containers of spaghetti sauce to use for pizza, larger containers for an entrée.

■ To reduce frozen-food casualties, put a rug in front of the freezer to cushion the fall in case of an avalanche.

■ Aim to use all frozen produce before summer to make room for more.

■ Clean out the freezer annually, preferably late spring when the inventory is lowest.

Avoiding Investment Losses

Develop a plan for power outages. The first step is to keep your cool. If a power outage is anticipated, set the freezer control to the lowest setting. The colder the foods, the longer they stay frozen.

Do not open the freezer, as it allows cold air to escape and warm air to enter. Wait until power is restored before assessing the situation.

Food in a full freezer will usually stay frozen for two to four days. A half-filled freezer will stay frozen for a much shorter time, about 24 hours. These approximate times involve many variables, including the size of the freezer, types of food, outside temperature, and number of times the door is opened.

To prolong thawing, cover the freezer with layers of newspaper and blankets. Keep the insulating layers away from freezer air vents, which are needed when power is restored. Dry ice may be used to keep foods cold longer.

When power returns, the food is safe to refreeze if it contains ice crystals and the thermometer registers 40°F or lower. If it is safe to eat, it is safe to refreeze. Quality diminishes, so plan to eat refrozen foods as soon as practical.

If the freezer temperature is above 45°F and no ice crystals remain in the food, all food should be thrown out.

Tracking Investments

A user-friendly tracking system makes frozen investments more convenient and valuable. Here are some ideas to try:

■ Post an erasable message board on the freezer for logging entrées. Use tally marks to indicate quantity, making it easy to erase when an item is removed.

■ Attach paper to the freezer door with magnets, and keep a pencil handy for marking additions and subtractions.

■ Use a graph paper grid, outlining or highlighting one box for each package placed in the freezer. Mark off one square each time you remove a container from the freezer.

■ Draw a freezer map, and group items by storage location.

■ Develop a master freezer-inventory log, organized by categories. Include description, quantity, date, and use-by date. Laminate the log for reusability. See Table 10 for a sample freezer-inventory log.

Investment Resources

For more information about safely freezing foods, contact your county Cooperative Extension office, and refer to the resources section in the appendix. The National Food Safety Database (www.foodsafety.org), operated by the United States Department of Agriculture, is an excellent Internet resource.

Fight the Time Squeeze

You can create reserves of ready-made food (frozen assets) by investing time in freezing foods ahead. Then, whenever you choose, you can cash in on your investments and enjoy delicious dividends.

Table 9: How Freezing Affects Foods

Food	Quality After Freezing
Dairy Products	
Cheese	Crumbles unless grated (OK as ingredient)
Cottage cheese, creamed	Separates, mushy (OK as ingredient)
Cream cheese	Texture changes (OK as ingredient)
Cream pie	Watery, soggy crust
Milk- or cream-based sauce	Separates, curdles (use Clear Jel to prevent separation)
Sour cream	Separates (OK as ingredient)
Yogurt	Separates, watery (OK as ingredient or eat partially thawed)
Eggs	
Custard	Watery
Egg white, cooked	Rubbery
Egg, yolk or whole	Gummy (sugar or salt prevents this)
Egg-based sauce	Separates, curdles
Seasonings	
Celery seasonings	Flavor intensifies
Cloves	Flavor intensifies
Curry	Flavor changes
Paprika	Flavor changes
Parsley and other fresh herbs	Flavor diminishes, becomes limp
Pepper	Flavor intensifies
Salt	Flavor diminishes
Vanilla, imitation	Flavor intensifies
Miscellaneous	
Bread crumb topping	Gets soggy
Brown rice, instant, cooked	Disintegrates
Fried food	Gets soggy
Gelatin	Weeps
Gravy and sauce thickened with wheat flour	Separates (whisk when reheating or use Clear Jel to prevent separation)

Icing made with egg white	Gets foamy
Jelly on bread	May soak into bread
Mayonnaise	Separates
Pasta in soup	Loses shape (undercook or use thick pasta)
Pie, fruit (baked)	Soggy when thawed; reheat to refresh (use Instant Clear Jel to prevent sogginess)
Soup thickened with wheat flour	Separates (whisk when reheating)
Spaghetti noodles, cooked	Mushy (undercook to use as ingredient)
Tofu (fresh, not silken)	Spongy texture
Vegetables	
Celery	Flavor intensifies
Cucumber	Watery, limp
Garlic	Flavor intensifies
Green onions	Watery and limp (OK for cooking)
Green pepper	Flavor intensifies
Lettuce and salad greens	Gets limp
Olives, ripe	Texture changes (OK as ingredient)
Onion	Flavor intensifies
Pepper	Flavor intensifies
Potato, cooked	Watery, mealy, disintegrates (mashed OK)
Potato, raw	Texture changes, may darken
Radish	Poor texture, pithy
Sweet potato, raw	Darkens, bitter flavor
Sweet potato, cooked	Discolors (add lemon juice to retain color)
Tomato, raw	Watery, limp (OK for cooking)
Unblanched vegetables	Color and flavor changes (onions, bell peppers, and celery OK without blanching)

Table 10: Freezer Inventory Log

Food	Date	Quantity	Use By

CHAPTER 8

FIX A MIX

One Sunday afternoon Seth asked, "Mom, can we have enchiladas for dinner tonight?"

"I'm sorry, but we don't have any enchilada sauce—not even a seasoning mix," Lisa answered, after checking the cupboards.

What could Lisa do?

- Make a trip to the store to buy enchilada sauce.
- Take the family to a Mexican restaurant for dinner.
- Say "Let's have spaghetti instead."
- Make enchilada sauce using a mix recipe from this cookbook.

A mix—whether for enchilada sauce, pancakes, or gravy—gives a jump start and allows us to accelerate past the thinking, assembling, and measuring. Then with the simple addition of liquid ingredients, we're cooking! Mixes are a great shortcut, usually saving at least half the preparation time, sometimes even more.

No wonder mixes have gained such popularity since 1932, when several women developed the first just-add-water piecrust mix, calling it Krusteaz. Walk down supermarket aisles and look at the proliferation of mixes—muffins, cookies, pancakes, gravy, salad dressings, to name a few.

Mixed Blessings

But some mixes are a mixed blessing. While they offer convenience, many commercial mixes contain long lists of hard-to-pronounce ingredients. Table 11 (p. 79) lists the ingredients of two creamy salad dressing mixes. Compared to the homemade mix, the commercial mix looks embalmed.

Advantages of Homemade Mixes

Making our own mixes allows us to spend money on nourishment—rather than chemical concoctions, multimedia advertising, and high-profile packaging. Homemade mixes save us half (or more) of the cost of their commercial counterparts, because we provide the labor and packaging.

Make-it-your-way mixes boost real home-cooked food with fresher flavor, flexibility, and wholesome ingredients. We get the *ease* of fast food without the *disease*-producing side effects.

Homemade mixes put us in the driver's seat, providing an easy and economical way to be nutritionally responsible. We choose the standards and control the food quality. The versatility of mixes allows us to accommodate preferences, food allergies, and special dietary needs.

Easily personalized, mixes offer unlimited potential for creative gift giving. Children enjoy making mixes to present to someone special in their lives. For more gift-giving ideas, see Chapter 15, "Gifts From the Kitchen" (p. 125). Mixes travel well and keep well, making them a wonderful convenience for camping and camp meetings.

Do-it-yourself mixes are easy and simple—just measure, mix, and package them. Because most mixes require five minutes or less to assemble, this type of investment cooking can be done easily in tiny intervals.

The Magic of Mixes

The magic of mixes comes from three concepts: time shifting, time efficiency, and timeliness.

1. Time-shifting. We use this principle when we program the VCR to record a TV program. This enables us to watch the recorded show at our convenience. Time shifting in the kitchen means a forward-thinking investment of time to prepare mixes for our cooking convenience.

2. Time efficiency. When we prepare mixes in quantity, the

improved efficiency compounds our time savings. To make one soup mix on six different occasions would require a total of 30 minutes. Assembling all the mixes at once uses time-and-motion economy to our advantage and reduces the preparation time to 10 minutes.

3. Timeliness. Using our kitchen provisions (p. 49), we can create almost any mix on the spur of the moment. Lisa decided to use the enchilada sauce mix recipe to make her own, and discovered how the fix-a-mix strategy can avoid last-minute trips to the grocery store.

Table 11: Ingredient Comparison of Mixes

Commercial Mix Ranch Salad Dressing Mix	Homemade Mix Creamy Herb Salad Dressing Mix
Maltodextrin	Dehydrated parsley
Salt	Dehydrated onion
Monosodium glutamate	Onion powder
Buttermilk solids	Dehydrated garlic
Whey solids	Salt
Dehydrated garlic	
Dehydrated onion	
Lactic acid	
Modified food starch	
Spices	
Citric acid	
Calcium lactate	
Casein	
Hydroxypropyl methylcellulose	
Whole milk solids	
Artificial flavor	
Guar gum	
Calcium stearate	

Healthy Dividends

The fix-a-mix strategy pays healthy dividends at mealtime. What could be faster than pouring Lentil-Barley Soup Mix into the slow cooker and adding water, olive oil, and a can of tomatoes? Just cover and cook eight to 10 hours while you work or play. Stir milk, margarine, and egg (or substitute) into Corn Bread Mix and bake. Use a prewashed salad mix to make a salad and dinner is done in a mere 12 minutes of hands-on time! Is it fast food? You bet. Does it taste good? Of course. Is it good for you? Indeed.

Types of Mixes

There are two basic types of mixes: bulk and premeasured. In bulk mixes, such as Mexican Seasoning or Tofu Seasoning, the ingredients remain evenly distributed throughout. Quantity preparation provides versatility and allows bulk mixes to be used to your taste in cooking.

The bulk recipes in this cookbook include mini mixes—scaled-down versions. Try the mini mixes first and decide if they match your expectations for taste and convenience. Make modifications if necessary. When you are happy with the results, expand to the mega mixes.

Some mixes require specific amounts of ingredients and work better stored in premeasured amounts. For example, the salt settles to the bottom of the Split Pea Soup seasoning mix. This uneven distribution remains after stirring, producing inconsistent seasoning—sometimes salty and other times bland. Packaging the seasonings into premeasured amounts for each recipe solves this problem. Zip-top snack bags work well for this purpose. Craft and packaging stores sell smaller bags, but determine if they are approved for food storage before purchasing.

Sometimes premeasured storage makes a bulk mix more convenient. Individually packaged servings of Microwave Oatmeal Mix make them easier to take to the office or for a child to use.

Where to Start

Are you all mixed up and wondering where to start? Here's how to begin:

1. Choose one mix from this cookbook that will simplify your life—one you'll use the most.

2. Take a kitchen inventory and purchase any needed ingredients.

3. Set aside five minutes to fix a mix. Use the mini mix first, if applicable.

4. If not using immediately, label, date, and store according to directions.

5. Use the mix to prepare tasty food at your convenience.

Most likely you'll love the mix so much that you'll go stir-crazy mixing up more to keep on hand.

Tips for Preparing Homemade Mixes

- Use a clear bowl for mixing, to assure thorough mixing.
- Measure dry ingredients accurately by leveling the measuring spoon or cup.
- Use a wire whisk for blending dry ingredients.
- Package dry beans separately from seasoning mixes. This allows rinsing of beans prior to cooking without washing away the seasonings.
- Buy ingredients in bulk and on sale whenever possible. Dried celery costs more than $6.00 per ounce when purchased in half-ounce jars. Purchased in bulk through a food co-op the price drops to $.50 per ounce.
- Dehydrate your own foods when possible. If you don't own a dehydrator, arrange to borrow one from a friend in exchange for some homemade mixes.
- Store mixes in airtight containers such as zip-top bags, plastic containers, or jars.

- Label with name of mix, date, and/or use-by date. Include directions or page number of the cookbook.
- Type frequently used mix recipes into the word processor. Tape a copy to the side of the mix container for added convenience when refilling.
- Store mixes according to recipe directions.

Guidelines for Converting Recipes

- See Table 12 ("Converting a Conventional Recipe to a Dry Mix," p. 83) for an example of a conventional mix recipe converted to a dry mix.
- Dehydration changes the texture of some foods. Expect a mix to produce a slightly different product than a conventional recipe. I like to use dehydrated zucchini slices in minestrone because they don't disintegrate like fresh ones.
- Dehydration diminishes the taste of some foods. Adjust seasonings accordingly. If time allows, add a few fresh ingredients when using the mix.
- Some recipes, such as corn bread, allow a range of possibilities. Do you prefer to include milk powder in the mix and add water later? Or would you prefer to add liquid milk or buttermilk when using the mix? The choice of sweetener and egg (or substitute) presents additional options. Experiment to see what works best for you.
- See Table 13 (p. 84) for an ingredient conversion guide.
- Store whole-grain flours for only a short time at room temperature. For longer storage, refrigerate or freeze.

Table 12: Converting a Conventional Recipe to a Dry Mix
Lentil-Barley Soup

Conventional	Mix	Comments
1½ cups lentils	1½ cups lentils	Package separately from the seasonings to allow rinsing of beans before cooking.
½ cup barley	½ cup barley	
1½ cups chopped onion	⅓ cup dried onion	
1 cup chopped celery	¼ cup dried celery	Expensive unless purchased in bulk. May omit or add fresh celery when cooking.
¼ cup minced fresh parsley	2 tablespoons dried parsley	
2 teaspoons salt	2 teaspoons salt	
½ teaspoon oregano	½ teaspoon oregano	
¼ teaspoon thyme	¼ teaspoon thyme	
1 can (14½ oz.) diced tomatoes		Add when cooking.
2 tablespoons olive oil		Add when cooking.
2 medium carrots, shredded, optional		If used, add when cooking or add ½ cup dried carrots to the mix.
1 package (10 oz.) frozen chopped spinach, optional.		If used, add when cooking.

home•made mix \(´home ´made ´miks\ noun **1:** an ingenious, almost instantaneous method of avoiding monotonous meals by preparing marvelous, salubrious convenience foods for ravenous appetites without laborious effort, hazardous additives, or ridiculous prices. **2:** a timesaving kitchen shortcut.

Make-your-own mixes are not only delicious, nutritious, and expeditious, they are a judicious use of resources, saving time, money, energy, and our health.

Table 13: Ingredient Conversion Guide for Dry Mixes
Amounts are approximate. Products vary; consult label for directions.

Conventional Recipe Ingredients		Approximate Dry Mix Equivalents	
1 cup	Applesauce	½ cup	Apple granules + ½ cup water
1 cup	Beef-style broth	1 tsp.	Beef-style seasoning + 1 cup water
1 cup	Bread crumbs, soft	½ cup	Dry bread crumbs, ground
1 cup	Buttermilk	¼ cup	Dried buttermilk powder + 1 cup water
1 cup	Carrots, diced	½ cup	Dried diced carrots + 1½ cups water. Simmer 15 min.
1 cup	Celery, chopped	¼ cup	Dried chopped celery + ½ cup water
1 cup	Chicken-style broth	1 tsp.	Chicken-style seasoning + 1 cup water
1 oz.	Chocolate, unsweetened	3 tbsp.	Cocoa powder + 1 tablespoon oil or margarine
		3 tbsp.	Carob powder + 1 tablespoon oil or margarine
1 cup	Corn	½ cup	Dried corn + 1½ cups water. Simmer 30-35 min.
1	Egg, whole	1 tbsp.	Pasteurized dried whole eggs + 2 tbsp. water
		1 tbsp.	Soy flour + 2 tbsp. water
		1½ tsp.	Ener-G Egg Replacer + 2 tbsp. water
1	Egg white	2 tsp.	Pasteurized dried egg white powder + 2 tbsp. water
1 clove	Garlic (medium)	⅛ tsp.	Garlic powder, granulated or minced garlic
1 tbsp.	Herbs, fresh, chopped	1 tsp.	Dried herbs
1 cup	Honey	1 cup	Honey Sweet or date sugar
1 tsp.	Lecithin, liquid	1 tsp.	Granular lecithin
1 cup	Milk	⅓ cup	Instant nonfat milk powder + about ¾ cup water
		2½ tbsp.	Noninstant milk powder + 1 cup water
		2 tbsp.	Soy milk powder + 1 cup water
1 cup	Onions, chopped	¼ cup	Minced dried onion + ¼ cup water
		1 tbsp.	Onion powder
1 cup	Peppers, bell, red or green	¼ cup	Dried bell pepper flakes + ¼ cup water
1 cup	Potatoes, diced	Scant 1 cup	Dried diced potato + scant 1½ cups water. Simmer 10-15 minutes.
1 cup	Potatoes, grated	½ cup	Dried grated potatoes +1½ cups salted boiling water
1 cup	Potatoes, mashed	1 cup	Dried potato flakes + 1 cup water
1 cup	Potatoes, sliced	½ cup	Dried potato slices + water to cover. Simmer 10-15 minutes.

1 cup	Sugar, granulated or brown	½ cup	Crystalline fructose
		1¼ cup	Granular FruitSource
		1 cup	Sucanat, evaporated cane juice, date sugar, or Honey Sweet
1 cup	Tomatoes, chopped	¼ cup	Sun-dried tomato flakes + ¼ cup water
1 cup	Tomato sauce	½ cup	Tomato powder + 1 cup water
1 tsp.	Vanilla extract	1 tsp.	Vanilla powder
1 cup	Vegetable Broth	1 tsp.	Instant vegetable broth granules + 1 cup water

CHAPTER 9

FIX AND FORGET

Deena glanced at the clock and sighed. *Five o'clock. What should I fix for dinner? Since I'm home all day, it seems as though I shouldn't be dealing with this question. But now that I'm home-schooling Benjamin and Joshua, I am busier than ever. Plus I'm trying to keep up with Alanna toddling everywhere.*

In desperation Deena picked up the cordless telephone and dialed. "Hi, Kelly. What are you having for dinner? I mean, do you have any fast ideas for me? Brian will be home any minute."

"I'm serving black beans with cilantro and lime," Kelly replied. "It's fast."

"Sounds good—you know how I love cilantro. Could I get your recipe right now? I've got to get dinner going before Brian gets home."

"This *is* fast. It only took me five minutes to start it." Then Kelly laughed. "But it's slow food."

"Slow food?"

"It's been simmering in my slow cooker all day. I put it in right after breakfast."

"Oh, guess that won't help me now." Disappointment rang through Deena's voice. "Uh-oh, Brian just drove in. Got to go."

"Wait! I have an idea," Kelly exclaimed. "Why don't you come eat dinner with us tonight? If you like the black beans, I'll give you the recipe and show you how to make slow food."

"Thanks, Kelly. We'll be right over."

How can something so slow be so fast? It requires only five minutes to combine dry black beans (no presoaking needed) and seasonings in the slow cooker, put the lid on, and select the temperature setting. Let the slow cooker do its job while you do yours. When you come back in eight to 10 hours, the wonderful aroma of simmering black beans will greet you. Add a salad and bread to complete the meal. Couldn't be much simpler, yet it's delicious, nutritious, and expeditious.

The slow cooker is an easy timesaving investment strategy for preparing healthy foods. It requires no stirring or critical timing, making it perfect for busy, tired, and lazy cooks. Just fill it and forget it. Here's a quartet of reasons to use a slow cooker:

- No fret: needs no tending once the lid goes on
- No threat: of overcooked, scorched food
- No sweat: avoids heating the kitchen
- No regret: of not having dinner ready on time

Slow Cooker Trivia

Irving Naxon invented the slow cooker many years ago, calling it the Naxon Beanery. When he retired, he sold his small appliance company to Rival Manufacturing, which renamed it the Crock-Pot in the early 1970s. Now 61 percent of households own a slow cooker, according to the Association of Home Appliance Manufacturers. Another survey showed slow cookers as the top appliance given as wedding gifts.

Slow cookers have maintained their popularity over the years because they help busy people get good food on the table in a hurry. The one-step convenience of slow cooking reduces preparation time and produces fewer dishes to wash. Much like the pot on the back burner of the wood-burning stove, the slow cooker's long simmering time and moist, even distribution of heat combine to work wonders on a variety of foods. Slow cookers offer these additional advantages:

- Economical: low setting draws less electricity than a 100-watt light bulb
- Portable: perfect for keeping food warm at a potluck
- Flexible timing: helpful for families who eat in shifts
- Versatile: useful for cooking beans, soups, cereals, potatoes,

and one-dish meals, and baking bread and cakes

Tips for Using a Slow Cooker

- No peeking during the first three quarters of cooking time. Removing the lid allows heat to escape, taking up to 20 minutes to regain the lost heat.

- Check for doneness at minimum cooking time, replacing the lid quickly.

- When cooking on the high setting, lift the lid long enough to give the food a quick stir occasionally during the second half of the cooking time to improve the distribution of flavors and prevent sticking.

- Slow cookers cook more efficiently when at least half full. Smaller amounts cook faster. Fill no higher than one inch from the top.

- Presoaking beans is not necessary, but does shorten cooking time.

- Add dairy products, such as milk, cheese, sour cream, or yogurt, near the end of cooking time to prevent separation.

- If possible, purchase a slow cooker with a removable crock. It is easier to wash and more attractive for serving. It also allows you to microwave onions in the crock prior to cooking in the slow cooker, if desired.

- To reduce excess liquid, uncover the slow cooker and cook food on high about 45 minutes.

- For frozen foods, increase cooking time by two to three hours, or start on high for the first hour and a half.

- Vegetable colors fade with long slow cooking. A garnish of freshly chopped parsley or other complementary herbs adds color and flavor.

- If the suggested cooking time is shorter than the time you will be away, you can use an automatic timer (often used to turn lights on and off) to delay the start time. Plan the timing so food will remain at room temperature no more than two hours. Thoroughly chill the ingredients for several hours or overnight. You can also use ice cubes as part of the liquid. This works well for overnight cooking also.

- If time is limited in the morning, jump-start the preparation the night before. Chop vegetables, measure ingredients, assemble, and refrigerate overnight.

- Shorter-cooking recipes (several hours) may be cooked the night before serving. Allow them to cool up to two hours and refrigerate. Microwave to reheat.

- For the ultimate in convenience, pair a mix with the slow cooker. For example, try Lentil-Barley Soup Mix (p. 379), Split Pea Soup Mix (p. 390), or Five-Bean Chili Mix (p. 306).

- To bake breads and cakes in the slow cooker, use the insert available from the manufacturer or a large metal can.

Adapting a Recipe to the Slow Cooker

- As a rule, reduce the amount of water, because less moisture is lost, especially when using the low setting. In many recipes, reduce liquid by about half, except for soups and beans. For soups, add water to cover.

- Use extra care with dry beans, because they vary in moisture content with age, variety, and storage. Especially when cooking them on high, err on the side of using too much water rather than scorching the beans.

- Two hours before the end of cooking time, add: rice, noodles, macaroni, Chinese vegetables. When cooking on high, add them one hour before the end of cooking time.

- Sautéing vegetables is not necessary but does improve the flavor in blander foods such as potato soup.

- Slow cooking may intensify or dilute the flavor of herbs and spices. Basil and garlic often become less pungent. Before serving, taste and season to taste.

- Leaf or whole herbs are preferable to ground, since they release their flavors more slowly. If you use ground herbs, add them during the last hour for best flavor retention.

- Not all foods adapt well to long slow cooking. If in doubt, try it out. If results are less than optimal, choose other cooking methods (pressure cooking, microwaving) or stick with conventional cooking.

- The low setting is about 200° F (just below boiling). The high setting is about 300° F.
- One hour on high equals about two hours on low.
- Many factors affect cooking time, including the type, temperature, amount, and size of the food.
- Time conversion guidelines: To convert from conventional to slow cooker time on the low setting, quadruple the time. To cook on high, double the conventional time (Table 14, below). These conversion times are approximate.

Table 14: Cooking Time Conversion Guide
(Approximate Times)

Conventional	Slow Cooker: High	Slow Cooker: Low
½ hour	1 hour	2 hours
1 hour	2 hours	4 hours
1½ hours	3 hours	6 hours
2 hours	4 hours	8 hours
2½ hours	5 hours	10 hours
3 hours	6 hours	12 hours

Slow Cooker Solution

Need a solution to the quick-meal hurdle?
Try a slow cooker, which plods like a turtle.
Slowly and steadily, it simmers all day,
While the busy cook is at work or at play.
Remember: Good things come to those who wait.

Table 15: Slow Cooker Start Times

Choose the desired finish time on the left. Across the top, locate the appropriate hours of cooking for the recipe. The intersecting point indicates the slow cooker starting time.

Finish	Hours of Cooking											
	1	2	3	4	5	6	7	8	9	10	11	12
5:00	4:00	3:00	2:00	1:00	12:00	11:00	10:00	9:00	8:00	7:00	6:00	5:00
6:00	5:00	4:00	3:00	2:00	1:00	12:00	11:00	10:00	9:00	8:00	7:00	6:00
7:00	6:00	5:00	4:00	3:00	2:00	1:00	12:00	11:00	10:00	9:00	8:00	7:00
8:00	7:00	6:00	5:00	4:00	3:00	2:00	1:00	12:00	11:00	10:00	9:00	8:00
9:00	8:00	7:00	6:00	5:00	4:00	3:00	2:00	1:00	12:00	11:00	10:00	9:00
10:00	9:00	8:00	7:00	6:00	5:00	4:00	3:00	2:00	1:00	12:00	11:00	10:00
11:00	10:00	9:00	8:00	7:00	6:00	5:00	4:00	3:00	2:00	1:00	12:00	11:00
12:00	11:00	10:00	9:00	8:00	7:00	6:00	5:00	4:00	3:00	2:00	1:00	12:00
1:00	12:00	11:00	10:00	9:00	8:00	7:00	6:00	5:00	4:00	3:00	2:00	1:00
2:00	1:00	12:00	11:00	10:00	9:00	8:00	7:00	6:00	5:00	4:00	3:00	2:00
3:00	2:00	1:00	12:00	11:00	10:00	9:00	8:00	7:00	6:00	5:00	4:00	3:00
4:00	3:00	2:00	1:00	12:00	11:00	10:00	9:00	8:00	7:00	6:00	5:00	4:00

CHAPTER 10

FIX IT FAST

Bob dropped his briefcase with a thud in the entryway. *Two hungry kids will be home anytime. Guess I'd better get dinner going.* He pulled off his tie and walked into the kitchen.

Glancing at the stopwatch on the counter, Bob mused. *I don't know anyone else who has one of these in their kitchen.* An amateur bicycle racer, he loved the challenge of trying to beat his previous time. Now, as a single dad, he used his stopwatch to turn meal preparation into a game. *Twenty-four minutes yesterday. I can beat that.*

While Bob washed and dried his hands, he quickly reviewed the strategy he devised while driving home. *Here goes another record breaker.* He reset the stopwatch and began.

Placing a nonstick skillet on the burner, he drizzled in a small amount of olive oil and added chopped onions from the freezer. *Hope I get these cooked before Erica sees them. Hating onions is such a culinary handicap.* Bob spooned minced garlic out of the jar and stirred it into the onions. *Off to a good start. Aunt Christy always says onions, garlic, and olive oil are the beginning of a tasty dish.*

Soon Erica and Jared burst in the door from after-school activities. "Smells good, Dad," Erica declared.

"How soon till dinner?" Jared asked.

Bob glanced at the stopwatch. "Let's see. Nineteen minutes left—if we're going to beat last night's time." His eyes sparkled. "Wash up and come help me." Bob reached for the box of instant brown rice and studied the directions. *Guess I'll do it in the microwave.* Stirring the rice and water together in a casserole dish, he placed it in the microwave and punched the buttons.

Erica and Jared returned with clean hands.

"Erica, if you set the table and Jared makes the salad, dinner will be ready soon."

"OK, Dad," Erica and Jared answered in unison.

Bob opened two cans of black beans and stirred them in the skillet with a sprinkling of Mexican seasoning mix. Next he placed baby carrots in the pressure cooker to start cooking. Just then the microwave beeped. Bob took out the rice, set it on the table, and glanced at the stopwatch.

"I'm done setting the table. What's next?" Erica asked.

"Get the salad dressing and sunflower seeds out. We're getting close to the finish line," Bob answered

"I'm done with the salad." Jared placed the last tomato wedge on top.

"Let's get the rest of the food on the table." Bob carried the skillet to the table, then returned to get the carrots. It's ready . . . in record time!" He clicked off the stopwatch. "Twenty-one minutes and 12 seconds. Can we beat that tomorrow?"

When the Pressure Is On

As Bob discovered, pressure cookers make healthy food faster. They provide "two-hour taste in 10 minutes," according to Lorna J. Sass, author of *Great Vegetarian Cooking Under Pressure* (William Morrow, 1994). Quicker than microwaves, pressure cookers prove indispensable by producing rapid dividends:

> Sliced carrots: one minute
> Sliced potatoes: two minutes
> Soaked pinto beans: five minutes
> Lentil soup: seven minutes

Don't let your jiggle-top pressure cooker sit idle in the back of the cupboard. If you don't own one, make a "safe" investment by purchasing a new-generation model equipped with additional safety features. Then explore the pressure cooker's versatility and experience the fix-it-fast benefits for yourself.

Store-bought Convenience

Keeping the kitchen stocked with healthy convenience foods enables us to prepare delicious, nutritious, and expeditious meals. We've focused on homemade convenience foods: fix-and-freeze, fix-a-mix, and fix-and-forget. Now let's look at store-bought fix-it-fast solutions. Table 16 (p. 100), "Healthy Convenience From the Supermarket," demonstrates the wide variety of foods available for purchase.

Store-bought convenience foods expand the possibilities for quick culinary creations. By using these "quick tricks" we can work magic in the kitchen, producing meatless meals in minutes without advance planning.

Nutritional Compromise

The manufacturers of many store-bought convenience foods may use different nutrition standards than we choose for our definition of healthy. While a large number of foods contain less-than-optimal ingredients, we need to keep our perspective. For example, pasta made from white flour does not make the list of Top 10 superfoods. Nor does it fit with the worst. But it is quick, convenient, and easily enhanced with nutrient-rich foods, just what's needed for a fix-it-fast meal. To summarize: When time problems arise, we sometimes compromise.

The convenience foods found at natural food stores usually involve less compromise. Generally they are manufactured to meet higher nutritional standards, using more whole foods and fewer additives.

Homemade convenience foods require the least nutritional compromise by allowing us to take full control of the ingredients. But we don't always have time to implement other investment cooking strategies, leaving us to choose the best of the rest of the options: store-bought convenience foods.

Fix-It-Fast Formula

Here's a successful fix-it-fast formula: Convenience foods + natural foods = a quick and healthy meal.

For example, use a seasoned noodle mix as a meal starter, add protein, such as canned beans, and a vegetable to prepare a quick and easy one-dish meal. This homemade meal rivals most fast food for flavor and nutrition. Add "good fast food," such as a salad mix, whole-grain bread, and fresh fruit (the original fast food), and this meal provides more nutritional value.

The following fix-it-fast ideas use store-bought convenience foods for preparing meals in a hurry, but homemade convenience foods work just as well:

Meatless Meals in Minutes

- **Bean Burritos:** Spread canned refried beans on a flour tortilla. Sprinkle with grated cheese, if desired. Microwave 30 seconds. Add chopped tomatoes, shredded lettuce, sour cream, and salsa. Roll up and serve with low-fat tortilla chips, salsa, and raw vegetables.

- **Beans and Couscous:** Sauté onions, garlic, and green pepper in olive oil. Add canned pinto beans and seasonings. Serve with whole-wheat couscous, green beans, a green salad, and sliced oranges sprinkled with coconut.

- **Baked Beans:** Heat canned vegetarian baked beans and serve with microwave-baked potatoes, mixed vegetables, and Waldorf salad.

- **Tofu Cutlets:** Cut extra-firm tofu into thin slices, about one-quarter-inch thick. Dip both sides in Braggs Liquid Aminos or soy sauce. Coat with nutritional yeast mixed with chicken-style seasoning. Fry in a small amount of oil until lightly browned on both sides. Serve with spinach noodles, peas and carrots, sliced tomatoes, and cucumbers.

- **Chili:** Open a can of vegetarian chili and microwave until hot. Top with chopped onions. Serve with corn bread muffins made from a mix, cooked spinach, a green salad, and grapes.

- **Kids' Favorite—Packaged Macaroni and Cheese:** Use low-fat milk and less margarine. Serve with peas, celery stuffed with peanut butter, and chocolate chip cookies.

- *Hot Dogs:* Heat meatless hot dogs and serve on whole-wheat hot dog buns with favorite condiments. Serve with corn, raw vegetables, dip, and orange wedges.

- *One-Dish Meal:* Prepare a seasoned noodle mix, adding cubed chicken-flavored meat substitute. Stir in peas near the end of cooking. Complete with a tossed salad and blueberries.

- *Pita Pizza:* Spread pizza sauce on whole-wheat pocket bread and top with olives, mushrooms, onions, bell pepper, and zucchini. Bake at 450°F until steaming, about five minutes. Sprinkle with grated reduced-fat mozzarella cheese (or nondairy cheese). Return to the oven until cheese is melted, about two minutes. Serve with crisp raw vegetables and pineapple for dessert.

- *Potatoes and Tofu:* Brown frozen hash browns in a little oil in a nonstick skillet. Add cubes of firm tofu and season with chicken-style seasoning and turmeric. Heat until hot. Serve with an "everything-but-the-kitchen-sink" salad.

- *Potatoes and Toppings:* Cook potatoes in microwave. Top with favorite toppings, such as chili, canned beans, sour cream, green onions, peas, cottage cheese, scrambled tofu, cheese or nondairy cheese, salsa, or chopped tomatoes. Serve with a salad and fruit smoothie.

- *Sloppy Joes:* Add meatless burger to canned sloppy joe sauce or a mix, and serve on whole-wheat burger buns. Complete the meal with peas, baby carrots, and apple slices.

- *Souper Simple:* Heat a can of lentil soup. Serve with whole-grain crackers, carrot-raisin salad, and oatmeal cookies.

- *Spaghetti:* Cook artichoke pasta and top with canned spaghetti sauce. Serve with broccoli, green salad, and garlic bread made with whole-wheat sourdough bread.

- *Speedy Stir-fry:* Prepare a package of frozen stir-fry vegetables, using a stir-fry seasoning sauce mix. Add cubes of extra-firm tofu and garnish with roasted cashews. Serve over instant brown rice.

- *Toasted Cheese Sandwiches and Tomato Soup:* Place cheese

(or nondairy cheese) between two slices of whole-wheat bread. Coat both sides of bread with cooking spray and brown in skillet. Heat a can of tomato soup. Serve with cantaloupe and blueberries.

- *Vegetable Soup and Tofu Sandwich:* While canned vegetable soup is heating, mash firm silken tofu with mayonnaise, salt, onion powder, and chopped celery and pickles. Serve tofu sandwich filling in whole-wheat pocket bread. Add watermelon for dessert.
- *Veggie Burgers:* Broil veggie burgers on both sides until edges darken, or according to package directions. Serve on whole-wheat buns with trimmings, coleslaw, and fig bars.

Fast-Food Alternatives

Rebecca and the children are driving home from a doctor's appointment. They are 20 minutes from home at lunchtime, and the children are begging for food. What should she do?

- Make the children wait until they get home.
- Buy fast food and supplement it with food from the snack box.
- Give the children food from the snack box, and finish feeding them at home.

Fast foods provide convenient meal options, but because of their nutritional deficits and high cost, they are not the best daily fare. With a small investment of time, we can create a stash of quick and healthy foods to keep in the car as an alternative or supplement to fast food.

Before fast-food restaurants sprang up on every block, my mother kept a metal lunch box or a lidded plastic pitcher in the trunk of the car. Her "survival kit," as she called it, included dried fruit, canned vegetarian baked beans, and canned Boston brown bread. It also contained eating utensils, a paring knife, and a can opener.

After fast-food restaurants gained popularity, Mother continued her survival kit strategy for a number of reasons. A survival kit in the car:

- Outfits us with healthy choices for nutritional survival when we are on the go.
- Helps hungry tummies last until a real meal.
- Rounds out a fast-food meal.
- Equips us with supplies for creating a simple, inexpensive meal with fresh food from the grocery store (especially helpful when traveling long distances).

For my survival kit, I use two plastic containers—a snack box and a supply box. I stock the snack box with finger foods, individually wrapped when possible. With our frequent car trips and my children's hearty appetites, I rarely deal with stale food. The less-frequently used items go in the supply box. Here are some ideas for stocking survival kits for cars:

Table 17: Car Survival Kit Suggestions

Snack Box	Supply Box
Bite-size whole-grain cereal	Paper cups
Cereal bars	Paper plates
Fruit leather	Plastic ware
Graham crackers	Can opener
Granola bars	Paring knife
Nuts	
Peanut butter crackers	**Optional**
Pretzels	Canned fruit
Raisins or other dried fruits	Canned meat substitute
Moistened towelettes and antibacterial hand cleaner	Canned vegetarian beans
Napkins	Shelf-stable packages of juice or milk

Nutritional Preparedness

Mark is working late, but his hunger makes concentration difficult. He doesn't have money for fast food. What else can he do?

- Scrounge up some change for something from the vending machine
- Tell himself, "I'm not hungry."

- Eat food from his office survival kit

Jennifer dashes off to work, forgetting her lunch. She is tired of fast food. What can she do?

- Skip lunch
- Beg food from a friend who brought lunch
- Eat food from her office survival kit

The disaster preparedness plan at Greg's school requires each student to have an emergency kit consisting of snack foods for one meal (e.g., a package of cheese and crackers, dried fruit roll, juice). These kits are intended for use if students get stuck at school during a natural disaster or emergency situation.

In my opinion, *any*time without nutritious food is a disaster and an emergency! The long hours demanded by Greg's teacher/principal job often leave him "stranded" at work during dinnertime. So I developed a "nutritional preparedness" plan for Greg, which involves keeping a survival kit at school. Office survival kits include the same items as for car kits, plus microwave-safe foods (if a microwave is available).

Office Survival Kit Suggestions

- Items for Snack Box and Supply Box (Table 17, p. 98)
- Canned and dry soups
- Canned vegetarian baked beans
- Canned vegetarian chili
- Canned fruits
- Microwave popcorn

Fix-it-fast investment strategies give us nutritious resources to use when we are racing the clock (or stopwatch) at home, or racing around town.

Table 16: Healthy Convenience From the Supermarket

Baked Goods	Frozen, continued
Baked pizza crusts	Veggie burgers
Whole-grain breads	Whole-wheat bread dough
Whole-wheat English muffins	
Whole-wheat pocket bread	**Grocery**
Whole-wheat tortillas	Bread crumbs
	Dried tomatoes
Canned Foods	Fruit spreads
Beans	Instant brown rice
Fruits	Pasta
Pumpkin	Pasta and rice mixes
Refried beans	Pasta and pizza sauces
Sloppy joe sauce	Potato flakes
Soups	Roasted red peppers
Vegetables	Salad dressing mixes
Vegetarian baked beans	Seasoning mixes
	Sliced olives
Delicatessen	Soup mixes
Salsa	Vegetable broth
Salads	Wheat bread mix
	Whole-grain cereals (hot and cold)
Frozen	
Cholesterol-free egg product	**Meatless Entrées**
Chopped onions	Bacon
Fruits	Burger
Juices	Chicken
Meal starters	Frozen entrées
Pearl onions	Vegetarian chili
Phyllo dough	Hot dogs
Pizza crust	Sandwich slices
Potatoes	Seitan (wheat meat)
Vegetables	Sausage

Meatless Entrées, continued

Tuna

Natural Foods

Bean dips

Gravy mixes

Naturally sweetened desserts

Organic meal starters (dry and frozen)

Precooked bean flakes

Tofu pudding mixes

Tofu seasoning mixes

Whole-grain baking mixes

Whole-grain cereals

Whole-grain pastas

Whole-grain tortilla chips

Whole-wheat couscous

Produce

Broccoli flowerets

Produce, continued

Cauliflower flowerets

Minced garlic

Organic vegetables

Peeled baby carrots

Peeled pineapple

Salad mixes

Sliced mushrooms

Washed spinach

Refrigerated

Pasta sauces

Salsa

Seasoned tofu

Tofu

Whole-wheat biscuit dough

Salad Bar

Chopped lettuce

Cut and sliced vegetables

CHAPTER 11

THE EIGHT TRAITS
OF GREAT COOKS

Anyone can become a great cook. Cooking is a learned skill, like driving a car or skiing. While it's true that some cooks excel, basic cooking is something everyone—men, women, and children—can master. What qualities distinguish the great cooks?

Let's look at the eight traits of great cooks.

1. Plan Proactively

Great cooks understand the principle of thinking ahead. Delicious, nutritious food doesn't just happen. It requires a plan in the same way that a well-built house needs a blueprint. Developing a menu—a written food plan—places these cooks in a nutritionally proactive position and lays the foundation for nutritious food.

Great cooks anticipate the unexpected and maintain a cache of quick tricks in the pantry for last-minute meals, guests, and power outages. Julia, one of my mentors, never knows if she'll serve five or 15 for lunch after church, so she keeps versatile, quick-to-fix foods on hand to supplement her menu. Like the five wise virgins who possessed extra oil for their lamps (Matthew 25:1-13), Julia stocks extra food in her pantry.

2. Prepare Nutritious Food

Great cooks prepare real food, which satisfies the body better than nutritionally anemic concoctions. Good health depends on good blood, which depends on good food, which depends on good cooking.

This tribute to cooks, penned in 1901, summarizes it well:

"Cooking . . . is a science in value above all other sciences. . . . [God] places a high estimate on those who do faithful service in preparing wholesome, palatable food. The one who understands the art of properly preparing food, and who uses this knowledge, is worthy of higher commendation than those engaged in any other line of work. This talent should be regarded as equal in value to ten talents; for its right use has much to do with keeping the human organism in health" (Ellen G. White, *Counsels on Diet and Foods,* p. 251).

3. Produce Delicious Food

Great cooks possess a passion for palatability. They know it's futile to serve nutrition-packed food if it doesn't get eaten because of poor taste. Great cooks are adept at making tasty food. Some have the ability to use a pinch of this and a bit of that to produce wonderful food. Others follow good recipes.

Almost anyone can create a good taste by smothering food with cheese, butter, cream, or sugar. Even breaded-and-fried dog food would be almost edible! It takes skill to make tasty food that is healthy, too.

4. Preserve Simplicity

Great cooks understand the elegance of simplicity. They often apply the KISS principle: keep it simple and short. And food preparation and menu planning results in less-complicated recipes and meals. Natural foods with minimal processing retain the most nutrition, color, and flavor.

"Cooks should know how to prepare simple food in a simple and healthful manner, and so that it will be found more palatable, as well as more wholesome, because of its simplicity" (*ibid.,* p. 257).

5. Prize Beauty

Great cooks know beautiful food brings enjoyment. Sometimes they serve a picturesque palette of edible art designed for the most particular palates. But most of the time they create beauty with little touches that transform simple fare into a feast for the eyes. They pay attention to color combinations and add flair by using garnishes. Sue, a cook who excels at creating beauty, frequently prays, "God, show me how to make this meal beautiful, so the people I'm serving will know how special they are."

6. Pursue Timesaving Strategies

Great cooks work smarter, not harder, by using shortcut preparation methods to streamline kitchen time. They create healthy convenience foods by using investment-cooking strategies (pp. 64-73) to produce delicious dividends. Great cooks use timesaving kitchen equipment. My friend Ronda says, "I don't know what I'd do without my slow cooker."

7. Practice Ingenuity

Great cooks continually seek improvement. They modify recipes to increase nutritional value and to speed preparation. They enhance their skills through experimentation. Julia, widely known as a great cook, says, "Don't be intimidated. Don't be afraid to have flops."

"Without continually exercising ingenuity, no one can excel in healthful cookery, but those whose hearts are open to impressions and suggestions from the Great Teacher will learn many things, and will be able also to teach others; for He will give them skill and understanding" (*ibid.,* p. 254).

8. Persevere at Learning

Great cooks value learning. They realize the time invested in mastering the art (and science) of preparing healthy food is not wasted. They hunger for knowledge and find food for thought everywhere possible—other cooks, videos, taking cooking classes, to name a few. They learn by doing, observing, and studying. Not content to stagnate, they continually search for fresh approaches.

With practice and persistence, anyone can become a great cook.

CHAPTER 12

MORE MARY, LESS MARTHA

As Friday's sun dropped behind the horizon, bringing with it the sacred Sabbath hours, Jennifer slipped into her favorite chair to relax and recharge. The sound of inspirational music lifted her spirit. Basking in God's presence, she felt like Mary sitting at the feet of Jesus.

Suddenly the peacefulness was shattered by a voice asking, "Is supper ready?"

The "day of rest and gladness" turned into another round of cooking and kitchen cleanup. Begrudgingly she performed the Martha duties, grumbling, "Everyone gets a Sabbath rest but me."

A Different Paradigm

A proper perspective, planning, and preparation can transform a Martha's experience into a Mary's on the Sabbath. Begin with a refreshingly different paradigm and consider the following: "We should not provide for the Sabbath a more liberal supply or a greater variety of food than for other days. Instead of this *the food should be more simple,* and less should be eaten in order that the mind may be clear and vigorous to comprehend spiritual things" (Ellen G. White, *The Ministry of Healing,* p. 307, italics supplied).

Perspective

Simplifying changes the focus from the food to fellowship with God, family, and friends. Simplicity liberates us by saving time, energy, and stress. It means a change of thinking, and disentangling ourselves from unrealistic expectations: "Do not conform any longer to the pattern of this world, but be transformed by the renewing of your mind" (Romans 12:2).

The principle of simplicity may reduce the temptation to

overeat. Eating less food results in a clearer mind for understanding spiritual truths.

However we approach it, the formula remains the same: Good Food – Fuss + Fellowship = Sabbath blessings multiplied by God.

Planning

With some forethought, you can make tasty, enjoyable food to enhance the Sabbath's delight. Keeping simplicity in mind, plan one Sabbath surprise—something out of the ordinary. It needn't be complicated, extravagant, or expensive to seem special. For breakfast, try fresh pineapple or raisin-nut bread. For lunch, serve a distinctive dessert or a favorite food. Fresh artichokes or asparagus always receive rave reviews in my home.

Extras such as candlelight or fresh flowers add elegance to the simplest meal. Dress the table with a tablecloth, your best dishes, and cloth napkins. Inspirational music adds to the ambience.

Instead of an elaborate dinner, plan a menu of only a few items. Feature natural foods, simply prepared. For example, try stir-fried tofu and vegetables, brown rice, and sorbet.

Streamline Friday supper by establishing a tradition of serving the same menu every week. Try haystacks (make-your-own layered taco salads), spaghetti, or soup simmered in the slow cooker.

Plan Sabbath menus around family favorites, or foods you usually don't eat during the week. Write menus on separate 3" x 5" cards, so they're reusable and flexible. On Sunday or Monday choose the next Sabbath's meal. If you want to invite guests over after church, include that in your planning too. And while you're at it, think through the meals for the rest of the week (Chapter 4). Next, organize a shopping list and purchase the needed groceries early in the week. Some cooks aim to complete the shopping by Tuesday.

Preparation

Use investment–cooking strategies to prepare food ahead. If possible, try to have most of the cooking done *before* Friday. Cooking the food on Wednesday or Thursday works for many people. Others cook early in the week and freeze the food.

Cooks Need the Sabbath Rest Too

What can we do when Sabbath finds us unprepared? Relax and remind yourself of the proper perspective—the principle of simplicity. Focus on fellowship, not food. Serve peanut butter sandwiches, or microwave-baked potatoes and toppings (or if you have it, food from the freezer). "Better a dry crust with peace and quiet than a house full of feasting, with strife" (Proverbs 17:1).

Preparing food ahead maximizes the Sabbath rest and minimizes the rush. Then, like Mary, we can sit at the feet of Jesus, our heavenly Friend.

CHAPTER 13

SHARING DELICIOUS DIVIDENDS

Would you like to join us for lunch today?" Sandy asked after church.

Surprised, I replied, "I'd be glad to." I smiled and slipped my coat on. *It will be a welcome change from eating alone,* I thought.

Ed and Sandy led me to their small home, a short distance from the church. Ed, obviously comfortable in the kitchen, prepared the salad, while Sandy heated the soup and filled a basket with bread. We got better acquainted as we chatted about our families, where we grew up, and working together at the hospital.

After Sandy set the table, we sat down to eat. The simple food, instead of being the focus, became the forum for friendship.

Several years later, when I read *Open Heart, Open Home,* by Karen Mains, I realized why Ed and Sandy's spontaneous invitation impacted me so deeply. Their hospitality said, "You're important to us. We're not trying to impress you. Welcome to our home and into our hearts."

Hospitality, spontaneous or planned, fosters friendship, fellowship, and family relationships. It shifts our attention from things and schedules to the people who bring meaning and perspective to our lives.

Spontaneous Hospitality

Investment cooking provides us with quick solutions for spontaneous hospitality.

- "Let's invite Hank and Kathy over tonight." A spur-of-the-moment invitation is not a problem with investment cooking. We can use mixes and kitchen provisions to produce a quick meal.

- ▪ "Hi. We were in the area and thought we'd stop in." Unexpected company is not a problem with investment cooking. We can offer an enthusiastic "Come right in" and cash in some of our frozen assets.
- ▪ "I forgot! Potluck is tomorrow!" A forgotten meal obligation is not a problem with investment cooking. We can create a slow cooker solution.

Planned Hospitality

"I invited a few more people over for lunch," John announced. He closed the back door behind him.

Julia looked up from washing lettuce in the sink. Since they were responsible for the hospitality meal after church, she had come home earlier to get lunch started. "How many does that make now?"

"Let's see. Two of us, the six visitors we already had, plus the Kings makes 12."

"OK. We'll need more food," Julia replied matter-of-factly.

"Let's cook more spuds in the microwave, then finish them in the oven," added John. "And we can cook more frozen peas."

"Could you grab another loaf of bread and the fruit crumble topping from the freezer, please? Then we can open the huge can of apple slices. The crisp will be baked by dessert time. I'd rather prepare too much food than not enough."

"And I'll build a bigger salad," John said. He rolled up his sleeves and washed his hands.

John and Julia started out with planned hospitality and added spontaneous hospitality. By relying on their kitchen provisions, they expanded the amount of food to feed more guests.

If you're not sure how many you will be feeding, have a create-a-solution like John and Julia, or plan a menu that easily accommodates additional guests, such as haystacks, spaghetti, or baked potatoes with toppings.

Susan Whitted, a full-time dietitian and one of my college class-mates, uses an organized approach for after-church hospitality. These steps can be easily adapted to other occasions. In an article called "Simple Hospitality" (*Adventist Review,* June 12, 1997) Susan describes her strategy:

- Extend the invitation early in the week.
- Plan the menu and purchase groceries by Monday or Tuesday.
- Prepare the entrée and dessert, and clean house on Wednesday and Thursday.
- Complete the finishing touches on Friday.

There are many options for planned hospitality with ready-to-heat entrées in the freezer, homemade mixes in the pantry, and ample kitchen provisions. Make the food at your convenience and serve it later.

Hospitality to Go

Keep a picnic basket stocked with a tablecloth, napkins, disposable dishes, and plastic ware. Add sandwiches, coleslaw, cookies, and fruit and meet a friend for lunch.

Give a stay-at-home mother a couple of hours of solitude by picking up her preschool children for a picnic in the park. Take along a basket filled with meatless hot dogs, whole-wheat buns, vegetarian baked beans, fresh vegetables and dip, and watermelon.

Deliver dinner to friends who are in the process of moving. Pack the picnic basket with Spinach-Tofu Calzones (p. 335), pasta salad, pumpkin muffins, and grapes. Spread a blanket on the floor, and share the gift of hospitality in the midst of boxes.

Have Food, Will Travel

We can provide portable hospitality and good nutrition by sharing food with an aging parent, a stressed single mother, a friend recovering from surgery, a grieving neighbor, a disabled relative, or the family of a newborn. Whether it's an entrée or a complete meal, the investment cooking dividends we share with others bring satisfying rewards.

Whenever possible, deliver the food in disposable dishes to minimize the cleanup and avoid the need to return dishes. Take the food ready to serve or include preparation instructions.

"I used to enjoy cooking," my 83-year-old father told me. "But I'm alone now and don't feel like cooking anymore. It's too much bother."

I was concerned about his limited diet but felt helpless, as I lived three hours away. With investment cooking, I freeze small portions of leftover entrées in disposable containers. Whenever I visit my father I take the frozen entrées for him to reheat in the microwave.

Tips for Caregivers

Perhaps you're a volunteer or hired caregiver and unfamiliar with the eating patterns of the person you prepare food for. Take time to learn about food allergies, dietary restrictions, and food preferences. Food does more than nourish. It also nurtures. Find out about the psychological meaning the person attaches to food. If appropriate, ask family members, and talk to their friends for more information. Use the reproducible food preference questionnaire (p. 115) as a guide.

Dietitians use this approach in health-care facilities to maximize the nutritional potential of each resident. Graham Kerr uses a similar strategy for individualizing recipe makeovers. Even if you think you know a person well, take time to complete the food preference questionnaire. You're likely to find surprises. After nine years of marriage, I discovered last week how much my husband enjoys dried figs.

Dealing With Dietary Differences

Just before Thanksgiving, Justin, a high school junior, announced to his family, "I've decided to become a vegetarian."

His family tried to change his mind, but nothing could sway Justin.

His mother, Sherri, wondered, *What do I feed him? How do I make sure he gets all the nutrients he needs? Will I always have to cook two meals?*

Sherri consulted a dietitian specializing in vegetarian nutrition. She found answers to her questions and could finally accept Justin's choice to go "veggie."

Studying Justin's completed food preference questionnaire, Sherri and Justin worked together to make a list of meatless meal possibilities. They started with his favorites—bean burritos and pizza—and froze large quantities of them. Next they added cooked beans and grains to the freezer. They continued to add to the frozen inventory as they discovered new foods. They keep the freezer stocked with a variety of vegetarian entrées divided into servings for a ravenous teen.

Team Cuisine

Meal co-ops and food swaps offer synergistic ways to team up for greater efficiency. Meal co-ops involve a group of people meeting together in a home or church kitchen to prepare a quantity of food to be divided among the participants. Also called cooking bees, they provide social interaction and teamwork while making meals ahead.

Meal exchanges similarly focus on teamwork and sharing. Several families coordinate a meal exchange schedule. Each family is responsible for delivering dinner on a specified day. By rotating the responsibility, the families are able to enjoy good meals while spending less time in the kitchen. This type of meal exchange works best for families with similar eating styles who live in close proximity.

Food swaps can provide nutritional variety for those who don't have the desire or energy to cook. Here's one way to do it: Senior citizens meet weekly at a community center at noon. They tell stories, laugh, and trade lunches like schoolchildren. Each person also brings four entrée servings individually packaged in zip-top bags or disposable containers. They swap entrées and take home four different entrées to eat during the week.

Holiday Hospitality

Is there a way to prepare and serve Thanksgiving dinner and still spend time with our relatives? Delegate parts of the meal to lighten the load, and turn it into team cuisine. (If you prefer to cook the meal yourself, use investment-cooking strategies to cook ahead and minimize last-minute preparations.)

The following are some of my favorite vegetarian holiday menus (see index for recipes):

Thanksgiving
Bread Dressing With FriChik and Gravy
Sweet Potatoes
Mashed Potatoes and Gravy
Vegetable Platter and Dill Dip
Cranberry Salad
Pumpkin Pie With Whipped Topping

Christmas Eve
Broccoli-Potato Soup
Spinach Dip in a Bread Bowl
Fresh Vegetable Platter
Assorted Crackers
Apple Cranberry Crumble With Whipped Topping

Christmas
Wheat Meat in Gravy
Garlic Mashed Potatoes
Green Beans With Almonds
Spinach Salad
Molded Cranberry Salad
Refrigerator Rolls
Pumpkin Pie

"I've discovered that if you wait until you have time to prepare gourmet meals in a spotless, quiet home, you'll never do it. Don't wait until your circumstances are perfect to reach out to others. Instead, ask God to show you ways to nurture your friendships," writes Lettie J. Kirkpatrick ("Hospitality on the Run," *Women of Spirit,* July/August 1998).

When we invest in planning and cooking ahead, we have the time and energy left to invest in our guests. We are blessed and grow richer when we share our delicious dividends with friends.

Reproducible Food Preference Questionnaire

Name _____ Date _____

Food allergies _____

Food intolerances _____

What foods do you avoid and why? _____

_____

What food-related goals do you have? _____

_____

Please list your favorites and dislikes in the following categories:

FOOD CATEGORY	FAVORITES	DISLIKES
Entrées		
Casseroles		
Meat/Meat Alternatives		
Cheese		
Eggs		
Beans		
Nuts		

FOOD CATEGORY	FAVORITES	DISLIKES
Grains		
Pasta		
Potatoes		
Vegetables		
Salads		
Soups		
Breads		
Sandwiches		
Beverages		
Milk		
Milk Products		
Breakfast Foods		

FOOD CATEGORY	FAVORITES	DISLIKES
Desserts		
Snacks		
Condiments		
Seasonings		
Ethnic Foods		
Other		

Please list your favorite menus and food combinations:

Favorite Menus	1	2	3
Breakfast			
Lunch			
Dinner			
Thanksgiving			
Christmas			
Birthday			

Favorite Menus	1	2	3
Anniversary			
Special Occasion			
Other			
Other			

CHAPTER 14

KEYS TO CONDUCTING A FIRST-RATE COOKING CLASS

Tracy loved to cook and to collect cookbooks, especially vegetarian ones. Even though she'd been a vegetarian all her life, she kept looking for more ideas and recipes. *Fix-It-Fast Vegetarian Cookbook,* Tracy's newest cookbook, excited her as she tried its timesaving concepts.

She called her friend Heidi. "Did you know you could make bean burritos ahead and freeze them?" Without pausing for a response, Tracy chattered on. "I used to make burritos almost daily for my children's lunches. Now about once a month I set up an assembly line and mass-produce them. The children help too. I only have to clean up one mess! Whenever I need burritos for lunches, I take them out of the freezer and put them in the lunch boxes. It's a 10-second job.

"Could you teach me to do that?" Heidi asked. "I bet Barb would like to know too. Why don't you teach a class? Since you're into saving time, you could show us all at once."

"That's a great idea," Tracy agreed. "But how would I go about teaching a cooking class?"

A cooking class provides an excellent venue for sharing vegetarian cooking techniques. You don't need a college degree to share recipes and ideas. The most essential qualities include vegetarian cooking experience, a desire to help others, and the ability to communicate. Based on my experience and interviews with others, I offer the following proven advice to help you conduct a first-rate cooking class.

Collaborate. Collaborate with people who can contribute complementary abilities and knowledge. Look for health professionals, great cooks (see "The Eight Traits of Great Cooks" in Chapter 11), and dependable helpers. Also locate people who are adept at organizing, delegating, communicating, and advertising.

Delegate. Adequate organization and delegation make the difference between perpetual disasters and a smooth-running class. Decide on leadership, and assign people to take charge of various duties such as planning, advertising, locating supplies, cooking, artistically arranging food, and cleaning up.

Affiliate With Health-Care Professionals. If you want to include nutrition and health lectures, ask a qualified health-care professional to speak. You could also use video presentations (see sources) or concentrate only on cooking.

Formulate a Plan. Here are the steps to take:

- Choose the focus of the class. Will it be timesaving strategies, freeze-ahead meals, homemade mixes, slow cooking, or fix-it-fast meals? Will it be entrées, dinners, breakfasts, lunches, low-sugar desserts, whole-grain breads, or holiday meals?

- Choose the frequency of the class. Will it be a onetime class or a series of classes meeting once a week?

- Choose the type of class. For example, consider a come-and-go tasting event with food samples and accompanying recipes, a demonstration class, or a hands-on class.

- Choose the location. Will the class meet in a home, fellowship hall, gymnasium, classroom, or public meeting room? Keep in mind it is helpful to have a location with kitchen appliances and sink.

- Choose the day and time. Will the class be conducted in the evening, during the day, or on the weekend?

- Choose the length. Will it last for two hours, three hours, or longer?

- Choose when and how to serve samples. A cooking class needs samples. Decide if you want to serve samples at the beginning, during, or at the end of class. Consider if you want to serve bite-sized samples or an entire meal to show how a meal is put together.

- Choose a registration fee. Estimate your expenses for food, advertising, handouts, and supplies, and charge accordingly. In most cases a cooking class should be self-supporting. Will a cookbook be included in the fee or available for purchase separately? Will you offer a family discount or an early registration discount?
- Choose a preregistration deadline. Preregistration is necessary for planning the amount of food. If possible, make the deadline one week before the class starts for adequate preparation time.

Communicate News About the Class. The effort you expend to conduct a cooking class remains about the same whether you teach five or 25 people, because most of the time goes into the planning process. Advertise widely so as many as possible will have the opportunity to attend.

Personal invitations from enthusiastic people are the cheapest and most effective advertising. Use your creativity with other ways to spread the word. Distribute flyers to natural food stores, fitness centers, and offices of health-care providers who are supportive of a vegetarian lifestyle. Place an ad in the newspaper if your budget allows. Submit a listing for the newspaper's food event column, if available.

Accommodate Differences. Accommodate differences of opinion among the cooking class presenters. Practice tolerance, and find ways to work together even if you agree to disagree. There is not one right way. Avoid imposing your beliefs on others. Your job is to educate, not legislate.

Anticipate Diversity. Anticipate diversity. Your audience will likely include a wide range of people—from lifelong vegetarians to those who want to include meatless meals in their diets. Plan a variety of recipes designed to appeal to a wide spectrum of people. Vegans will want recipes without dairy products, eggs, and honey. For the greatest versatility, include nondairy and egg alternatives in recipes that include milk and eggs.

Accentuate the Positive. Accentuate healthy, tasty foods attractively served. Decorate the serving table and garnish the food. Emphasize a realistic, gradual approach to lifestyle changes (Chapter 1, "Climbing Out of Food Ruts").

Discriminate. Discriminate between reliable facts and sensational information from questionable origins. Present proven principles, emphasizing balance and moderation. Guard against extremes. Avoid promoting specific products that may involve a conflict of interest or financial gain for one individual.

Evaluate the Needs. At the beginning of your cooking class, take time to survey the participants. Find out their experience with vegetarian cooking and what they hope to gain. Then tailor the class to meet their needs.

Facilitate Learning With Demonstrations. Demonstrations involve a teacher showing the audience step-by-step methods to prepare a recipe. The demonstrator can use an overhead demonstration mirror, if available, to provide better visibility for the audience. A videotaped demonstration allows the camera to zoom in from a variety of angles to provide better viewing than the demonstration mirror. The advantages of a videotaped demonstration include less stress during the cooking class (unless the equipment malfunctions) and the ability to videotape until you get it right ("take two"). Cooking demonstrations on video can be purchased (see sources).

Facilitate Learning With Participation. To facilitate multisensory learning, incorporate hands-on participation. Hands-on classes work best with small groups. The more relaxed setting helps participants feel more comfortable asking questions. Participants gain confidence for cooking at home after experiencing hands-on learning opportunities in classes.

The smallest groups can use a home kitchen. Divide larger classes into small groups so everyone has a chance to participate. Arrange different learning stations in a large room. Use portable appliances such as electric skillets or hot plates. Have each group prepare one recipe or component of the meal. Groups may also rotate from one station to another after a predetermined time.

Facilitate Learning With Written Materials. Consider including a copy of this or another cookbook as a class textbook. Include the cost of the cookbook in the registration fee. This minimizes your duplicating costs and provides a quality reference for class members to use for the future. For example, in class summarize the meal-planning concepts from Chapter 4. The participants can read the chapter for homework.

Provide visually attractive handouts at your class. Credit the source for recipes other than your own. Obtain proper permission before duplicating copyrighted recipes and materials.

Reevaluate Effectiveness. Give participants an evaluation form to complete at the end of the class. Ask them to give feedback about the most helpful aspects, favorite samples, and suggestions for improvement. On a separate paper, offer participants the opportunity to indicate their interest in receiving information about future classes.

Collaborate Again. After the cooking class is completed, collaborate to review evaluations. Affirm the positive feedback, and try to think of ways to incorporate suggestions for improvement. Express appreciation to all who helped. Celebrate the successful completion of a first-rate cooking class, then start making plans for the next one.

Sources for More Information

- Adventist Book Centers, (800) 765-6955.
- Health Ministries Department, General Conference of Seventh-day Adventists
  12501 Old Columbia Pike, Silver Spring, MD 20904-6600; (301) 680-6702.
- Health ministries director, local conference of Seventh-day Adventists.
- Local Seventh-day Adventist hospital.
- American Dietetic Association, Vegetarian Practice Group, 216 W. Jackson Boulevard, Chicago, IL 60606-6995; (800) 877-1600; www.eatright.org.

- The Vegetarian Resource Group, P.O. Box 1463, Baltimore, MD 21203; (410) 366-8343; www.vrg.org.
- *Cooking by the Book,* by Marcella Lynch, video cooking class demonstrations, available at Adventist Book Centers, (800) 765-6955.
- Weimar Institute, Weimar, California 95736; (530) 637-4111. Video nutrition and health lectures.

CHAPTER 15

GIFTS FROM THE KITCHEN

Gina tied the bow on the last jar of soup mix and surveyed the crowded counter. She counted the containers one more time. *Well, that takes care of most of my Christmas list,* she mused. *Now I don't have to fight the crowds at the mall looking for those elusive "perfect" gifts, . . . and I saved money, too.* She smiled as she admired her afternoon's work: attractively topped jars of lentil-barley soup mix, containers of fruit-and-nut-studded granola, decorative tins of pilaf mix, and the basket brimming with breakfast foods. *Oh, I can't wait! Uncle Dave's going to love this!*

Gifts from the kitchen are like care packages, tangible and edible demonstrations of love. They're portable hospitality for every season and sentiment. Homemade food gifts nourish the body and warm the hearts of the recipients. Who wouldn't enjoy receiving home-baked bread or cookies or jars of ready-to-cook soup mix? Such personalized presents make great gifts for the hard-to-buy-for person—better than adding dust collectors to their houses. "Tasteful" gifts can delight any food lovers. With them, you can

- Show appreciation to a host or a coworker
- Welcome a neighbor
- Thank a friend for a favor
- Cheer a sick friend or shut-in
- Comfort the bereaved
- Celebrate a birthday or special occasion
- Surprise a dormitory student
- Encourage a teacher or pastor
- Show support for a caregiver
- Relieve the stressed

- Amaze a friend
- Pamper yourself

Foods to Give

The possibilities are endless. Whether you're a kitchen klutz or a gourmet cook, it's easy, rewarding, and downright fun to surprise someone with an original gift of food you've made yourself. Do you have a signature dish—one that you are known for? See if you can turn it into an edible gift. Your gift can be as simple and spur-of-the-moment as pouring granola or a soup mix into a container, or as elaborate and carefully planned as creating a specialty basket for Valentine's Day.

Many of the recipes in this cookbook work well as food gifts. The types of food you give depend largely on where the person lives. A package to be mailed needs nonperishable foods that can withstand the rigors of shipping—granola, soup mix, or cookie mix. (See Chapter 8 for more on mixes.) Foods in glass jars, such as peaches, jam, or blueberry pie filling require careful packaging to avoid breakage. A birthday gift basket you deliver can include perishable foods such as casseroles, freezer jam, or whole-grain bread—plain or formed into fancy shapes.

Tailor your food gifts to fit the recipients' taste buds and lifestyle choices. Are these people fond of blueberries, allergic to milk, or avoiding sugar? Do they dislike nuts, love chocolate, or hate to cook? If you're not sure of the answers, do some detective work.

Packaging Food Gifts

Creative packaging can transform simple foods into elegant masterpieces. If you are adept at crafts, that's a plus. But don't despair if you're artistically challenged. Do the best with what you know, and be willing to experiment. Follow the goof-proof ideas below for starters. Check your local library for books with step-by-step packaging instructions. (See the appendix for some additional resources.)

Team up with a friend who excels at crafts. Look in specialty stores and catalogs for ideas.

You can find a variety of decorative jars, tins, containers, bags, boxes, and baskets at craft, discount department, specialty, and packaging supply stores. Scout out containers at yard sales and second-hand stores.

Look at the variety of food containers in your kitchen and think of innovative recycling. For example, transform a large clear plastic container into a canister. Peel and soak as much of the label off as possible, removing the remainder with a nontoxic solvent such as De-Solv-It. After washing and drying the container, add granola or other food. Wrap in tulle and tie with a ribbon for a glamorous makeover.

Finishing Touches

With a little imagination, you can add personalized finishing touches to greatly enhance the gifts. Use stickers, rubber stamps, and computer graphics to decorate labels. Or buy ready-made labels. Look how easy it is to dress up a quart jar with a jar topper:

1. Fill the jar with food, such as soup mix, and screw on the lid.
2. Cut a 14-inch square of fabric (or textured paper), using pinking shears if desired.
3. Center the fabric square, wrong side up, over the top of the jar.
4. Pull the fabric square down over the top of the jar and tightly tie a string beneath the lip of the jar neck.
5. Gather the fabric above the top of the jar and tie with ribbon or raffia.
6. Attach a gift tag or label.

Food Gift Ideas

To get your creative juices going, salivary glands flowing, and heart glowing, try these food gift ideas for starters:

- **Entrée to Go:** a casserole accompanied by the recipe

- **Pastabilities:** a basket filled with a jar of spaghetti sauce, a package of pasta, a crusty loaf of bread, a bulb of garlic, and a bottle of sparkling cider
- **Soup's On:** a soup mix in a jar, a package of corn bread mix, and a sturdy wooden spoon
- **Cook's Delight:** a favorite cookbook with notes written beside the best recipes, accompanied by a dish made from it
- **Old-fashioned Goodness:** homemade bread and a jar of jam in a basket
- **Breakfast Bounty:** whole-grain pancake mix, muffin mix, microwave oatmeal mix, a jar of applesauce, granola, a bottle of pure maple syrup, and fresh grapefruit.
- **Tea Time:** muffins or muffin mix, local honey, and herbal tea in a basket lined with a colorful napkin
- **Holiday Cheer:** pumpkin bread topped with a plaid ribbon and an evergreen sprig
- **Savor the Summer Flavor:** whole-grain bread, fresh-off-the-vine tomatoes (from your garden or a farmer's market), and a sweet onion
- **Side Dish Delicacy:** uniquely shaped pasta and Pasta Seasoning Mix With Basil and Garlic (p. 315).
- **Cookies Galore:** homemade cookies on a platter or in a tin, or a cookie mix in a jar
- **Basil-lover's Special:** a jar of pesto, a package of pasta, and a basil plant

Gifts made in the kitchen bring raves for little "dough." A few hours devoted to assembling food gifts can make a big dent in your gift list with minimal impact on your pocketbook. Most ingredients are relatively inexpensive, but you can save even more by watching for sales or buying in bulk. Since you do the processing and packaging, you'll save a bundle compared to supermarket and gift-shop prices. But what about the time invested? Adding your time makes the gift more valuable to the recipient.

It's fun to give homemade delicious, nutritious, and expeditious gifts from the kitchen. Whatever your time, money, and imagination produce, package with love, and your "work of heart" will be appealing, appreciated . . . and devoured. And don't forget to make extra for you and your family to enjoy.

RECIPES

ABOUT MAKING WHOLE-GRAIN BREADS

"It is a sacred duty for those who cook to learn how to prepare healthful food. . . . It takes thought and care to make good bread; but there is more religion in a loaf of good bread than many think" (Ellen G. White, *The Ministry of Healing,* p. 302).

Light whole-grain bread need not be an oxymoron. Whole-wheat bread can "rise to the occasion" instead of resembling a doorstop. Try these tips if you "knead" help.

About Flour

Use whole-wheat bread flour with at least four grams of protein per quarter cup.

Measure the ingredients accurately. Use standard measuring cups and spoons and level off the dry ingredients.

Spoon the flour into the measuring cup (instead of scooping) and level off with a straightedge.

Expect slight variations with different brands of flour (or with each bag of wheat if using a grain mill).

Try white whole-wheat flour, available in some stores and by mail order. Many people prefer its light color and mild taste.

Experiment with different flours and yeasts until you find the best combination. White whole-wheat flour, bread machine yeast, or instant yeast such as SAF yeast work best for me.

If you grind wheat, choose a variety with at least 14 percent protein. Freshly ground flour is fluffier than purchased flour. To measure, scoop the flour into the measuring cup and tap once before leveling off.

Limit nonwheat flours to less than one third of the total amount of flour.

About Liquids

Use a liquid measure for the water, checking the measurement at eye level.

Use purified water for the best flavor and results. Water that's too hard (alkaline) interferes with the fermentation of yeast. Water that's too soft (acidic) may produce a sticky dough.

The higher the gluten content, the more water the dough will absorb.

Dough Enhancers

Vital wheat gluten improves the rising by making the dough more elastic. When bread rises, the gluten forms an elastic framework that holds the gas bubbles formed by the yeast (much like bubble gum). Without enough gluten, the bubbles pop, resulting in a dense loaf. Too much vital wheat gluten can cause the bread to be tough and chewy. As a guideline, use one and a half to two teaspoons per cup of whole-grain flour. If omitting vital wheat gluten, decrease the water by an equal amount.

Lecithin, in combination with vital wheat gluten, improves the rising ability, produces a softer loaf, and improves shelf life. Use one to two tablespoons to replace an equal amount of oil in a large loaf. It is available in liquid and granular forms. When using the liquid form, which is very sticky, measure the oil first in the same measuring spoon so the lecithin will slide out easier. The granules are easy to measure and work well in dry mixes, but usually cost more and are harder to find. If you don't use the lecithin called for in a recipe, increase the oil by an equal amount.

Ascorbic acid (vitamin C) strengthens the gluten and promotes yeast growth. Use approximately one sixteenth teaspoon vitamin C crystals (varies by brand), or crush part of a tablet to get 250 milligrams.

Barley malt syrup contains active enzymes that enhance the growth of yeast by converting some of the starch into sugar and creating additional food for the yeast. It improves the flavor, texture, appearance, and keep quality of bread. One teaspoon barley malt syrup will replace one tablespoon sugar or honey. Use about one teaspoon for three cups of flour. If you don't use barley malt syrup called for in a recipe, add one tablespoon evaporated cane juice or sugar. Look for barley malt syrup at natural food stores. It requires refrigeration after opening. Since barley malt syrup is very sticky, coat the measuring spoon with oil or cooking spray before measuring.

Diastatic malt is a powder derived from barley, which performs the same functions as barley malt syrup. It is more difficult to locate, but more convenient for measuring.

Nonfat milk powder produces a more tender crumb and a higher rise. Nondairy milk powders may be substituted.

Most commercial dough enhancers contain whey. If you want to avoid dairy products, look for Lora Brody's Bread Dough Enhancer, which contains only ascorbic acid, diastatic malt, and vital wheat gluten.

Other Tips

The type of salt may make a difference. You may want to try sea salt or mineral rock salt such as Real Salt, since the additional minerals can improve gluten development.

Check the amount of salt. Salt enhances flavor, controls bacteria, and strengthens dough by tightening gluten. But too much salt (more than one third teaspoon of salt per cup of flour) significantly slows yeast fermentation. Experiment to find the compromise between the amount of salt for optimal rising and your taste buds.

If you have problems with heavy whole-grain breads after trying the tips listed here, start with the Wheat Bread recipe. Gradually increase the amount of whole-wheat flour until you find the combination that works best for you.

Use a small amount of oil or vegetable cooking spray when working with dough to prevent adding too much flour, the most common bread-making mistake.

Fat-free breads such as French Bread will stale and dry out more quickly.

For an attractive soft crust, lightly coat the top of the hot bread with cooking spray.

While you are measuring dry ingredients, assemble several mixes to speed the process next time you make bread.

Baking Tips

Take the bread's temperature. Bake bread until it reaches an internal temperature of 205°F, a more reliable test for thorough baking than tapping the bottom of the loaf. Insert an instant-read thermometer in the end of the loaf to check the temperature. If temperature is low, return to the oven and continue baking.

Additional Tips for Bread Machines

Precise measuring of ingredients is essential.

Heat the water to 95-100°F (about 30 seconds in the microwave for one and a quarter cups water). Check the temperature with an instant-read thermometer, or test it on your wrist. Like checking a baby bottle, it should not feel hot or cold but match the temperature of your skin.

Check the dough's consistency after about five minutes of kneading, since bread machines cannot automatically adjust for variables such as humidity or gluten content of flour. The ball of dough should be soft, smooth, supple, and slightly sticky or tacky (like a freshly painted wall). When you touch it, a small amount of the dough should come off on your finger.

If the dough is not soft to the touch but is stiff, or if the machine is struggling to knead the dough, add one tablespoon of water. Allow time for the water to be thoroughly kneaded in and absorbed before rechecking. If more liquid is needed, add one tablespoon of water at a time until the dough is smooth and soft.

If the dough is wet and sticky and not forming a ball, add one tablespoon flour at a time until the dough is smooth yet soft to the touch.

The amount of water may vary depending on the humidity and the bread machine. If the top of the finished loaf falls and/or the loaf contains large holes, decrease the water by one to two tablespoons. If the top of the baked loaf is rough and/or the loaf is compact and dense, increase the water by one to two tablespoons.

Most bread machines, even many with whole-wheat cycles, do not adequately knead whole-grain breads. Try a double knead to see if it improves your results. After the completion of the first kneading cycle (about 10 minutes), reset the machine and start again. This extra kneading better develops the gluten, often resulting in a lighter, higher-rising, and better-shaped loaf. (Some machines won't restart unless the bread pan is removed and allowed to cool for a few minutes. With other machines with long preheat cycles, this may not work.) Another option is to purchase a programmable bread machine that allows you to choose the length of kneading and rising times.

Keep in mind that bread machines excel at kneading but not at baking. For superior results, use the dough cycle with the extra kneading, and bake the bread in the oven. A standard 8½" x 4½" x 2½" pan is a good size for a loaf containing three to three and a half cups of flour.

Not all bread machines are created equal. Some models do a much better job with whole-grain breads than others. The same recipe may produce a light, beautiful loaf in one machine and a compact loaf in another. Experiment until you discover how to get the best product from your bread machine. If you are considering purchasing a bread machine, do adequate research to assure you're getting what you want. Bread machines with programmable cycles allow you to control length of kneading and rising times, often with improved results.

Kneading Options

The advantage with hand kneading or using a standing mixer is that you can double or quadruple the recipe and make extra bread or pizza crusts to freeze.

Food Processor Method: Place all ingredients except water in a food processor fitted with a plastic or metal blade. Pulse the food processor on and off several times to mix. With machine running, slowly pour in water through the feed tube, and process until ball forms. Let rest three to five minutes to allow the flour to absorb the moisture. Check the dough consistency, and adjust with additional water or flour, if needed. (If the food processor capacity is smaller than 10 cups, proceed with half the dough at a time.) Process about 30 seconds to form a smooth ball. Do not overprocess. Remove from food processor and place on an oiled work surface. Let rest two minutes. Repeat with remaining portion if needed. Oil hands and knead dough for approximately four minutes until dough is elastic and springs back when poked with a finger. Tuck the dough into a tight smooth ball and place in a heatproof bowl. Cover with a damp towel. Turn the oven on for exactly one and a half minutes, then turn it off. Place the bowl in the oven, and let rise about 30-40 minutes until doubled (about 60 minutes at room temperature). Proceed with oven method.

Hand-kneaded Method: Combine all ingredients except flour in a mixing bowl. Stir in about one-half the flour until a pancake batter consistency is reached. Beat with an electric mixer for three minutes (or a spoon for five minutes). Stir in the remaining flour. Turn dough onto an oiled work surface. Oil hands and knead dough for two to three minutes. Adjust consistency of dough, adding more water or flour as needed to achieve a soft, supple dough. Avoid adding too much flour and allowing the dough to get too stiff. Knead another three to seven minutes or until dough is smooth and elastic. Coat the inside of a four-quart bowl with straight sides with cooking spray. Place the dough in the prepared bowl, and turn it over to coat the surface. Tuck the dough into a tight, smooth ball. Cover with plastic wrap. Turn the oven on for exactly one and a half minutes, then off. Place the bowl in the oven and let dough rise about 30-40 minutes until doubled (about 60 minutes at room temperature.) Proceed with oven method.

Standing Mixer Method: Combine ingredients in mixing

bowl of a standing mixer (such as Bosch or KitchenAid). Using dough hook, knead on low speed for two to three minutes. Adjust consistency of dough, adding more water or flour as needed to achieve a soft, supple dough. Avoid adding too much flour and allowing the dough to get too stiff. Knead about six to seven more minutes until dough is smooth and elastic. Allow dough to rise in mixer for 20–30 minutes. Proceed with oven method.

Shaping Options

Twisted Loaf: Divide dough in half, and roll each piece into a 9- to 10-inch long roll. Place side by side, wrapping one around the other to form a twist. Place in loaf pan, gently pressing down to evenly distribute dough. Sprinkle with poppy or sesame seeds, if desired. Proceed with oven method.

Braided Loaf: Divide dough into three pieces. Roll each piece into a 14-inch rope. Braid ropes, and pinch ends to seal. Place in prepared baking pan or on baking sheet. Proceed with oven method.

Pan Rolls: Divide dough into 18 equal pieces. Roll into balls, and place nine in each of two sprayed eight-inch baking pans. Let rise 20–30 minutes until doubled in bulk. Bake at 375°F for 15–20 minutes until golden brown. Cool on wire rack.

Dinner Rolls: Divide dough into eight equal pieces. Roll each piece into a ball. Place on baking sheet and cover loosely with plastic wrap. Let rise approximately 20–30 minutes until doubled. Use kitchen scissors to make five cuts like the spokes of a wheel on each roll. Bake 15–20 minutes at 375°F until golden brown. Cool on wire rack.

CORN BREAD

For the best flavor, texture, and nutritional value, choose whole-grain cornmeal. Delicious with chili or soup.

PREP:
5 MINUTES

BAKE:
25–30 MINUTES

YIELD:
9 SERVINGS

1 cup stone-ground cornmeal

1 cup unbleached all-purpose flour

2-4 tablespoons granulated sugar or other sweetener

2 teaspoons baking powder, preferably aluminum-free

¼ teaspoon baking soda

½ teaspoon salt

⅔ cup low-fat buttermilk or plain yogurt

⅔ cup low-fat milk or nondairy milk

¼ cup cholesterol-free egg product

OR

1 egg

OR

2 egg whites

¼ cup oil or melted margarine

Preheat the oven to 425°F (400°F for a glass baking pan). Coat an 8" x 8" x 2" baking pan with cooking spray. In a medium bowl, combine the cornmeal, flour, sugar (or other sweetener), baking powder, baking soda, and salt, mixing thoroughly.

Stir the milk, egg, and oil in a liquid measuring cup. Add the liquid ingredients to the dry ingredients, stirring just until combined. Pour batter into the prepared pan.

Bake at 425° F (400° F for a glass pan) 25 to 30 minutes or until lightly browned.

Nutrition Facts per Serving (1 piece): 190 calories, 7 g. total fat (0.5 g. saturated fat), 0 mg. cholesterol, 310 mg. sodium, 27 g. carbohydrate, 0 g. fiber, 5 g. sugars, 5 g. protein. **Daily Values:** 2% vitamin A, 0% vitamin C, 15% calcium, 6% iron. **Diabetic Exchanges:** 2 breads, 1 fat.

Additions: 1½ cups corn, one 4-ounce can green chiles, ¼ cup shredded carrots, ¼ cup shredded zucchini, or ¼ cup green onion.

Blue Corn Bread: Use whole-grain blue cornmeal.

Corn Bread Made With Milk: Replace the buttermilk with 1 cup plus 2 tablespoons low-fat milk and 1 tablespoon lemon juice.

Corn Bread Mix: Store the dry ingredients in an airtight container at room temperature for 2 weeks or up to 3 months in the refrigerator or freezer; label with instructions. For a more complete mix, add 4 teaspoons powdered egg whites. Add ¼ cup water with liquid ingredients.

Corn Muffins or Corn Sticks: Spoon the batter into sprayed muffin or cornstick pans. Bake for 12 to 15 minutes or until browned. Makes 12 muffins or 24 sticks.

Crusty Corn Bread: Bake in a preheated 8-inch cast-iron skillet.

Vegan Corn Bread: Replace the egg with 1 tablespoon egg-replacement powder. Replace the buttermilk with 1 cup plus 2 tablespoons nondairy milk and 1 tablespoon lemon juice. Decrease oil to 2 tablespoons. Stir batter for 30 seconds.

100 PERCENT WHOLE-WHEAT BREAD

Nothing beats the aroma, taste, and nutrition!

PREP:
5 MINUTES

BAKE:
(BREAD MACHINE):
3½–4½ HOURS

YIELD:
1 (1½- OR
2-POUND) LOAF

Large Loaf (1½ pounds)

1¼ cups (10 ounces) warm water

1¼ teaspoons salt

1 tablespoon oil

2 tablespoons honey or molasses

1½ tablespoons lecithin

1 teaspoon barley-malt syrup

3 cups whole-wheat bread flour

2 tablespoons vital wheat gluten

250 milligrams vitamin C

1½ tablespoons nonfat dry milk

1½ teaspoons instant yeast

OR

2½ teaspoons active dry yeast

Extra-large Loaf (2 pounds)

1½ cups (12 ounces) warm water

1½ teaspoons salt

4 teaspoons oil

2½ tablespoons honey or molasses

2 tablespoons lecithin

1½ teaspoons barley-malt syrup

4 cups whole-wheat bread flour

2½ tablespoons vital wheat gluten

250 milligrams vitamin C

2 tablespoons nonfat dry milk

1½ teaspoons instant yeast

OR

2½ teaspoons active dry yeast

Place ingredients in the bread-machine pan in the order listed or as recommended in the manufacturer's guidelines. Select the whole-wheat cycle, if available. Check dough after 5 minutes of kneading; adjust consistency as necessary to produce a soft, slightly tacky ball of dough (see "About Making Whole-Grain Breads," p. 133). Remove bread from the machine as soon as the baking cycle is complete.

Cool the bread on a wire rack for 30 minutes. Place bread in an airtight container and store at room temperature for up to 5 days, or the bread can be sliced, wrapped well, and stored in the freezer for up to 3 months.

Nutrition Facts per Serving (⅟₁₆ large loaf): 110 calories, 2.5 g. total fat (0 g. saturated fat), 0 mg. cholesterol, 190 mg. sodium, 20 g. carbohydrate, 3 g. fiber, 3 g. sugars, 4 g. protein. **Daily Values:** 0% vitamin A, 0 % vitamin C, 2% calcium, 6% iron. **Diabetic Exchanges:** 1 bread, 1/2 fat.

Oven Method: Spray an 8½" x 4½" x 2½" bread pan. At the end of the dough cycle, transfer the dough to the prepared bread pan. Lightly coat a sheet of plastic wrap with cooking spray and cover the pan. Let dough rise for 40 minutes or until it nearly doubles and crowns 2 inches over the rim of the pan. Preheat the oven to 375° F. Remove the plastic wrap, and bake the loaf at 375° F for 35 to 40 minutes or until its internal temperature reaches 205° F.

100 Percent Whole-Wheat Bread Mix: Store the dry ingredients in an airtight container for up to 1 month or in the refrigerator or freezer for up to 3 months.

Nondairy Bread: Omit nonfat dry milk and decrease water by 1 tablespoon.

Other Variations: See Wheat Bread recipe (p. 146) for more kneading and flavoring options.

SESAME CRACKERS

Good with soup or in lunches.

Prep:
10 minutes

Bake:
30–40 minutes

Yield:
140 crackers

4 cups whole-wheat pastry flour

½ cup sesame seeds

1 teaspoon salt

½ cup oil

¾ cup plus 2 tablespoons water

¼ teaspoon salt

Preheat the oven to 350° F. Combine the flour, sesame seeds, and salt in a bowl. Add the oil to the dry ingredients, stirring until well mixed. Stir in the water. Shape the dough into a ball and divide it in half. Place each dough-half on a separate baking sheet or the bottom side of a jelly roll pan. Roll the dough to a thickness of ⅛ inch. Using a pizza cutter or knife, cut the dough into 2" x 1" strips. Sprinkle the strips with salt.

Bake the crackers for 15 to 20 minutes or until the edges of the crackers are dry, light brown, and pull away from the others. After 10 minutes, reverse the sheets top to bottom and front to back; remove the browned crackers. Return sheets to the oven and bake an additional 15 to 20 minutes, rotating the sheets every 5 minutes; remove the browned crackers.

Store the cooled crackers in an airtight container at room temperature for up to 2 weeks or in the freezer for up to 3 months.

Nutrition Facts per Serving (5 crackers): 80 calories, 4.5 g. total fat (0 g. saturated fat), 0 mg. cholesterol, 85 mg. sodium, 8 g. carbohydrate, 1 g. fiber, 0 g. sugars, 2 g. protein. **Daily Values:** 0% vitamin A, 0% vitamin C, 2% calcium, 4% iron. **Diabetic Exchanges:** ½ bread, 1 fat.

Wheat Flour: Replace whole-wheat pastry flour with 2 cups whole-wheat flour and 2 cups unbleached all-purpose flour. Increase the water by 2 tablespoons. (Crackers will not be as tender.)

WHEAT BREAD

PREP:
5 MINUTES

BAKE:
(BREAD
MACHINE):
3½–4 HOURS

YIELD:
1 LOAF

Large Loaf (1½ pounds)

  1 cup plus 2 tablespoons (9 ounces) warm
    water

1¼ teaspoons salt

  1 tablespoon oil

  2 tablespoons honey or molasses

  1 tablespoon lecithin

  2 cups whole-wheat bread flour

  1 cup unbleached bread flour

  1 tablespoon vital wheat gluten

250 milligrams vitamin C, optional

1½ tablespoons nonfat dry milk, optional

1½ teaspoons instant yeast

OR

2½ teaspoons active dry yeast

Extra-large Loaf (2 pounds)

1¼ cups plus 2 tablespoons (11 ounces)
    warm water

1½ teaspoons salt

  4 teaspoons oil

2½ tablespoons honey or molasses

  2 tablespoons lecithin

2¾ cups whole-wheat bread flour

1⅓ cups unbleached bread flour

1½ tablespoons vital wheat gluten

250 milligrams vitamin C, optional

  2 tablespoons nonfat dry milk

1½ teaspoons instant yeast

OR

2½ teaspoons active dry yeast

Place ingredients in the bread-machine baking pan in the order listed or as recommended in the manufacturer's guidelines. Select the whole-wheat cycle, if available. Check dough after 5 minutes of kneading; adjust consistency as necessary to produce a soft, slightly tacky ball of dough (see "About Making Whole-Grain Breads," p. 133). Remove bread from the machine as soon as the baking cycle is complete.

Cool the bread on a wire rack for 30 minutes. Place bread in an airtight container and store at room temperature for up to 5 days; or the bread can be sliced, wrapped well, and stored in the freezer for up to 3 months.

Nutrition Facts per Serving (¹⁄₁₆ medium loaf): 100 calories, 2 g. total fat (0 g. saturated fat), 0 mg. cholesterol, 190 mg sodium, 19 g. carbohydrate, 2 g. fiber, 3 g. sugars, 3 g. protein. **Daily Values:** 0% vitamin A, 0% vitamin C, 2 % calcium, 6% iron. **Diabetic Exchanges:** 1 bread, ½ fat.

Oven Method: Spray an 8½" x 4½" x 2½" bread pan. At the end of the dough cycle, transfer the dough to the prepared bread pan. Lightly coat a sheet of plastic wrap with cooking spray and cover the pan. Let dough rise for 40 minutes or until it nearly doubles and crowns 2 inches over the rim of the pan. Preheat the oven to 375° F. Remove the plastic wrap, and bake the loaf for 35 to 40 minutes or until its internal temperature reaches 205° F.

Herb Bread (large loaf): Add 2 teaspoons dried chives, 2 teaspoons dried basil, and 2 teaspoons dried oregano. **Extra-large loaf:** Add 1 tablespoon dried chives, 1 tablespoon dried basil, and 1 tablespoon dried oregano.

Onion–Dill Bread (large loaf): Add 2 tablespoons dried minced onion and 3 tablespoons dillweed, and 1 tablespoon dried parsley. Increase water by 1½ tablespoons.

Pesto Bread (large loaf): Replace oil with ¼ cup pesto.

Maple–Walnut Bread (large loaf): Decrease water by 2 tablespoons and add 2 tablespoons pure maple syrup (optional). Add 2 tablespoons natural maple flavoring or 1 tablespoon imitation maple flavoring. Near the end of the kneading cycle, add ½ cup chopped walnuts.

Cinnamon–Raisin Bread (large loaf): Add to dry ingredients 1 tablespoon brown sugar or other sweetener and 1 teaspoon cinnamon. Near the end of the kneading cycle, add 1½ cups raisins and 1 tablespoon water.

Multigrain Bread With Nuts (large loaf): Decrease wholewheat flour to 1½ cups and add ¾ cup rolled five-grain cereal (for more texture, use cracked-grain cereal). Increase vital wheat gluten to 2 tablespoons. Near the end of the kneading cycle, add ½ cup chopped walnuts, slivered almonds, or sunflower seeds.

Whole–Wheat Bread Mix: Combine the dry ingredients and store them in an airtight container at room temperature for up to 1 month or in the refrigerator or freezer for up to 3 months.

Nondairy Bread: Omit the nonfat dry milk and reduce water by one tablespoon.

WHOLE-WHEAT BISCUITS

*This extra-moist dough produces steam in a hot oven,
creating tender and fluffy biscuits.*

1¾ cups whole-wheat pastry flour

1 tablespoon granulated sugar or other
sweetener

1½ teaspoons baking powder, preferably
aluminum-free

¼ (heaping) teaspoon salt

⅛ teaspoon baking soda

1 cup low-fat buttermilk or nonfat plain
yogurt

2 tablespoons oil

PREP:
10 MINUTES

BAKE:
18–20 MINUTES

YIELD:
9 BISCUITS

Position the rack slightly above the center of the oven. Preheat the oven to 425°F. Coat an 8-inch cake pan or square baking pan with cooking spray. Combine the dry ingredients. Stir the buttermilk and oil, and add to the dry ingredients, stirring to combine. Drop by spoonfuls onto prepared pan. Bake 18 to 20 minutes or until lightly browned. Cool biscuits in the pan for 1 to 2 minutes before serving.

When the biscuits are cool, store them in an airtight container at room temperature for up to 2 days, in the refrigerator for up to 5 days, or in the freezer for up to 3 months.

Nutrition Facts per Serving (1 biscuit): 100 calories, 3.5 g. total fat (0 g. saturated fat), 0 mg. cholesterol, 200 mg. sodium, 16 g. carbohydrate, 2 g. fiber, 3 g. sugars, 3 g. protein. **Daily Values:** 0% vitamin A, 0% vitamin C, 8% calcium, 2% iron. **Diabetic Exchanges:** 1 bread, ½ fat.

Serving Idea: For breakfast, top biscuits with margarine and fruit-sweetened jam and serve with five-grain cereal and fresh grapefruit. For any meal, top with chicken-style gravy.

Cornmeal Biscuits: Decrease whole-wheat pastry flour to 1⅓ cups. Add ¼ cup stone-ground cornmeal. Stir batter for 30 seconds. If desired, add ¼ cup finely chopped sun-dried tomatoes, 3 tablespoons snipped fresh chives, or ¼ cup drained and diced canned green chiles.

Milk Variation: Replace buttermilk with ⅔ cup milk or nondairy milk mixed with 1 tablespoon lemon juice.

Strawberry Shortcakes: Increase sweetener to ¼ cup. Split the baked biscuits and top them with sliced strawberries and whipped topping or vanilla yogurt.

Surprise Biscuits: Place a dollop of jam or pesto between two small portions of dough and bake.

WHOLE-WHEAT FRENCH BREAD

Extra rising develops a wonderful flavor in this chewy, fat-free, sugar-free bread. From start to finish this bread takes 5 to 6 hours, but the hands-on time is only 10 minutes.

1 tablespoon stone-ground cornmeal

1½ cups water

1½ teaspoons salt

2 cups whole-wheat bread flour

2 cups unbleached bread flour

1 pinch vitamin C powder, optional

2 teaspoons instant yeast

OR

2½ teaspoons active dry yeast

PREP:
10 MINUTES

KNEADING (BREAD MACHINE):
1½–2 HOURS

RISING:
3–3½ HOURS

BAKE (OVEN):
25–30 MINUTES

YIELD:
1 EXTRA-LARGE (2-POUND) LOAF
OR
2 (14-OUNCE) LOAVES

Coat a pizza peel or flat baking sheet with cornmeal. Place the remaining ingredients in the bread-machine pan in the order listed or as recommended in the manufacturer's guidelines. Select the dough cycle. Check the dough after 5 minutes of kneading; adjust kneading time as necessary to produce soft-ball consistency. Leave the dough in the machine after the dough cycle ends, and let it rise for 1 hour. Punch down the dough and let it rise an additional 1 hour.

Lightly flour a work surface; remove the dough from the bread machine and knead it to remove the air bubbles. Shape the dough into a round ball or two long loaves. Transfer the dough to the prepared pizza peel, covering it with a damp kitchen towel. Place the dough in a warm place to rise until it nearly doubles, about 1 to 1½ hours. About 30 minutes prior to baking, place baking stone, tiles, or baking sheet in the oven; preheat the oven to 450°F. Set a small baking pan on the bottom rack of the oven.

Using a sharp knife, make several ½-inch-deep slashes on top of the loaf. Slide the loaf off the peel and onto the preheated baking stone. Pour ¾ cup water into the empty baking pan. Bake the bread until the crust is brown and an instant-read thermometer inserted in the bottom of the loaf registers 190°-200°F, 30 to 35 minutes.

Cool the bread on a wire rack. To maintain a crisp crust, store the bread in a cloth or paper bag for up to 2 days.

Nutrition Facts per Serving (¹⁄₂₀ extra-large loaf): 80 calories, 0 g. total fat (0 g. saturated fat), 0 mg. cholesterol, 180 mg. sodium, 18 g. carbohydrate, 2 g. fiber, 0 g. sugars, 3 g. protein. **Daily Values:** 0% vitamin A, 0% vitamin C, 0% calcium, 8% iron. **Diabetic Exchanges:** 1 bread.

Serving Idea: Make into garlic bread; serve with pesto and angel hair pasta.

Hand or Mixer Method: Combine ingredients. Knead dough until it becomes elastic (by hand, about 10 minutes; with a standing mixer, about 5 minutes). Preheat the oven to 200°F and turn it off. Form dough into a ball; place dough in a large bowl, and cover it with a damp towel. Allow dough to rise until it nearly doubles, about 2 to 3 hours. Punch down, form into a ball to rise again, about 1½ to 2 hours. Proceed with the remainder of the recipe.

Simple French Bread: Select the dough cycle on the bread machine. After the dough cycle ends, remove the dough from the pan and shape it into 2 long loaves or 1 round loaf; let the dough rise until it nearly doubles. About 30 minutes prior to baking, preheat the oven to 450°F. Bake the bread on a preheated baking stone until a thermometer inserted in the bottom of the bread registers 190–200°F, 25 to 35 minutes.

Super Simple French Bread: Select the whole-wheat cycle and let the bread machine do the baking.

Herbed French Bread: Add 1 tablespoon Italian seasoning mix.

French Bread Mix: Store the dry ingredients in an airtight container at room temperature for up to 1 month; refrigerate or freeze them for up to 3 months.

Italian Bread: While mixing, add 2 tablespoons extra-virgin olive oil.

BREAKFAST
CEREALS

BREAKFAST BARLEY

Start the barley in the slow cooker in the evening for a delicious hot cereal in the morning. Dried fruit gives this cereal a festive look. Use any combination of dried fruit.

6 cups water

1 cup pearl barley

1 teaspoon salt

¼ cup raisins

¼ cup chopped dates

¼ cup chopped dried apricots

¼ cup dried cranberries

½ teaspoon ground cinnamon

¼ cup slivered almonds, optional

PREP:
10 MINUTES

SLOW COOKER:
8–10 HOURS

STOVE TOP:
50–60 MINUTES

YIELD:
6 (1-CUP)
SERVINGS

Stir together the water, barley, and salt in a 3½-quart slow cooker. Cover and cook on low for 8 to 9 hours or until the barley is tender. About 15 to 60 minutes before serving, stir in the dried fruit and cinnamon. Continue cooking on low until serving time. Sprinkle with slivered almonds, if using. Serve hot. Refrigerate for up to 1 week, or freeze for up to 6 months.

Nutrition Facts per Serving (½ cup): 110 calories, 1.5 g. total fat (0 g. saturated fat), 0 mg. cholesterol, 200 mg. sodium, 23 g. carbohydrate, 4 g. fiber, 8 g. sugars, 2 g. protein. **Daily Values:** 6% vitamin A, 0% vitamin C, 2% calcium, 4% iron. **Diabetic Exchanges:** 1 bread, ½ fruit.

Stove Top: Bring to boiling 3 to 3½ cups water, 1 cup pearl barley, and ¾ teaspoon salt. Reduce heat; cover and simmer 40 minutes. Stir in dried fruit and cinnamon. Continue cooking 10 to 20 minutes or until the barley is tender and most of the liquid is absorbed.

GRANOLA WITH ALMONDS

Bake it overnight and wake up to a wonderful aroma.

PREP:
10 MINUTES

BAKE:
9–10 HOURS

YIELD:
18 CUPS;
36 (½-CUP)
SERVINGS

16 cups rolled oats

2 cups slivered or sliced almonds

1-2 cups unsweetened shredded coconut

1 cup honey or concentrated fruit sweetener

½ cup oil

1 tablespoon vanilla

1 teaspoon natural almond flavoring

OR

½ teaspoon almond extract

½ teaspoon salt

Position the racks in the center of the oven. Preheat the oven to 325°F (300°F for dark pans).

Place two baking pans on the counter. Mix the oats, almonds, and coconut in a very large mixing bowl. Stir the remaining ingredients together. Pour the liquid ingredients over the dry ingredients and mix thoroughly (hands work best). Divide the mixture between the two baking pans, spreading evenly. Bake for 20 minutes, stirring mixture and rotating the pans every 10 minutes. Reduce heat to 175°F (150°F for dark pans). Bake for 8 to 10 hours until dry and golden brown.

Nutrition Facts per Serving (½ cup): 240 calories, 9 g. total fat (2 g. saturated fat), 0 mg. cholesterol, 36 mg. sodium, 33 g. carbohydrate, 5 g. fiber, 8 g. sugars, 7 g. protein. **Daily Values:** 0% vitamin A, 0% vitamin C, 4% calcium, 8% iron. **Diabetic Exchanges:** ¼ cup = 1 bread, 1 fat.

Granola With Cinnamon: Add 2 teaspoons cinnamon.

Fruited Granola: After baking, add dried fruit, such as raisins, cranberries, chopped apricots, blueberries, pineapple, or papaya.

Chunky Granola: Add 2 cups wheat germ and 1 cup whole-wheat flour to the dry ingredients. Add ¾ cup water to the liquid ingredients.

Chewy Granola: Use 4 cups rolled five-grain cereal instead of 4 cups rolled oats.

Maple–Nut Granola: Replace the almond flavoring with 1½ tablespoons natural maple flavoring or imitation maple flavoring. If desired, replace the honey with pure maple syrup and add ½ cup brown sugar.

Orange–Almond Granola: Replace the almond flavoring with 3 tablespoons natural orange flavoring.

Vary the Nuts: Replace the almonds with any combination of raw nuts, such as walnuts, pecans, cashews, sunflower seeds, or sesame seeds. Add unsalted roasted nuts after baking.

Traditional Baking Method: Bake at 325°F (300°F for dark pans) for 20 minutes, stirring mixture and rotating the pans every 10 minutes. Reduce heat to 250°F (225°F for dark pans) and bake, stirring mixture and rotating pans every 10 minutes, until golden brown and dry, about 40 to 50 minutes.

MICROWAVE OATMEAL MIX

Making your own mix allows you to control what goes into your bowl.

PREP:
5 MINUTES

YIELD:
MINI MIX: ⅔ CUP
(2 SERVINGS)
MEGA MIX:
5½ CUPS
(16 SERVINGS)

½ **cup** *(4 cups)* **quick oats**

3 **tablespoons** *(1½ cups)* **raisins**

⅛ **teaspoon** *(1 teaspoon)* **salt**

⅛ **teaspoon** *(1 teaspoon)* **cinnamon**

Combine the ingredients in an airtight container and store for up to 3 months (for convenience, store a ⅔-cup measure inside). Label the container with Microwave Oatmeal cooking directions (recipe follows).

Nutrition Facts per Serving (⅓ cup dry): 120 calories, 1.5 g. total fat (0 g. saturated fat), 0 mg. cholesterol, 150 mg. sodium, 24 g. carbohydrate, 3 g. fiber, 9 g. sugars, 4 g. protein. **Daily Values:** 0 % vitamin A, 0% vitamin C, 2% calcium, 6% iron. **Diabetic Exchanges:** 1 bread, ½ fruit

Other Fruits: Use any combination of chopped dried fruit: dates, apricots, papaya, golden raisins, cranberries, or fruit mix.

Nuts: Decrease dried fruit to 1 cup and add ½ cup slivered almonds, chopped walnuts, pecans, or shredded coconut.

Sweeter Mix: Add 1½ tablespoons (or to taste) date sugar, Sucanat, granulated or brown sugar.

Rolled Oats: Replace quick oats with rolled oats. Follow cooking directions for rolled oats.

Five- or Seven-Grain Cereal: Replace quick oats with rolled five- or seven-grain cereal. Follow cooking directions for five- or seven-grain cereal.

MICROWAVE OATMEAL

A microwave turns the mix into a quick, whole-grain cereal.

⅔ **cup Microwave Oatmeal Mix**

1 cup water

Stir the mix to distribute seasonings before measuring. Combine the ingredients in a large microwave-safe cereal bowl. Microwave 1½ to 2 minutes on high. Let stand 1 minute. Stir. Serve hot.

PREP:
1 MINUTE

COOK:
2 MINUTES

YIELD:
2 SERVINGS OR
1 HEARTY
SERVING

Nutrition Facts per Serving (½ cup): 110 calories, 1 g. total fat (0 g. saturated fat), 0 mg. cholesterol, 150 mg. sodium, 24 g. carbohydrate, 3 g. fiber, 9 g. sugars, 3 g. protein. **Daily Values:** 0 % vitamin A, 0% vitamin C, 2% calcium, 6% iron. **Diabetic Exchanges:** 1 bread, ½ fruit.

One Serving: Use ⅓ cup oatmeal mix and ½ cup water. Microwave 1 to 1½ minutes.

Thicker Oatmeal: Use less water.

Thinner Oatmeal: Use more water.

Stove Top: Bring the water to boil in a small saucepan. Stir in the oatmeal mix, and cook 1 minute, stirring occasionally. Cover and remove from heat; serve in 2 to 3 minutes.

Rice Cooker: Coat rice cooker with cooking spray. Add oatmeal mix and water. Stir and cover. Turn cooker on and cook until it turns off, about 12 to 15 minutes.

Rolled Oats: Microwave at 50 percent power for 5 minutes.

Rolled Five- or Seven-Grain Cereal: Microwave at 50 percent power for 7 minutes. Let stand 2 minutes.

Stove Top: Bring the water to boil. Stir in mix. Return to a boil; reduce heat, cover, and simmer 10 minutes, or until desired thickness.

Sweeter Oatmeal: Stir in low-sugar jam, pure maple syrup, honey, or other sweetener, or replace water with apple juice.

BREAKFAST
BREADS

ABOUT SWEET ROLLS

- This dough can also be made with a bread machine: After about 5 minutes of kneading, turn off the machine; allow the dough to rise until it doubles, about 1 hour.
- Whole-wheat pastry flour and minimal kneading produce a softer, less chewy dough.
- For softer dough, replace 2 tablespoons of the unbleached all-purpose flour with 2 tablespoons potato flour or ¼ cup instant potato flakes.
- See Tips for Making Whole-Grain Breads (p. 133).

APPLE-GLAZED CINNAMON ROLLS

Shape the rolls in the evening, let them rise overnight in the refrigerator, and bake them in the morning—truly a taste and aroma worth waking up for!

PREP:
30 MINUTES

FIRST RISING:
1 HOUR

SECOND RISING:
1 HOUR
(OR OVERNIGHT IN THE REFRIGERATOR)

BAKE:
30 MINUTES

YIELD:
16 ROLLS

Sweet Dough:

1 cup warm water

1 teaspoon salt

2 tablespoons oil

2 tablespoons lecithin

3 tablespoons honey or other sweetener

1 teaspoon vanilla

1¾ cups unbleached all-purpose flour

1½ cups whole-wheat pastry flour

2 tablespoons soy flour

2 tablespoons nonfat dry milk

OR

1 tablespoon nondairy milk powder

2 teaspoons instant yeast

OR

1 tablespoon active dry yeast

Filling:

2 cups chopped peeled apple

¾ cup raisins

½ **cup chopped walnuts or pecans, optional**

¼ **cup honey or other sweetener**

1 tablespoon cinnamon

Glaze:

⅔ **cup apple juice concentrate**

2 tablespoons margarine or butter

2 tablespoons honey or other sweetener

Sweet Dough: Combine the sweet dough ingredients in a large mixing bowl. Knead the dough 1 to 2 minutes until a soft, smooth ball forms. If the dough is too dry, add water 1 tablespoon at a time. If the dough is too moist, add flour 1 tablespoon at a time. For best results, keep the dough on the sticky side, and oil your hands to prevent sticking, rather than add more flour. Coat a bowl with cooking spray. Place dough in the prepared bowl and turn it over to coat. Tuck the dough into a tight, smooth ball, and cover it with a damp towel or plastic wrap. Let the dough rise in a warm place 1 hour, or until it nearly doubles.

Filling: Combine the filling ingredients and set them aside.

Glaze: Microwave the glaze ingredients until the margarine melts, about 1 to 2 minutes, or heat them in a small saucepan on the stove top. Coat two 9-inch round cake pans or one 14-inch round or one 12-inch square pan with cooking spray. Pour half the glaze in each pan. Set aside.

Assembly: Punch down the dough, kneading it to remove air bubbles. Roll the dough on a lightly floured surface to a 20" x 12" rectangle. Spread filling evenly over the dough, leaving a ½-inch margin on one long side. Beginning with the opposite long side, roll the dough snugly into a log, pinching the seam to seal. Using a sharp, serrated knife or dental floss, cut the dough into 16 equal pieces. Place 8 pieces in each prepared pan. Cover the pans with plastic wrap or aluminum foil and refrigerate at least 10 to 14 hours. (See To Bake the Same Day or To Freeze Before Baking, below.) Bake at 350°F (325°F for glass pans) for 30 to 35 minutes, or until golden brown. Immediately turn pans upside down onto cooling racks or serving platters.

Nutrition Facts per Serving (1 roll): 240 calories, 8 g. total fat (1 g. saturated fat), 0 mg. cholesterol, 170 mg. sodium, 41 g. carbohydrate, 2 g. fiber, 20 g. sugars, 5 g. protein. **Daily Values:** 2% vitamin A, 2% vitamin C, 2% calcium, 8% iron. **Diabetic Exchanges:** 1 bread, 1 fruit, 1 other carbohydrate, 1 fat.

To Bake the Same Day: Cover the dough loosely with plastic wrap or a damp towel and let rise in a warm place until it doubles in size, about 1 hour. Bake 25 to 30 minutes.

To Freeze Before Baking: Wrap the dough securely with plastic wrap, making the package airtight; cover with foil. Store in the freezer for up to 4 weeks. To bake, remove from the freezer; unwrap. Thaw at room temperature 1 to 2 hours. Let the dough rise in a warm place until it doubles, about 1½ hours. Bake as directed.

Orange-Date Sweet Rolls: Replace apple juice concentrate in glaze with ⅓ cup orange juice concentrate and ⅓ cup water. Replace filling ingredients with 2 cups chopped dates, 1 tablespoon orange juice concentrate, 1½ teaspoons minced orange zest, and 1 teaspoon cardamom.

Cinnamon Rolls: Omit glaze and filling. Mix ⅓ cup granulated sugar or other sweetener with 1 tablespoon cinnamon. Roll dough into a 12" x 16" rectangle. Brush with 1 tablespoon milk and sprinkle with cinnamon sugar, leaving a ½-inch border along one long side. Sprinkle with ¾ cup raisins, ¾ cup chopped, pitted dates; and ½ cup chopped nuts (optional). Roll up and cut into 16 pieces. Spray two 9-inch round baking pans, or a 14-inch round or 12-inch square baking pan; place dough in the pan and let it rise, as for apple-glazed rolls. Bake 25 to 30 minutes, or until golden brown (a thermometer inserted into a roll should register 185°-188° F). Invert onto a wire rack to cool. Turn over to serve.

Other Fillings: Use pureed prunes, dates, or apricots with crushed pineapple.

Other Shapes of Pans: Bake rolls in a heart- or star-shaped pan.

Sweet Dough Mix: Store the dry ingredients in an airtight container at room temperature for up to 1 month; refrigerate or freeze them for up to 3 months. Label and date the container with baking directions.

Sticky Buns: Follow recipe for Cinnamon Rolls, except place 2 tablespoons melted margarine, ⅔ cup brown sugar or other sweetener, and ⅔ cup chopped pecans in bottom of pan before adding rolls. Immediately after baking, invert onto a wire rack with a baking sheet underneath to catch the drips.

BUTTERMILK PANCAKES

The acidity of the buttermilk combined with low-gluten flour produce tender, light, and fluffy whole-grain pancakes with a minimum of fat.

PREP:
5 MINUTES

COOK:
10 MINUTES

YIELD:
14 (4-INCH)
PANCAKES

---

1 cup whole-wheat flour

1 cup whole-wheat pastry, barley, or all-purpose flour, or quick oats

1 tablespoon brown sugar or other sweetener

1 teaspoon salt

1 teaspoon baking powder, preferably aluminum-free

½ teaspoon baking soda

1½ cups low-fat buttermilk

½ cup low-fat milk

1 tablespoon oil, melted margarine, or butter

¼ cup cholesterol-free egg product

OR

1 egg

OR

2 egg whites

Preheat a nonstick skillet over medium-high heat, or griddle to 375° F. Mix the dry ingredients.

Combine the liquid ingredients, and whisk them into the dry ingredients just until mixed (the batter will be thick). Test skillet or griddle readiness by sprinkling water on it: If the water dances, the temperature is hot enough. Pour ½–cup portions of batter onto the hot skillet; cook until the bottom is browned and bubbles begin to form on top. Turn the pancakes and cook until they are browned. Serve hot.

Layer pancakes with wax paper to prevent sticking, and store them in an airtight container in the refrigerator for up to 1 week or in the freezer for up to 3 months.

Nutrition Facts per Serving (1 pancake): 80 calories, 1.5 g. total fat (0 g. saturated fat), 0 mg. cholesterol, 290 mg. sodium, 13 g. carbohydrate, 2 g. fiber, 2 g. sugars, 4 g. protein. **Daily Values:** 2% vitamin A, 0% vitamin C, 8% calcium, 4% iron. **Diabetic Exchanges:** 1 bread.

Serving Idea: Spread peanut butter or almond butter on pancakes if desired. Serve with pure maple syrup or blueberry sauce.

Spelt Pancakes: Replace whole-wheat flour with 1¼ cups spelt flour.

Kamut Pancakes: Replace whole-wheat flour with 1 cup plus 2 tablespoons kamut flour. Increase oil to 2 tablespoons.

Cornmeal Pancakes: Omit whole-wheat pastry flour and increase whole-wheat flour to ⅔ cup. Add ⅔ cup stone-ground cornmeal.

Multigrain Pancakes: Replace whole-wheat and pastry flours with 1¼ cups whole-wheat flour, ¼ cup oat bran or quick oats, ¼ cup wheat germ, and 2 tablespoons rye, rice, barley, or buckwheat flour.

Almond Pancakes: Add 3 tablespoons finely ground almonds.

Pancakes Made With Milk: Replace buttermilk and milk with 1½ cups low-fat milk and 2 tablespoons lemon juice.

Nondairy Pancakes: Replace buttermilk and milk with 1½ cups nondairy milk and 2 tablespoons lemon juice.

Egg-free Pancakes: Replace egg with 1 tablespoon egg-replacement powder, 1 tablespoon soy flour, or 1 teaspoon Egz-Actor. The batter will be extra thick, but do not thin it.

Orange Pancakes: Omit the sugar. Replace the buttermilk and low-fat milk with 1½ cups orange juice.

Additions: 1. One half to 1 cup blueberries, diced apples, or dates. **2.** One quarter cup nuts, trail mix, or granola. **3.** One half teaspoon cinnamon.

Buttermilk Waffles: Increase oil to 2 tablespoons. Heat waffle iron on medium heat. For 7-inch round waffles, pour ⅔-cup batter into the center of hot waffle iron, spreading batter out to the edges. Bake waffle about 6 minutes, until golden brown; serve hot.

Pancake and Waffle Mix: Store the dry ingredients in labeled and dated airtight container at room temperature for up to 2 weeks, or in the refrigerator or freezer for up to 3 months. For a more complete mix, add 4 teaspoons pasteurized dried egg whites, replacing fluid eggs with ¼ cup water when adding liquid ingredients.

ABOUT WHOLE-GRAIN MUFFINS

- The easiest way to make a quantity of chopped orange peel is to peel a washed orange (preferably organic) with a vegetable peeler. Process the strips of orange peel in a blender until finely ground. Measure the amount needed and freeze the extra orange peel for up to 6 months.

- Fill muffin cups so the curve of the batter is slightly above the rim.

- Use a spring-handled scoop for quickly forming evenly shaped muffins. You can purchase scoops at restaurant supply or kitchen specialty stores. Use a No. 16 scoop (¼ cup) for regular muffins or a No. 40 scoop (1½ tablespoons) for mini muffins.

- Chill extra batter immediately for the best leavening and keeping quality.
- Refrigerator muffin batters work best if they are thick, contain a small amount of baking soda, and include an acidic ingredient such as citrus, yogurt, or buttermilk.
- For convenience, label extra batter with a use-by date.

ORANGE-DATE-PUMPKIN MUFFINS

Make muffins at a moment's notice with this make-ahead batter.

1 (15-ounce) can pumpkin puree (about 1¾ cups)

OR

2 cups homemade pumpkin puree

1½ cups chopped pitted dates

½ cup orange juice concentrate

¼ cup water

2 teaspoons vanilla

1½ tablespoons finely chopped orange peel

2 cups whole-wheat pastry flour or whole-wheat flour

PREP:
15 MINUTES

BAKE:
12–20 MINUTES, DEPENDING ON SIZE

YIELD:
22 MUFFINS OR 44 MINI MUFFINS

2 cups unbleached all-purpose flour

½ cup chopped walnuts or pecans

4 teaspoons baking powder, preferably aluminum-free

1 teaspoon salt

2 teaspoons cinnamon or pumpkin pie spice

¼ teaspoon baking soda

1 cup brown sugar or other sweetener

⅓ cup oil

½ cup cholesterol-free egg product

OR

2 eggs

OR

3 egg whites

Preheat the oven to 400° F. Coat muffin pans with cooking spray. Combine the pumpkin, dates, orange juice concentrate, water, vanilla, and orange peel; set aside. In a separate bowl, combine the flour, nuts, baking powder, salt, cinnamon or pumpkin pie spice, and baking soda; set aside. In a large bowl, stir the sugar, oil and eggs. Stir in half the dry ingredients. Stir in half the pumpkin mixture. Working in batches, stir in the remaining ingredients, alternating the dry and wet ingredients. Batter will be fairly thick. Scoop the batter into muffin pans. Promptly refrigerate unused batter in an airtight container that has been labeled and dated. Bake within 7 days (for best results, within 3 to 4 days).

Bake for 15 to 18 minutes (11 to 13 minutes for mini muffins), or until a wooden pick comes out dry when inserted in the center. Store muffins, covered, at room temperature for up to 3 days, or in the freezer for up to 3 months.

Nutrition Facts per Serving (1 muffin): 200 calories, 5 g. total fat (0 g. saturated fat), 0 mg. cholesterol, 220 mg. sodium, 37 g. carbohydrate, 3 g. fiber, 19 g. sugars, 4 g. protein. **Daily Values:** 60% vitamin A, 8% vitamin C, 10% calcium, 8% iron. **Diabetic Exchanges:** 1 bread, 1 fruit, ½ other carbohydrate, 1 fat.

Serving Idea: Serve for breakfast with five-grain cereal and fresh strawberries. For lunch or dinner, serve with lentil soup and a salad.

Orange–Cranberry Muffins: Replace: pumpkin with 1½ cups unsweetened applesauce; dates with dried cranberries.

Cherry-Almond Muffins: Replace: pumpkin with 1½ cups unsweetened applesauce; orange juice concentrate with ½ cup buttermilk or plain nonfat yogurt; dates with dried cherries; and walnuts with sliced almonds. Omit orange rind, and replace vanilla with 1 teaspoon natural almond flavoring (or ½ teaspoon almond extract.)

Banana Muffins: Replace: pumpkin with 2 cups mashed banana (about 3 large). Replace dates with raisins. Omit orange peel. Replace cinnamon with 1 teaspoon grated nutmeg. Decrease sugar to ¾ cup. Replace orange juice concentrate and water with ⅔ cup milk and 1 tablespoon lemon juice.

Lemon–Zucchini Muffins: Replace: pumpkin with grated zucchini; dates with currants; orange juice concentrate with ¼ cup lemon juice and 1 cup milk; orange rind with lemon rind; cinnamon with ½ teaspoon ginger and ½ teaspoon nutmeg. Increase sweetening to 1⅓ cups.

Whole-Grain Muffins: Replace unbleached all-purpose flour with whole-wheat flour, or use 2 cups whole-wheat flour and 2 cups barley flour.

Egg-free Muffins: Omit cholesterol-free egg product or eggs (works best for mini muffins) or add 1 tablespoon egg-replacement powder.

Wheat-free Muffins: Replace flour with 1 cup brown rice flour,

½ cup white rice flour, and ½ cup tapioca flour.

Muffin Mix: Stir together dry ingredients. Add dried fruit and nuts, if desired. For a more complete mix, add 1 tablespoon dried egg whites and 1 teaspoon vanilla powder. Add remaining ingredients when preparing muffins.

Nut Topping: Before baking, sprinkle muffins with finely chopped walnuts or pecans.

Quick Bread: Coat an 8½" x 4½" x 2½" loaf pan with cooking spray. Spoon in 3 cups batter. Bake at 350° F for 50 to 60 minutes until wooden pick comes out dry when inserted in center. Cool completely on wire rack before slicing.

Lemon–Blueberry Muffins: Replace pumpkin, orange juice concentrate, and water with 1¼ cups unsweetened applesauce and 2 tablespoons lemon juice. Replace orange peel with lemon peel. Omit cinnamon. Stir in 1½ cups fresh or frozen blueberries tossed with 1 tablespoon all-purpose flour. Use within 3 days.

BREAKFAST ENTRÉES

HEARTY MUFFIN SANDWICHES

Great for breakfast, brunch, or lunch. Quick and easy, especially if your freezer is stocked with English muffins and grated cheese.

4 meatless breakfast links, frozen or canned

2 cups Scrambled Tofu (p. 182)

¼ cup chopped tomato

¼ cup reduced-fat mozzarella cheese or nondairy cheese

4 whole-wheat English muffins

PREP:
10 MINUTES

COOK:
5 MINUTES

YIELD:
4 SERVINGS

Prepare one recipe Scrambled Tofu. Cook the breakfast links according to package directions. Stir tomato and cheese into the tofu; heat over medium heat until the cheese melts. (Or cover and microwave on high 2 to 3 minutes, or until hot.) Split and toast English muffins. Cut the links in half, lengthwise.

Assembly: Place on each toasted muffin-bottom: ¼ cup Scrambled Tofu, 2 link halves, and muffin top.

Nutrition Facts per Serving (1 sandwich): 260 calories, 7 g. total fat (1.5 g. saturated fat), 5 mg. cholesterol, 1,090 mg. sodium, 32 g. carbohydrate, 4 g. fiber, 3 g. sugars, 19 g. protein. **Daily Values:** 2% vitamin A, 4% vitamin C, 20% calcium, 25% iron. **Diabetic Exchanges:** ½ sandwich = 1 lean meat, 1 protein.

Serving Idea: Good with oven-browned red potato

wedges and cantaloupe cubes mixed with fresh blueberries.

Hearty Muffin Sandwiches With Salsa: Replace tomatoes with salsa.

Additions: Cook with the Scrambled Tofu: ½ cup coarsely chopped zucchini and ¼ teaspoon dried basil.

Hearty Breakfast Burrito: Omit English muffins. Wrap ingredients in flour tortillas.

ABOUT SCRAMBLED TOFU

- Try the mini mix version of the seasoning mix before making the mega mix.
- Tofu packages come in a variety of sizes. Use these Scrambled Tofu Seasoning amounts as a guide:

Tofu Package	Scrambled Tofu Seasoning
12.3-ounce shelf-stable extra firm	1 tablespoon plus 2¼ teaspoons
14-ounce water pack	2 tablespoons
16-ounce water pack	2 tablespoons plus ¾ teaspoon
19-ounce water pack	2 tablespoons plus 2 teaspoons

- If the Scrambled Tofu is too watery, stir in 1 teaspoon flour and cook longer.
- Do not add frozen chopped onion unless sautéed first, because freezing intensifies the flavor and overwhelms the delicate flavors of the scrambled tofu.
- Scrambled tofu becomes more chewy and watery if frozen.

SCRAMBLED TOFU SEASONING MIX

Convenient and versatile, this mix even tastes good on popcorn!

4 teaspoons *(⅓ cup)* **vegetarian chicken-style seasoning**

4 teaspoons *(⅓ cup)* **nutritional yeast flakes**

1 teaspoon *(4 teaspoons)* **whole-wheat or brown rice flour**

1 teaspoon *(4 teaspoons)* **onion powder**

½ teaspoon *(2 teaspoons)* **salt**

¼ teaspoon *(1 teaspoon)* **garlic powder**

¼ teaspoon *(1 teaspoon)* **turmeric**

PREP:
5 MINUTES

YIELD:
¼ CUP (MINI MIX)
1 CUP (MEGA MIX)

Combine ingredients in an airtight container; label and date. Store in a cool, dry place for up to 6 months.

Nutrition Facts per Serving (1 teaspoon): 10 calories, 0 g. total fat (0 g. saturated fat), 0 mg. cholesterol, 420 mg. sodium, 2 g. carbohydrate, 0 g. fiber, 1 g. sugars, 1 g. protein. **Daily Values:** 0% vitamin A, 0% vitamin C, 0% calcium, 0% iron. **Diabetic Exchanges:** free.

SCRAMBLED TOFU

Delicious served hot as an entrée for breakfast . . . or any meal! Use it any way you would use scrambled eggs—with no cholesterol!

PREP:
5 MINUTES

COOK:
5 MINUTES

YIELD:
4 (½-CUP)
SERVINGS

1 (14-ounce) package firm tofu

2 tablespoons Scrambled Tofu Seasoning Mix

Drain the tofu well, and place it in a large non-stick skillet. Mash the tofu into even-sized pieces and add the seasoning, mixing until evenly distributed. Over medium-high heat, stir mixture occasionally; cook until the tofu turns bright yellow and the liquid is absorbed, about 4 to 5 minutes. Taste and adjust seasoning. Serve hot.

Store in an airtight container in the refrigerator for up to 5 days or in the freezer for up to 3 months.

Nutrition Facts per Serving (½ cup): 80 calories, 3.5 g. total fat (0.5 g. saturated fat), 0 mg. cholesterol, 630 mg. sodium, 5 g. carbohydrate, 0 g. fiber, 1 g. sugars, 8 g. protein. **Daily Values:** 0% vitamin A, 0% vitamin C, 10% calcium, 8% iron. **Diabetic Exchanges:** 1 lean meat.

Serving Ideas: For breakfast, serve with oven fries, whole-wheat toast, and strawberries. For lunch or dinner, serve with steamed red potatoes, green beans, and a salad.

Fresh Herbs: Just before serving, stir in 1 tablespoon chopped fresh basil, cilantro, chives, or parsley.

Additions: ¼ cup sautéed chopped onions, chopped green onion, sliced mushrooms, chopped red or green bell pepper, chopped tomato or salsa, or 1 to 2 cups cooked diced potatoes.

Microwave: Pat tofu dry with a paper towel. Combine ingredients in a 1-quart microwave-safe dish. Cover, and cook on high for 3 minutes. Stir, and cook another 2 to 3 minutes, or until heated through.

Breakfast Burrito: Wrap ingredients in a whole-wheat tortilla and serve with salsa, cheese or nondairy cheese, and sliced green onions.

Pocket Sandwich Filling: Mix 1 cup Scrambled Tofu with 1 tablespoon low-fat mayonnaise. Add chopped pickles, diced celery, and onion. Serve in pocket bread topped with sliced cucumbers, alfalfa sprouts, or chopped lettuce. Good with tomato soup.

SCRAMBLED TOFU FIESTA

Ask your family or guests if they want more—and they're sure to say "¡Si!"

2 cups Scrambled Tofu (p. 182)

½ cup salsa

2 medium-size red potatoes, cooked and sliced (about 2 cups)

1 green onion, sliced (about ¼ cup)

¼ cup (1 ounce) reduced-fat mozzarella cheese or nondairy cheese

2 tablespoons chopped cilantro

PREP:
10 MINUTES

COOK:
5 MINUTES

YIELD:
4 (½-CUP)
SERVINGS

Prepare Scrambled Tofu in a large nonstick skillet. While tofu is cooking, stir in salsa, potatoes, and green onion; heat thoroughly. Stir in the cheese, and heat until it melts. Just before serving, stir in cilantro. Serve hot.

Nutrition Facts per Serving (1 cup): 180 calories, 5 g. total fat (1.5 g. saturated fat), 5 mg. cholesterol, 810 mg. sodium, 23 g. carbohydrate, 3 g. fiber, 2 g. sugars, 12 g. protein. **Daily Values:** 8% vitamin A, 30% vitamin C, 20 % calcium, 10% iron. **Diabetic Exchanges:** ⅔ cup = 1 medium-fat meat, 1 bread.

Serving Ideas: Serve with whole-grain muffins and grapefruit for breakfast or brunch. For lunch or dinner, serve with green beans and a salad.

Microwave: Prepare Scrambled Tofu in a 2-quart microwave-safe dish. Stir in salsa, potatoes, and green onion. Cover, and microwave on high 3 to 5 minutes, or until hot. Stir in cheese. Cook 1 minute, or until cheese melts. Stir in cilantro, and serve.

Frozen Potato Wedges: Cover, and increase cooking time by 5 minutes, or until potatoes are soft and hot.

Scrambled Tofu Fiesta Burrito: Omit potatoes and use as a filling for flour tortillas.

Fiesta Stuffed Potatoes: Cut open 4 hot baked potatoes. Place ¼ cup Scrambled Tofu on each potato, topping each with 1 tablespoon salsa, 1 tablespoon reduced-fat cheese or nondairy cheese, 1 tablespoon sliced green onions, 1½ teaspoons chopped cilantro, and 1 tablespoon reduced-fat sour cream or nondairy sour cream.

FRUIT
SPREADS
AND SAUCES

BLUEBERRY SAUCE

A scrumptious, low-sugar topping for pancakes or waffles.

1 cup apple juice

OR

¼ cup apple juice concentrate plus ¾ cup water

2 cups fresh or frozen blueberries

2 tablespoons cornstarch or modified cornstarch

1½ tablespoons water

1 tablespoon granulated sugar or other sweetener (or to taste)

PREP:
5 MINUTES

COOK:
5 MINUTES

YIELD:
8 (¼-CUP)
SERVINGS

Combine apple juice and blueberries in a saucepan and heat until boiling. Dissolve the cornstarch in water, and stir into boiling berries. Return to a boil, stirring constantly. Reduce heat, and simmer 1 to 2 minutes, stirring constantly until mixture is clear and thickened. Stir in sweetener. Taste, and adjust sweetness.

Nutrition Facts per Serving (¼ cup): 45 calories, 0 g. total fat (0 g. saturated fat), 0 mg. cholesterol, 0 mg. sodium, 11 g. carbohydrate, 1 g. fiber, 8 g. sugars, 0 g. protein. **Daily Values:** 0% vitamin A, 8% vitamin C, 0% calcium, 0% iron. **Diabetic Exchanges:** ¾ fruit (6 tablespoons = 1 fruit).

Serving Idea: Serve warm sauce over pancakes, waffles, or toast. Serve cool sauce over vanilla or tofu pudding. Stir leftovers into plain or vanilla yogurt.

Variations: ½ teaspoon grated lemon rind or orange rind; ½ teaspoon lemon juice to intensify the fruit flavor.

Fruit Juice-sweetened Sauce: Replace apple juice with ½ cup apple juice concentrate and ½ cup water. Omit sweetener.

Strawberry Sauce: Replace blueberries with sliced fresh or frozen strawberries,

Peach Sauce: Replace: blueberries with sliced, peeled peaches; apple juice with peach juice; and add ½ teaspoon natural almond flavoring or ¼ teaspoon almond extract.

Raspberry Sauce (1½ cups): Replace blueberries with fresh or frozen and thawed raspberries. In a blender, process raspberries for 1 minute. Pour sauce through strainer into a saucepan to remove seeds before proceeding with recipe. Increase sweetener to ¼ cup, or to taste.

Microwave: In a 4-cup liquid measure, microwave juice and fruit on high until hot, about 3 to 4 minutes. Stir in dissolved cornstarch. Microwave on high 1 to 2 minutes, stirring after each minute, until thickened.

FREEZER STRAWBERRY JAM

This easy no-cook jam uses a fraction of the sugar. (A traditional recipe uses four cups of sugar!) Sugar is best used as a flavor enhancer, not a food.

4 cups fresh strawberries, rinsed and hulled (or frozen and thawed)

½ cup granulated sugar or other sweetener, or to taste

¼ cup precooked cornstarch powder

1 teaspoon lemon juice

PREP:
10 MINUTES

YIELD:
2 CUPS

Using a potato masher or fork, mash strawberries in a bowl. Combine sweetener and cornstarch in a small bowl, stirring until thoroughly mixed; stir into strawberries. Stir lemon juice into strawberries; let stand 10 minutes. Check consistency and sweetness; adjust, if needed.

Pour the jam into freezer containers, leaving ½-inch headspace; label and date. Freeze jam for up to 1 year, or refrigerate for up to 2 weeks.

Nutrition Facts per Serving (1 tablespoon): 15 calories, 0 g. total fat (0 g. saturated fat), 0 mg. cholesterol, 0 mg. sodium, 3 g. carbohydrate, 0 g. fiber, 2 g. sugars, 0 g protein. **Daily Values:** 0% vitamin A, 15% vitamin C, 0% calcium, 0% iron. **Diabetic Exchanges:** free.

Blender Strawberry Jam (2 cups): Reduce strawberries to 3 cups and replace sugar with 1 cup apple juice concentrate. Process in blender or food processor until smooth.

> **Nutrition Facts per serving (1 tablespoon):** 20 calories, 0 g total fat (0 g saturated fat), 0 mg cholesterol, 0 mg sodium, 5 g carbohydrate, 0 g fiber, 4 g sugars, 0 g protein. **Daily Values:** 0% vitamin A, 15% vitamin C, 0% calcium, 0% iron. **Diabetic Exchanges:** free

Cooked Strawberry Jam: Replace precooked cornstarch powder with cornstarch or modified cornstarch. Stir and cook over medium heat until thickened. Remove from heat and stir in lemon juice. (Or microwave strawberries and sugar 2 minutes, or until hot. Dissolve cornstarch in equal amount of water and stir into strawberries. Microwave on high for about 5 minutes, or until thickened, stirring every minute. Stir in lemon juice.)

Freezer Peach Jam: Replace strawberries with peeled, chopped peaches. Add 1 teaspoon vitamin C to decrease browning.

MAPLE PANCAKE TOPPING

Great on pancakes and waffles.

1 cup apple juice

4 teaspoons natural maple flavoring

OR

½ teaspoon imitation maple flavoring

4 teaspoons cornstarch or modified
cornstarch

4 teaspoons water

1-4 tablespoons granulated sugar or other
sweetener

PREP:
5 MINUTES

YIELD:
1 CUP

Bring apple juice and maple flavoring to a boil in a saucepan. Dissolve cornstarch in water, then stir into boiling juice. Reduce heat, and simmer 1 to 2 minutes, stirring constantly, until slightly thickened. Remove from heat and stir in sweetener. Taste and adjust sweetening. Serve hot over pancakes, waffles, or French toast. Refrigerate for up to 1 week.

Nutrition Facts per Serving (2 tablespoons): 20 calories, 0 g. total fat (0 g. saturated fat), 0 mg. cholesterol, 0 mg. sodium, 5 g. carbohydrate, 0 g. fiber, 4 g. sugars, 0 g. protein. **Daily Values:** 0% vitamin A, 0% vitamin C, 0% calcium, 0% iron. **Diabetic Exchanges:** free.

MICROWAVE APPLESAUCE

*Great for breakfast. Sweeter varieties of apples such as
Golden Delicious often require no additional sweetening.*

PREP:
15 MINUTES

COOK:
10 MINUTES

YIELD:
2¼ CUPS

2½ pounds apples (about 8 medium)

1 teaspoon vanilla, optional

½ teaspoon cinnamon, optional

**granulated sugar or other sweetener,
optional**

Wash, peel, core, and slice apples (or use an apple
wedger to speed the process). Place 8 cups prepared
apples in a microwave-safe casserole dish. Cover and
microwave on high for 5 minutes. Stir apples and
rotate dish. Depending on variety of apple, microwave
5 minutes more, or until apples are tender. Let stand
2 to 3 minutes. If desired, stir in vanilla or cinnamon.
Taste and sweeten, if desired. Serve warm, or chill before serving. Cover and refrigerate for up to 1 week,
or freeze in an airtight container for up to 1 year.

Nutrition Facts per Serving (½ cup): 130 calories, 0 g.
total fat (0 g. saturated fat), 0 mg. cholesterol, 0 mg. sodium, 34 g.
carbohydrate, 7 g. fiber, 26 g. sugars, 1 g. protein. **Daily Values:**
2% vitamin A, 2% vitamin C, 2% calcium, 2% iron. **Diabetic
Exchanges:** 2 fruits.

Cranberry Applesauce: Add 1 cup fresh or frozen cranberries, and 2 tablespoons sugar, or to taste.

Raspberry Applesauce: Add 1 cup fresh or frozen raspberries, and 2 tablespoons sugar, or to taste.

Stove Top Applesauce: Heat apples in a saucepan over medium heat with ½ cup water (or as needed) until boiling. Cover and simmer, stirring occasionally, about 10 minutes, or until apples are tender.

Slow Cooker Applesauce: Place apples and ¼ to ½ cup water in slow cooker. Cover and cook on high 3 to 4 hours, or on low 6 to 8 hours, or until apples are tender. (Expect a darker applesauce.)

Food Mill Method: Do not peel apples. After they are cooked, process apples through a food mill to remove the peelings.

Pressure Cooker Applesauce: Place prepared apples and ½ cup water or apple juice in pressure cooker. Lock on lid and bring to high pressure over high heat. Remove from heat and allow pressure to drop naturally, about 10 minutes. Release any remaining steam. Remove lid and stir.

ORANGE-PINEAPPLE SAUCE

Especially attractive garnished with shredded coconut.

PREP:
5 MINUTES

COOK:
5 MINUTES

YIELD:
3 CUPS

2 cups orange juice

1 cup canned crushed pineapple

2 teaspoons grated orange rind, preferably organic

3 tablespoons cornstarch or modified cornstarch

3 tablespoon water

2-4 tablespoons granulated sugar or other sweetener

Bring orange juice, crushed pineapple, and orange rind to a boil in a saucepan. Dissolve cornstarch in water. Stir cornstarch mixture into saucepan, stirring constantly until thickened, about 1 minute. Taste and sweeten, as desired. Place in an airtight container, and store in the refrigerator for up to 1 week or in the freezer for up to 6 months.

Nutrition Facts per Serving (¼ cup): 40 calories, 0 g. total fat (0 g. saturated fat), 0 mg. cholesterol, 0 mg. sodium, 10 g. carbohydrate, 0 g. fiber, 8 g. sugars, 0 g. protein. **Daily Values:** 0% vitamin A, 30% vitamin C, 0% calcium, 0% iron. **Diabetic Exchanges:** 6 tablespoons = 1 fruit.

Serving Idea: Serve hot over pancakes, waffles, French toast, or toast.

Microwave: In a 4-cup liquid measure, microwave orange juice, pineapple, and orange rind on high for 3 to 4 minutes, or until hot. Stir in dissolved cornstarch. Microwave on high 3 to 5 minutes, stirring after each minute, until thickened. Stir in sweetening.

Orange Flavoring: Replace grated orange rind with 1 teaspoon natural orange flavoring or ½ teaspoon orange extract.

TROPICAL TOPPING

A quick sauce for waffles, pancakes, or toast.

1 (20-ounce) can crushed pineapple or pineapple chunks

1 medium peeled banana, fresh or frozen

¼ cup shredded coconut, preferably unsweetened

¼ teaspoon coconut flavoring

PREP:
5 MINUTES

YIELD:
2½ CUPS

Process ingredients in blender until smooth. Pour into a microwave-safe bowl and microwave on high for 3 minutes, or until hot. (Or heat in a saucepan over medium heat.) Serve hot over waffles, pancakes, or toast. Place in an airtight container, and store in the refrigerator for up to 1 week, or in the freezer for up to 6 months.

Nutrition Facts per Serving (¼ cup): 40 calories, 1.5 g. total fat (1 g. saturated fat), 0 mg. cholesterol, 0 mg. sodium, 8 g. carbohydrate, 1 g. fiber, 7 g. sugars, 0 g. protein. **Daily Values:** 0% vitamin A, 10% vitamin C, 0% calcium, 2% iron. **Diabetic Exchanges:** ½ fruit.

Piña Colada Topping: Omit the banana.

Thicker Sauce: Drain the pineapple juice, add 1½ teaspoons precooked cornstarch powder while blending, or dissolve 1½ teaspoons cornstarch in 1½ teaspoons water and add while heating.

Frozen Tropical Fruit Pops: Pour leftover sauce into fruit pop molds and freeze.

FRUITS AND
DESSERTS

APPLE PIE

An apple-wedger can speed the preparation. And you won't miss the refined sugar in this all-time favorite dessert.

Pastry dough for 9-inch double-crust pie

¾ cup apple juice concentrate, divided

¾ teaspoon cinnamon

1 teaspoon vanilla extract

¼ cup cornstarch or modified cornstarch

7½ cups Golden Delicious Apples (3 pounds)

PREP:
30 MINUTES

BAKE:
50 MINUTES

YIELD:
9-INCH PIE
(8 SERVINGS)

Combine apple juice concentrate, cinnamon, vanilla, and cornstarch in a large saucepan. Set aside. Peel, core, and cut apples into ½-inch slices. Add apple slices to saucepan and bring to a boil over high heat, stirring frequently. Boil, stirring constantly until the liquid is thickened and clear, about 1 minute. Remove pan from the heat.

Adjust oven racks to the low and middle position, and preheat oven to 375°F. Roll out 1 ball of dough between two sheets of lightly floured wax paper into a 12-inch circle, about ⅛-inch thick. Ease dough into a 9-inch glass pie pan. Fill the pie shell with apple filling. Brush the edge of the bottom crust with water. Roll out the remaining dough into a 10-inch circle and lay it on the top. Press the edges together and trim with kitchen scissors to ½-inch larger than the pie pan. Tuck the dough under so it is even with the pan lip. Flute or press with fork tines to seal. Cut 3 or 4 vent holes.

Place a foil-lined baking sheet on the lowest rack to catch drips. Bake the pie on the middle rack until the crust is golden and apples are tender when pierced with a knife, about 50 minutes. Tent the crust with aluminum foil if it starts to brown too quickly. Transfer the pie to a wire rack to cool.

Nutrition Facts per Serving (1 slice): 440 calories, 15 g. total fat (1 g. saturated fat), 0 mg. cholesterol, 160 mg. sodium, 72 g. carbohydrate, 5 g. fiber, 31 g. sugars, 6 g. protein. **Daily Values:** 2% vitamin A, 2% vitamin C, 2% calcium, 15% iron. **Diabetic Exchanges:** ½ slice = 1 bread, 1½ fruits, 1½ fats.

Sparkly Crust: Before baking, spray top of piecrust with cooking spray. Sprinkle with turbinado sugar.

Sweeter Apple Pie: Boil 1¼ cups apple juice concentrate until reduced to ¾ cup. Or add ¼ cup granulated sugar or other sweetener, or to taste.

BROWNIES

Double-chocolate, rich-tasting brownies, yet low in fat.

1¼ cups granulated sugar or other sweetener

¾ cup cake flour

⅔ cup semisweet chocolate chips

½ cup unsweetened Dutch-processed cocoa powder

½ teaspoon baking powder

½ teaspoon salt

½ cup cholesterol-free egg product

OR

2 eggs

OR

3 egg whites

¼ cup margarine, melted

1 tablespoon water

2 teaspoons vanilla extract

PREP:
10 MINUTES

BAKE:
30 MINUTES

YIELD:
16 SERVINGS

Preheat oven to 325°F. Coat a 9-inch square glass baking pan with cooking spray. Set aside. Whisk dry ingredients together in a mixing bowl. Stir liquid ingredients together, then stir into dry ingredients. Spoon batter into the prepared pan. Bake at 325°F for 30 minutes. Cool on a wire rack before cutting into squares. Store in an airtight container at room temperature for up to 5 days or in the refrigerator for up to 1 week or in the freezer for up to 6 months.

Nutrition Facts per Serving (1 brownie): 160 calories, 5 g. total fat (2 g. saturated fat), 0 mg. cholesterol, 135 mg. sodium, 27 g. carbohydrate, 1 g. fiber, 19 g. sugars, 2 g. protein. **Daily Values:** 4% vitamin A, 0% vitamin C, 2% calcium, 10% iron. **Diabetic Exchanges:** 2 other carbohydrate, 1 fat.

Nuts: Add ½ cup chopped walnuts, pecans, or macadamia nuts.

Mint: Add ¼ cup crushed hard peppermint candy or candy cane.

Whole-Grain Brownies: Replace the cake flour with whole-wheat pastry flour.

Brownie Mix: Combine the dry ingredients in an airtight container for up to 6 months. Label with instructions. (For a more complete mix, add 2 tablespoons powdered egg whites, 2 teaspoons vanilla powder. Before baking, increase the water to 3 tablespoons when adding liquid ingredients.)

Vegan Carob Brownies: Reduce sugar to 1 cup. Replace cake flour with whole-wheat pastry flour. Replace chocolate chips with carob chips. Replace cocoa powder with sifted carob powder. Replace eggs with 1 tablespoon egg-replacement powder and 3 tablespoons water. Increase melted margarine (vegan) to ⅓ cup.

CRISPY PEANUT BUTTER BARS

A kid-friendly dessert.

½ **cup honey or other liquid sweetener**

½ **cup peanut butter, preferably natural**

½–⅔ **cup nonfat dry milk**

OR

¼–⅓ **cup nondairy milk powder**

1 **teaspoon vanilla extract**

4 **cups crispy rice cereal**

PREP:
10 MINUTES

CHILL:
1 HOUR

YIELD:
16 SQUARES

Heat the honey in a microwave-safe mixing bowl for 1 to 1½ minutes or until bubbly. Add the peanut butter, milk powder, and vanilla. Stir in the cereal until uniformly coated. Press the mixture into an 8- or 9-inch square pan until evenly distributed. Refrigerate until firm, about 1 hour. Cut into 16 squares. Store in an airtight container at room temperature for up to 3 days, or refrigerate for up to 2 weeks, or freeze for up to 3 months.

Nutrition Facts per Serving (1 square): 110 calories, 4 g. total fat (0.5 g. saturated fat), 0 mg. cholesterol, 105 mg. sodium, 17 g. carbohydrate, 0 g. fiber, 11 g. sugars, 3 g. protein. **Daily Values:** 4% vitamin A, 6% vitamin C, 4% calcium, 4% iron. **Diabetic Exchanges:** 1 fat, 1 other carbohydrate.

Crispy Peanut Butter Bars With Chocolate: Allow mixture to cool for 30 minutes before stirring in ½ cup chocolate or carob chips.

Nuts: Stir in ⅓ cup chopped walnuts, pecans, or almonds.

Crispy Almond Butter Bars: Replace peanut butter with almond butter.

Crispy Balls: Chill mixture for 30 minutes, then form into balls.

Stove Top: Heat the honey in a medium saucepan over low heat until bubbly. Remove from heat and proceed with recipe.

Firmer Texture: For a firmer texture, add more milk powder and keep refrigerated.

FRUIT CRUMBLE

Oats in the topping make this a crumble rather than a crisp.
Keep extra topping in the refrigerator or freezer to
make a quick dessert (2 cups topping per fruit crumble).

PREP:
20 MINUTES

BAKE:
30-40 MINUTES

YIELD:
MINI MIX:
6 SERVINGS
(2 CUPS)
MEGA MIX:
24 SERVINGS
(8 CUPS)

6 tablespoons *(1½ cups)* **whole-wheat pastry flour or whole-wheat flour**

⅓ cup *(1⅓ cup)* **packed light brown sugar or other sweetener**

¼ teaspoon *(1 teaspoon)* **salt**

½ teaspoon *(2 teaspoons)* **cinnamon**

¾ cup *(3 cups)* **quick or rolled oats**

¼ cup *(1 cup)* **chopped pecans or walnuts**

¼ cup *(1 cup)* **softened margarine or butter**

6 cups *(24 cups)* **sliced apples, pears, peaches, nectarines, or plums**

2 tablespoons *(½ cup)* **granulated sugar or other sweetener**

Preheat the oven to 375°F. Combine flour, sugar, salt, cinnamon, oats, and nuts. Using a pastry blender or two table knives, mix in margarine or butter. Refrigerate the topping mixture while preparing fruit. Stored in an airtight container at this stage, the mixture may be refrigerated for up to 1 month or frozen for up to 3 months.

Combine the fruit and sugar in an 8-inch square baking pan (or a 13" x 9" pan for a double recipe, or two 13" x 9" pans for the mega mix). Sprinkle topping evenly over fruit. Bake at 375°F for 30 to 40 minutes or until fruit bubbles and the topping is light brown. Serve warm or at room temperature. Cover and refrigerate for up to 3 days.

Nutrition Facts per Serving (1 cup): 240 calories, 12 g. total fat (2 g. saturated fat), 0 mg. cholesterol, 190 mg. sodium, 33 g. carbohydrate, 4 g. fiber, 19 g. sugars, 3 g. protein. **Daily Values:** 8% vitamin A, 8% vitamin C, 2% calcium, 6% iron. **Diabetic Exchanges:** 1 bread, 1 fruit, 2 fats.

Apple-Raspberry: 5 cups peeled, sliced apples, and 1 cup raspberries.

Peach-Blueberry: 5 cups peeled, sliced peaches, and 1 cup blueberries.

Pear-Cranberry: 5 cups peeled, thick-sliced pears, ½ cup dried cranberries, and ½ teaspoon minced orange peel.

Strawberry-Rhubarb: 4 cups hulled and quartered strawberries, 2 cups ¼-inch slices rhubarb, and 1 tablespoon quick-cooking tapioca. Increase sugar to ⅓ cup.

Three-Berry: 3 cups blueberries, 2 cups raspberries, and 1 cup blackberries, and 1 tablespoon quick-cooking tapioca. Increase sugar to ¼ cup.

Plums or Berries: Thicken juicy fruits with 1 tablespoon quick-cooking tapioca.

FRUIT DESSERT IDEAS

Fruit is the natural dessert!

Baked Apples: Core 4 baking apples with a melon baller and place the apples in a casserole dish. Stuff dates or raisins in the center of each apple. Pour ¾ cup apple juice, or pineapple juice, or ½ cup pure maple syrup over apples. Bake, uncovered, at 425°F for 35 to 45 minutes, or until tender. (Or cover apples, and microwave on high for 5 minutes, rotating ¼ turn halfway through cooking.) Let apples rest, covered, for 5 minutes. Test for doneness. Cook 1 to 2 minutes longer if needed.

Smoothies: Pour a small amount of juice or milk into the blender. With the blender running, add frozen banana chunks, a few at a time, until smooth. Add fresh or frozen strawberries (or other fruit). Sweeten, if desired. Serve immediately. Options: freeze in popsicle molds or in an ice cream freezer, or freeze, and put through ice shaver.

Stuffed Dates: Select moist dates. Remove the pit, and stuff with a walnut or pecan half.

Grapesicles: Freeze seedless grapes on a cookie sheet; place them in freezer container. Eat frozen or slightly thawed. (Or freeze pitted cherries.)

Ambrosia: Combine fresh, cool, juicy fruit in a glass bowl. Garnish with coconut.

Fruit Pockets: Spread a thin layer of peanut butter and honey inside pocket bread. Add a few chopped dates, raisins, or dried figs. Fill pocket bread with sliced bananas.

Papaya: Cut a ripe papaya in half lengthwise. Fill with blueberries. Top with your favorite whipped topping. Garnish with a lime wedge.

Honeydew Berry Boats: Cut a ripe honeydew melon in half horizontally and remove the seeds. Cut each half into 3 wedges. Spoon sliced strawberries into the center of each wedge. Garnish with fresh mint sprigs.

Frozen Fruit Circles: Freeze an unopened can of juice-sweet-ened fruit cocktail. Just before serving, run hot water over the can briefly. Open both ends of the can, push contents from one end, and slice. Serve slices on a bed of green leaf lettuce.

Cantaloupe and Blueberries: Combine cantaloupe chunks and fresh blueberries.

Orange Slices: Slice oranges and place on lettuce leaf. Sprinkle with grated coconut.

Parfaits: Layer granola, fresh fruit, and your favorite whipped topping in parfait glasses or goblets.

Stuffed Apples: Combine ¼ cup each granola, milk powder, raisins, peanut butter, and honey. Stuff into 6 cored apples. Cover and refrigerate at least one hour. Great to pack in lunches. Or chill well, and slice into rounds to serve.

Fruit Kabobs: Prepare bite-size pieces of 4 or 5 varieties of fresh fruits, such as strawberries, pineapple, bananas, grapes, apples, or melons. Thread the fruit onto bamboo skewers, alternating colors and shapes; serve on a platter.

Edible Centerpiece: Cut fresh pineapple in half lengthwise, including leaves. Carve out the inside of the pineapple, and cut it into bite-size pieces. Stuff the pineapple shell with pieces of tightly wadded aluminum foil; place cut-side down on a platter lined with leaf lettuce. Insert about 12 fruit kabobs into each pineapple half.

Applesauce: Serve warm, freshly made applesauce with graham crackers or cookies.

FRUIT GELATIN

Kids' favorite—vegetarian version. Vary the flavors with your choice of fruit juice concentrate (grape, raspberry, cherry, and peach) or iced tea concentrate.

PREP:
5 MINUTES

CHILL:
2 HOURS

YIELD:
5 (½-CUP)
SERVINGS

1 cup boiling water

1⅓ tablespoons unflavored vegetarian gelatin

¾ cup fruit juice concentrate

¾ cup cold water

Combine boiling water and gelatin and stir until the gelatin dissolves. Stir in fruit juice concentrate and cold water. Pour into dessert dishes, mold, or bowl, and refrigerate 2 hours or until firm.

Nutrition Facts per Serving (½ cup): 70 calories, 0 g. total fat (0 g. saturated fat), 0 mg. cholesterol, 25 mg. sodium, 16 g. carbohydrate, 0 g. fiber, 15 g. sugars, 2 g. protein. **Daily Values:** 0% vitamin A, 50% vitamin C, 0% calcium, 2% iron. **Diabetic Exchanges:** 1 fruit.

Jiggly Gelatin Geometrics: Increase unflavored gelatin to 2 tablespoons. Omit cold water. Pour into an 8- or 9-inch square glass pan. Refrigerate 1 hour or until firm. Cut into squares, diamonds, or triangles.

Fruited Gelatin: After gelatin is partially set (about 15 minutes), stir in 1 cup chopped fruit.

Lemon Gelatin: Use white grape juice concentrate.

Decrease cold water to ½ cup. Add ¼ cup lemon juice, 1 tablespoon granulated sugar or other sweetener, and 1 teaspoon natural lemon flavoring (or ½ teaspoon lemon extract).

Double Recipe: Use a 12-ounce can of fruit juice concentrate.

FRUIT PIZZA

A picture-perfect dessert.

Icebox Cookie dough, ½ recipe (p. 213)
OR
  **1 (18-ounce) package purchased sugar-
  cookie dough**
  **¾ cup apple juice, light-colored fruit juice,
  or nectar**
  **1 tablespoon cornstarch or modified
  cornstarch**
  **2 tablespoons granulated sugar or other
  sweetener**
  **1 (8-ounce) package light cream cheese (or
  nondairy cream cheese), softened**
  **3 tablespoons granulated sugar or other
  sweetener**

PREP:
30 MINUTES

BAKE:
15–18 MINUTES

CHILL:
1 HOUR

YIELD:
12 SERVINGS

1½ **teaspoons minced orange peel**

1 **teaspoon coconut flavoring or vanilla extract**

2 **kiwifruit, peeled and sliced**

1 **cup fresh raspberries or sliced strawberries**

1 **peach, peeled and sliced**

OR

1 **(8-ounce) can mandarin oranges, drained**

If frozen, remove Icebox Cookie dough from the freezer and thaw it at room temperature for about 10 minutes. Preheat the oven to 350° F. Coat a pizza pan or baking sheet with cooking spray. Coat hands with cooking spray, and shape the dough into a ball. Place the dough on a prepared pan and pat it into a 10-inch circle to a thickness of ⅛ inch. Bake at 350° F 12 to 15 minutes, or until the dough is lightly browned and done in the middle. Let cool in the pan for 10 minutes; transfer to a cooling rack.

Combine the apple juice, cornstarch, and 2 tablespoons sugar in a small saucepan and bring to a boil, stirring frequently. After the mixture boils, cook and stir it for 1 minute. Remove the pan from heat and allow it to cool at least 5 minutes.

Using a hand-held mixer set at high speed, beat the cream cheese, 3 tablespoons sugar, orange peel, and coconut extract until smooth. Transfer the cookie crust to a serving platter. Spread the cream cheese filling evenly over the cooled cookie crust, leaving a ½-inch border around the outer edge. Using a pastry brush, spread a thin layer of the fruit juice glaze over the cream cheese filling. Arrange fruit on top. Brush fruit with the remaining glaze. Chill for 1 hour. Slice and serve.

Nutrition Facts per Serving (½): 130 calories, 4 g. total fat (0.5 g. saturated fat), 0 mg. cholesterol, 105 mg. sodium, 22 g. carbohydrate, 2 g. fiber, 13 g. sugars, 2 g. protein. **Daily Values:** 6% vitamin A, 25% vitamin C, 2% calcium, 4% iron. **Diabetic Exchanges:** 1 other carbohydrate, ½ bread, 1 fat.

Tofu Pudding Filling: Using a mix or your own recipe, replace cream cheese mixture with 1 cup tofu pudding.

Other Ideas: Use grape halves, blueberries, pineapple chunks, banana slices. Garnish with slivered almonds. Use a heart-shaped pan.

Apricot Glaze: Heat ½ cup fruit-sweetened apricot preserves until melted. Stir in 1 tablespoon fruit juice or water. Pour through a strainer for a smoother consistency, if desired. Use instead of fruit-juice glaze.

FRUITY NUGGETS

Naturally good. For an attractive serving or gift, place Fruity Nuggets in decorated petit four cups and arrange on a platter.
(Petit four cups are sold in the candy-making section of craft stores.)

1 cup raisins

1 cup pitted dates

1 cup dried apricots

½ cup toasted almonds

½ cup finely shredded unsweetened coconut

PREP:
20 MINUTES

YIELD:
36 NUGGETS

Combine raisins, dates, apricots, and almonds. Process in a food grinder, food processor, or blender, or chop with a knife until finely ground. Shape into 1-

inch balls. Roll in coconut. Place in an airtight container and store in the refrigerator for up to 3 months or in the freezer for up to 6 months.

Nutrition Facts per Serving (1 nugget): 50 calories, 2 g. total fat (0.5 g. saturated fat), 0 mg. cholesterol, 0 mg. sodium, 10 g. carbohydrate, 1 g. fiber, 8 g. sugars, 1 g. protein. **Daily Values:** 6% vitamin A, 0% vitamin C, 0% calcium, 2% iron. **Diabetic Exchanges:** 2 nuggets = 1 fruit, 1 fat.

Other Combinations: Dried pineapple, dried apples, raisins, and coconut; or raisins, dates, dried apples, and toasted walnuts. Use your imagination and what you have on hand.

Fruity Squares: Instead of forming balls, pat dried-fruit mixture evenly into an 8- or 9-inch square pan. Sprinkle with coconut. Refrigerate until cold, at least 2 hours. Cut into small squares.

Nuts: Instead of coconut, roll balls in finely chopped walnuts, pecans, or almonds.

ICEBOX COOKIES

Keep this easy slice-and-bake dough in the freezer for cookies or fruit pizza.

¾ **cup unbleached all-purpose flour**

¾ **cup quick oats**

½ **teaspoon baking soda**

¼ **teaspoon salt**

½ **cup (1 stick) margarine or butter, softened**

½ **cup granulated sugar or other sweetener**

½ **cup brown sugar or other sweetener**

2 **teaspoons vanilla extract**

¼ **cup cholesterol-free egg product**

OR

2 **egg whites**

OR

1 **egg**

PREP:
20 MINUTES

FREEZE:
3 HOURS

BAKE:
10 MINUTES
PER BATCH

YIELD:
4 DOZEN
COOKIES

Spoon the flour into a measuring cup and level it off with a knife (too much flour makes these cookies dry and crumbly). Combine flour, baking soda, and salt in a bowl; set aside. Using a hand mixer set at medium speed, beat the margarine until it is light and fluffy. Gradually add the sugar, beating until well blended. Beat in the vanilla and egg. Stir in the flour mixture; dough will be soft. Place the dough on wax paper or plastic wrap and shape it into a 12-inch log. Wrap dough tightly, twisting ends of the paper to prevent unrolling. Freeze the dough on a flat surface until it is very firm, at least 3 hours. For longer freezing, place the wrapped log in an airtight container (or wrap the dough in foil), and freeze for up to 3 months.

To bake: Preheat the oven to 350° F. Coat baking sheets or parchment paper with cooking spray. Unwrap the log and using a sharp knife, cut it into ¼-inch slices. After each slice, rotate the log one-quarter turn to prevent flattening on one side. Place slices 1 inch apart on baking sheet. Bake until the cookies are golden and slightly darker on the edges, about 8 to 10 minutes. (The longer the baking time, the crisper the cookies.) Remove from pan, and cool on wire racks.

Nutrition Facts per Serving (1 cookie): 60 calories, 2 g. total fat (0 g. saturated fat), 0 mg. cholesterol, 50 mg. sodium, 9 g. carbohydrate, 0 g. fiber, 5 g. sugars, 1 g. protein. **Daily Values:** 2% vitamin A, 0% vitamin C, 0% calcium, 2% iron. **Diabetic Exchanges:** 2 cookies = 1 other carbohydrate, 1 fat.

Peanut Butter Icebox Cookies: Decrease margarine to 6 tablespoons. Add ¼ cup peanut butter.

Additions: ½ teaspoon almond extract, 1 teaspoon natural lemon or orange flavoring, or ⅓ cup toasted coconut and finely chopped or ground pecans.

Lemon Icebox Cookies: Omit vanilla. Add 4 teaspoons finely chopped lemon peel and 2 teaspoons natural lemon flavoring.

Chocolate-Mint Icebox Cookies: Decrease all-purpose flour to 1½ cups. Add ½ cup unsweetened cocoa powder or sifted carob powder. Increase sugar and brown sugar to ⅔ cup each. Replace vanilla with peppermint extract. Roll the chilled dough in ¼ cup turbinado sugar for a sugary edge, if desired.

Raisin, Nut, or Coconut Icebox Cookies: Add ½ cup chopped nuts, raisins, or shredded coconut.

Almond Icebox Cookies: Add ½ cup ground almonds and replace vanilla with ½ teaspoon almond extract or natural flavoring.

Egg-free Cookies: Replace egg with 1½ teaspoons egg-replacement powder and 2 tablespoons water.

LAYERED DATE BARS

Good with other fillings, too.

3 cups date pieces, or snipped, pitted dates (about 1 pound)

1-1½ cups water

1 teaspoon vanilla extract

½ cup margarine or butter, softened

1½ cups whole-wheat pastry flour

OR

¾ cup whole-wheat flour plus ¾ cup unbleached all-purpose flour

1½ cups quick-cooking or rolled oats

¾ cup brown sugar or other sweetener

½ teaspoon salt

¼ teaspoon baking soda

PREP:
30 MINUTES

BAKE:
30–35 MINUTES

YIELD:
32 BARS

1½–2 tablespoons water

Preheat the oven to 350° F (325° F for glass pan). Coat a 13" x 9" baking pan with cooking spray; set aside. Microwave the dates and water in a microwave-safe bowl for 6 to 8 minutes, or until they are thickened and softened; stir halfway through cooking. (Start with a small amount of water and add more as needed.) Stir in vanilla. Spread the mixture on a dinner plate to cool.

Using a hand mixer set on medium speed, a pastry blender, or two knives, mix the margarine until fluffy. Add the flour, oats, sugar, salt, and baking soda, mixing on medium speed. Add the water, and stir until well mixed. Press half the crumb mixture evenly into the pan; reserve the other half for topping. Spread the date filling evenly over the crumb layer. Sprinkle the remaining crumb mixture evenly over the date filling, and press firmly. Bake 30 to 35 minutes or until light brown. Cool cookies (cover to soften); cut them into 32 bars. Store them in an airtight container at room temperature for up to 3 days, in the refrigerator for up to 2 weeks, or in the freezer for up to 6 months.

Nutrition Facts per Serving (1 bar): 120 calories, 3 g. total fat (0 g. saturated fat), 0 mg. cholesterol, 80 mg. sodium, 23 g. carbohydrate, 2 g. fiber, 6 g. sugars, 2 g. protein. **Daily Values:** 2% vitamin A, 2% vitamin C, 0% calcium, 4% iron. **Diabetic Exchanges:** ½ bread, 1 fruit, ½ fat.

Orange-Date Filling: Replace vanilla with 1 teaspoon natural orange flavoring or ½ teaspoon orange extract. Add 2 teaspoons minced orange peel (preferably organic), or replace ½ cup water with ½ cup orange juice concentrate.

Raspberry Filling: Replace date filling with one 10-ounce jar fruit-sweetened raspberry spread.

Tutti-frutti Filling: Decrease dates to ¾ cup, and add 1½ cups raisins, and ¾ cup chopped dried apricots.

Nuts: Add ½ cup chopped walnuts to filling or crumb mixture.

Layered Date Bar Mix: Stir together dry ingredients and place in a resealable bag. Place dates in a separate bag. Store in refrigerator or freezer up to 6 months.

OATMEAL-RAISIN COOKIE MIX

Making your own cookie mix saves time and increases the cookies' nutritional value. And the mix makes a great gift, too!

3 cups rolled or quick oats

1½ cups raisins

¾ cup brown sugar or other sweetener

¾ cup granulated sugar or other sweetener

¾ cup whole-wheat pastry flour or whole-wheat flour

¾ cup unbleached all-purpose flour

½ teaspoon baking powder, preferably aluminum free

½ teaspoon baking soda

½ teaspoon salt

¼ teaspoon nutmeg

PREP:
10 MINUTES

YIELD:
1 COOKIE MIX RECIPE (7½ CUPS) MAKES 4 DOZEN COOKIES

Place the oats and raisins in separate resealable bags. Combine the remaining ingredients in a separate bag. Place the three bags in a larger resealable bag. Store at room temperature for up to 3 months or in the refrigerator or freezer for up to 6 months.

Nutritional Facts per Serving (2½ tablespoons): 70 calories, 0 g. total fat (0.5 g. saturated fat), 0 mg. cholesterol, 45 mg. sodium, 16 g. carbohydrate, 0 g. fiber, 9 g. sugars, 1 g. protein. **Daily Values:** 0% vitamin A, 0% vitamin C, 2% calcium, 2% iron. **Diabetic Exchanges:** ½ bread, ½ other carbohydrates.

Chocolate-Chip Oatmeal Cookies: Replace the raisins with 1½ cups chocolate, carob, or butterscotch chips. Or use 1 cup chocolate chips and 1 cup raisins.

Cranberry-Pecan Cookies: Replace the raisins with dried cranberries. Add ½ cup chopped pecans. If desired, add 2 teaspoons minced orange rind and 1 teaspoon natural orange flavor or ½ teaspoon orange extract.

Oatmeal-Date Cookies: Replace the raisins with chopped dates. Add ½ cup chopped walnuts, if desired.

OATMEAL COOKIES

A satisfying sweet treat.

¾ cup margarine or butter, softened (1½ sticks)

1 recipe Oatmeal-Raisin Cookie Mix (7½ cups) (p. 217)

¼ cup cholesterol-free egg product

OR

2 egg whites

OR

1 egg

2 tablespoons water

1½ teaspoons vanilla extract

PREP:
15 MINUTES

BAKE:
11–13 MINUTES
PER BATCH

YIELD:
4 DOZEN (2½-
INCH) COOKIES

Preheat the oven to 350° F (325° F for dark pans). Using an electric mixer set on medium speed, cream the margarine for 2 minutes until fluffy and aerated. Add the flour and sugar mixture, and beat until thoroughly mixed. Mix the egg, water, and vanilla until fluffy. Using a spoon or rubber spatula, stir in the rolled oats and raisins. Drop by tablespoonfuls, 2 inches apart, onto a cookie sheet. Bake 8 minutes. Rotate pans. Bake an additional 3 to 5 minutes, or until the cookies are lightly browned on the edges. Let the cookies cool 2 to 3 minutes before transferring them to wire racks. Store in an airtight container at room temperature for up to 3 days or in the freezer for up to 3 months.

> **Nutrition Facts per Serving (1 cookie):** 100 calories, 3 g. total fat (0.5 g. saturated fat), 0 mg. cholesterol, 80 mg. sodium, 16 g. carbohydrate, 0 g. fiber, 9 g. sugars, 2 g. protein. **Daily Values:** 2% vitamin A, 0% vitamin C, 2% calcium, 2% iron. **Diabetic Exchanges:** ½ bread, ½ other carbohydrate, ½ fat.

Ready-to-Bake Frozen Cookie Dough: Spoon balls of cookie dough close together on a baking sheet and freeze. When dough is frozen firm, transfer it to an airtight container. Keep the dough frozen until ready to bake. Follow baking guidelines, extending baking time by 1 to 2 minutes, if necessary.

Vegan Oatmeal Cookies: Use vegan margarine. Replace egg with 1½ teaspoons egg-replacement powder (add with dry ingredients) and 3 tablespoons water. (Use 2 tablespoons water if using chocolate chips.)

PEANUT BUTTER TREATS

A yummy no-cook dessert.

1 cup peanut butter, preferably natural

½ cup honey or other liquid sweetener

¼ teaspoon vanilla

2 cups granola

1 cup raisins or chopped dried fruit

PREP:
5 MINUTES

YIELD:
32 SERVINGS

Combine peanut butter, honey, and vanilla in a mixing bowl. Stir in granola and raisins. Press into an 8- or 9-inch square pan. Refrigerate for 2 to 3 hours before cutting into 32 pieces. Store in an airtight container in the refrigerator for up to 3 months or in the freezer for up to 6 months.

Nutrition Facts per Serving (1 piece): 110 calories, 5 g. total fat (0 g. saturated fat), 0 mg. cholesterol, 25 mg. sodium, 14 g. carbohydrate, 1 g. fiber, 9 g. sugars, 3 g. protein. **Daily Values:** 0% vitamin A, 0% vitamin C, 2% calcium, 2% iron. **Diabetic Exchanges:** ½ bread, ½ other carbohydrate, 1 fat.

Peanut Butter Balls: Form into 1-inch balls.

PIECRUST

Surprisingly flaky for an oil crust.

PREP:
15 MINUTES

BAKE:
10–18 MINUTES

YIELD:
2 SINGLE
(9-INCH) CRUSTS
OR 1 DOUBLE
CRUST

2¼ cups unbleached all-purpose flour

½ cup wheat germ

2 tablespoons granulated sugar or other

sweetener

½ teaspoon salt

½ cup vegetable oil

2 tablespoons lemon juice

5–7 tablespoons water

For prebaked piecrusts:

Adjust the oven rack to the middle position and preheat the oven to 350°F. Measure the flour by spooning it into a measuring cup. Combine the flour, wheat germ, sugar, and salt in a mixing bowl. Stir in oil. Stir in lemon juice. Pour the water over the flour, stirring just until mixed and pastry forms a ball. Shape the dough into two balls. Place one ball of dough in the center of a sheet of waxed paper, plastic wrap, or parchment paper. (Before placing the paper down, first dampen the countertop to prevent the paper from shifting later as the dough is rolled.) Top the dough with another sheet of waxed paper. Using a rolling pin, roll the dough into a 12-inch circle. Occasionally flip the entire "sandwiched" pastry, loosening the waxed paper and preventing creases from forming. Remove the top sheet of waxed paper. Using the bottom waxed paper to lift the crust, carefully invert it into a glass pie pan, and remove the waxed paper.

For a single-crust pie, trim the overhanging edge of the pastry to within ½-inch of pie pan rim. Tuck the pastry under, even with pie pan. Flute the edge of the pastry or flatten it on the rim of the pie pan, pressing firmly with the tines of a fork. Repeat the process with the second ball of dough. Bake for 16 to 18 minutes or until the edges just begin to brown. Cool, and store in an airtight container at room temperature for up to 1 week or in the freezer for up to 3 months.

Nutrition Facts per Serving (1/16): 140 calories, 7 g. total fat (0 g. saturated fat), 0 mg. cholesterol, 75 mg. sodium, 17 g. carbohydrate, 0 g. fiber, 2 g. sugars, 3 g. protein. **Daily Values:** 0% vitamin A, 0% vitamin C, 0% calcium, 6% iron. **Diabetic Exchanges:** 1 bread, 1½ fats.

Wheat Piecrust: Stir 1½ cups whole-wheat pastry flour, 1 cup unbleached all-purpose flour, 1 tablespoon granulated sugar or other sweetener, and ½ teaspoon salt together. Stir in ½ cup oil. Stir in 2 tablespoons lemon juice. Stir water into flour mixture.

Piecrust Mix: Store the dry ingredients in an airtight container at room temperature for up to 1 month, in the refrigerator for up to 3 months, or in the freezer for up to 6 months.

PUMPKIN COOKIES

These cookies are rich in beta carotene. They freeze well too.

PREP:
15 MINUTES

BAKE:
12-14 MINUTES

YIELD:
4 DOZEN
COOKIES

1 cup pumpkin puree

1 cup raisins or golden raisins

1 cup brown sugar or other sweetener

½ cup chopped walnuts or pecans

½ cup oil

1 teaspoon vanilla extract

1 cup whole-wheat pastry flour or whole-wheat flour

1 cup unbleached all-purpose flour

2 teaspoons baking powder, preferably aluminum-free

¼ teaspoon baking soda

½ teaspoon salt

½ teaspoon cinnamon

½ teaspoon nutmeg

¼ teaspoon ginger

Preheat the oven to 350° F. Mix the pumpkin, raisins, sugar, walnuts, oil, and vanilla in a large mixing bowl. Stir in the remaining ingredients. Drop by tablespoons, 2 inches apart, onto a cookie sheet. Bake for 12 to 15 minutes, or until the cookies are brown on the edges. Don't overbake. Cool on a wire rack and store in an airtight container for up to 5 days at room temperature or in the freezer for up to 3 months.

Nutrition Facts per Serving (1 cookie): 60 calories, 3 g. total fat (0 g. saturated fat), 0 mg. cholesterol, 45 mg. sodium, 8 g. carbohydrate, 0 g. fiber, 3 g. sugars, 1g. protein. **Daily Values:** 25% vitamin A, 0% vitamin C, 2% calcium, 2% iron. **Diabetic Exchanges:** 2 cookies = 1 fruit, 1 fat.

Pumpkin-Date Cookies: Replace the raisins with chopped dates.
Triple Batch: Use a large (29-ounce) can of pumpkin.

PUMPKIN PIE

Creamy, moist, and flavorful. Shhh! Don't tell them it contains tofu!

1 (12.3-ounce) package silken extra firm tofu, drained

½ cup low-fat milk or nondairy milk

1 (29-ounce) can pumpkin puree (about 3½ cups)

2 cups low-fat milk or nondairy milk

1 cup brown sugar or other sweetener

½ cup cholesterol-free egg product

PREP: 10 MINUTES

BAKE: 30–35 MINUTES

YIELD: TWO (9-INCH) PIES

OR

3 egg whites

OR

2 eggs

2 teaspoons ground cinnamon

1 teaspoon ground ginger

1 teaspoon salt

¼ teaspoon ground cloves

2 unbaked 9-inch pie shells

Preheat the oven to 425°F. Using a blender or food processor, process the tofu and milk until smooth. Transfer the mixture to a bowl, and whisk in the remaining ingredients until well mixed. Divide the mixture evenly between pie shells. Bake for 15 minutes. Reduce the heat to 350°F, and bake 40 to 50 minutes, or until a knife inserted near the center comes out dry. Cool on wire rack for two hours. Serve, or refrigerate for up to 5 days.

Nutrition Facts per Serving (1/8 pie): 220 calories, 8 g. total fat (1 g. saturated fat), 0 mg. cholesterol, 260 mg. sodium, 34 g. carbohydrate, 3 g. fiber, 17 g. sugars, 6 g. protein. **Daily Values:** 240% vitamin A, 4% vitamin C, 8% calcium, 10% iron. **Diabetic Exchanges:** 1 bread, 2 fats, 1 other carbohydrate.

Eggless Pumpkin Pie: Replace the eggs with 3 tablespoons cornstarch. Bake at 425°F for 15 minutes. Reduce to 350°F and bake 30 to 35 minutes, or until small cracks begin to form in the filling. Cool on wire rack for two hours. Refrigerate until cold for firmer consistency.

Orange Pumpkin Pie: Omit the cinnamon, ginger, and cloves. Add 1 tablespoon minced orange peel and 2 teaspoons natural orange flavoring or 1 teaspoon orange extract.

SESAME BARS

Great to munch on while traveling.

2 cups whole-wheat pastry flour

2 cups rolled oats

1½ cups sesame seeds

¾ cup brown sugar or other sweetener

½ cup chopped walnuts

⅓ cup shredded coconut

½ teaspoon salt

¾ cup water

½ cup oil

PREP:
15 MINUTES

BAKE:
40 MINUTES

YIELD:
60 BARS

Preheat the oven to 325°F. Coat a large baking sheet (preferably without sides) with cooking spray; set aside. Combine the dry ingredients in a large mixing bowl. Combine the liquid ingredients in a liquid measuring cup, and stir them into the dry ingredients until thoroughly mixed. Using a rolling pin, roll out the dough evenly on the prepared baking sheet. Cut into 1" x 3" bars. Bake for 30 minutes. Remove the browned bars, and return the baking sheet to oven. Bake another 5 minutes, and remove the browned bars. Repeat until all the bars are a light brown. Remove bars from baking sheet while they are hot. Store in an airtight container in the refrigerator for up to 2 weeks or in the freezer for up to 3 months.

Nutrition Facts per serving (1 bar): 80 calories, 4.5 g.. total fat (0.5 g. saturated fat), 0 mg. cholesterol, 20 mg. sodium, 8 g. carbohydrate, 1 g. fiber, 3 g. sugars, 2 g. protein. **Daily Values:** 0% vitamin A, 0% vitamin C, 4% calcium, 4% iron. **Diabetic Exchanges:** ½ bread, 1 fat

Vary the Nuts: Replace walnuts with pecans, peanuts, almonds, or sunflower seeds.

ABOUT SMOOTHIES

- Bananas add creaminess and sweetness. The riper the banana, the sweeter and more pronounced the flavor. To freeze: peel, divide in half, and freeze in a resealable freezer bag for up to 3 months.
- This recipe uses 1 fresh fruit and 1 frozen. If both are frozen, you may need an additional 2 to 4 tablespoons liquid for blending. If both fruits are fresh, add 4 or more ice cubes to chill and thicken the smoothie.
- If you don't have milk powder, you can use fluid milk as the base, and juice concentrate to sweeten.
- For sweeter smoothies, add fruit juice concentrate, an extra banana, honey, granulated sugar, or other sweetener.
- Use your imagination to create a variety of flavor combinations with different fruits, juices, flavorings, yogurt, milk, or milk alternatives.
- Adding tofu, as in the Breakfast Smoothies below, is a good way to add more soy to your diet, and an easy way to use up a partial container of tofu. The milder flavor of the shelf-stable boxes works best, plus the aseptic packaging avoids bacterial contamination.

STRAWBERRY SMOOTHIES

Keep a variety of fruit in your freezer for this spur-of-the-moment dessert.
Also great for breakfast or a light supper.

½ **cup orange juice**

OR

2 **tablespoons orange juice concentrate plus**
    water to equal ½ cup

¼ **cup nonfat dry milk or 1–2 tablespoons**
    nondairy milk powder

½ **teaspoon vanilla**

¼ **teaspoon lemon juice**

1 **medium banana**

2 **cups frozen strawberries, partially thawed**

PREP:
5 MINUTES

YIELD:
2 SERVINGS

Pour the orange juice, milk powder, vanilla, and lemon juice into a blender. With blender running, gradually add the banana and strawberries. Process until smooth. If desired, sweeten to taste. Serve immediately. Store leftovers in an airtight container in the freezer for up to 3 months.

Nutrition Facts per Serving (1¼ cups): 170 calories, 0.5 g. total fat (0 g. saturated fat), 0 mg. cholesterol, 50 mg. sodium, 39 g. carbohydrate, 5 g. fiber, 32 g. sugars, 5 g. protein. **Daily Values:** 8% vitamin A, 150% vitamin C, 15% calcium, 8% iron. **Diabetic Exchanges:** 2 fruits, ½ skim milk.

Strawberry-Kiwi Smoothie: Decrease strawberries to 1 cup and add 2 peeled kiwifruit.

Peach Smoothie: Replace the orange juice with peach juice, and replace strawberries with fresh or frozen sliced peaches. To slow browning, add Fruit-Fresh or vitamin C, if desired.

Mango–Raspberry Smoothie: Replace the strawberries with 1 cup mango chunks and 1 cup raspberries. (If you prefer a seedless smoothie, blend the raspberries in juice, and strain the seeds before proceeding.)

Breakfast Smoothie With Tofu: Omit the milk powder and add ¾ cup silken tofu (half of a 12.3-ounce box).

Smoothie Pops: Freeze in frozen juice bar molds.

Smoothie Sorbet: Freeze in plastic containers and use an ice shaver. Or freeze in ice-cube trays and process through a heavy-duty juicer.

Smoothie Ice Cubes: Freeze in ice cube trays. Add to juice, punch, or to create additional smoothies.

Smoothie Concentrate Cubes: Use fresh fruit and omit juice. Freeze in ice cube trays. Store frozen cubes in resealable freezer bags. Blend smoothie cubes with ½ to 1 cup juice.

ZUCCHINI BREAD

Omitting the eggs in quick breads makes it possible to reduce the fat. Eggs toughen the structure of baked goods, as the protein coagulates during baking.

1 cup (packed) coarsely shredded zucchini

½ cup grated carrots

⅓ cup brown sugar or other sweetener

⅓ cup granulated sugar or other sweetener

½ cup chopped dates or raisins

½ cup low-fat or nondairy milk or orange juice

½ cup chopped walnuts, optional

3 tablespoons vegetable oil

1½ teaspoons vanilla extract

1 cup whole-wheat flour

1 cup unbleached all-purpose flour

2 teaspoons baking powder, preferably aluminum free

1 teaspoon cinnamon

½ teaspoon baking soda

½ teaspoon salt

PREP:
20 MINUTES

BAKE:
45 MINUTES

YIELD:
16 SLICES

Position rack in the center of the oven. Preheat the oven to 350°F. Combine the zucchini, carrots, sugars, dates, milk, walnuts, oil, and vanilla in a mixing bowl. Combine the dry ingredients in another large bowl. Pour the zucchini mixture over the dry ingredients, and stir until just moistened. Stir for 30 seconds. Coat an 8" x 4" loaf pan with cooking spray. Pour the batter into the prepared pan, spreading evenly. Bake for 50 to 60 minutes, or until a wooden pick inserted in center comes out dry. Place the pan on a wire rack to cool for 10 minutes; remove bread from the pan and let it cool on a wire rack. For a softer crust and easier slicing, wrap the bread in plastic wrap while it is slightly warm. Store the wrapped bread in an airtight container at room temperature for up to 3 days, in the refrigerator for up to 1 week, or in the freezer for up to 3 months.

Nutrition Facts per Serving (1 slice): 160 calories, 5 g. total fat (0 g. saturated fat), 0 mg. cholesterol, 170 mg. sodium, 26 g. carbohydrate, 2 g. fiber, 13 g. sugars, 3 g. protein. **Daily Values:** 20% vitamin A, 2% vitamin C, 6% calcium, 4% iron. **Diabetic Exchanges:** 1 bread, 1 other carbohydrate, 1 fat.

Fat-free: Omit oil and increase the milk to ¾ cup. Omit nuts.

Lemon Zest: Add 1 tablespoon organic lemon zest (or 1 teaspoon dried lemon zest).

ENTRÉES AND SIDE DISHES

BREAD DRESSING

Especially attractive served in baked acorn-squash halves.

12 cups unseasoned dried bread cubes, preferably whole-wheat

2 tablespoons olive oil

1½ cups chopped onion (1 large onion)

1½ cups diced celery (4 medium celery ribs)

¼ cup minced fresh parsley

OR

4 teaspoons dried parsley

1 teaspoon rubbed sage

¼ teaspoon dried thyme

¼ teaspoon marjoram

2 cups water

4 cups Cream Sauce (p. 241)

OR

1 (10¾-ounce) can condensed mushroom soup

2 teaspoons vegetarian chicken-style seasoning

½ teaspoon salt

PREP:
15 MINUTES

BAKE:
40–45 MINUTES

YIELD:
12 (1-CUP) SERVINGS

Preheat the oven to 400°F. Coat a 9" x 13" baking dish with cooking spray. Measure the bread cubes into a large mixing bowl; set aside. Heat the olive oil in a large skillet over medium-high heat. Stir in the onion and celery, and cook until they are tender and translucent, about 10 minutes. Stir in the herbs, and cook just until fragrant, about 1 minute. Transfer vegetables to the mixing bowl, and stir. Whisk together the water, cream sauce, chicken-style seasoning, and salt. Gently add the liquid ingredients to the bread cubes, tossing the cubes to coat them evenly. Transfer the mixture to the prepared dish; cover tightly with foil. Bake until fragrant, about 25 minutes. Remove the foil, and bake until the top is golden, 15 to 20 minutes.

Nutrition Facts per Serving (1 cup): 190 calories, 6 g. total fat (1 g. saturated fat), 0 mg. cholesterol, 540 mg. sodium, 30 g. carbohydrate, 4 g. fiber, 5 g. sugars, 6 g. protein. **Daily Values:** 2% vitamin A, 6% vitamin C, 8% calcium, 10% iron. **Diabetic Exchanges:** 2 breads, 1 fat.

Bread Dressing With Nuts: Add 1 cup pecan or walnut halves or slivered almonds.

Chicken-style Bread Dressing: Drain and reserve the liquid from a (12.5-ounce) can of vegetarian chicken alternative. Dice "chicken" into ½-inch pieces, or tear into bite-size pieces. Add water to the reserved liquid to make 1 cup; use the liquid in place of cream sauce or mushroom soup.

Bread Dressing With Mushrooms: Stir and cook 3 cups sliced fresh mushrooms (about 8 ounces) with the onions and celery.

Bread Dressing With Apples: Add 2 cups peeled and cored Granny Smith apples (2 apples), cut into ½-inch cubes, and cook with the onions and celery.

Bread Dressing With Cranberries: Add ½ cup dried cranberries.

Stove Top: Sauté vegetables and add liquid ingredients. Simmer 10 minutes. Drizzle vegetables and liquid ingredients over the bread mixture. Cover, and keep warm 5 minutes. Fluff with a fork before serving.

Microwave Instructions: Microwave on high 8 to 10 minutes, stirring halfway through cooking time. Stir in herbs. Let stand 3 to 5 minutes.

Slow Cooker: Coat the inside of the slow cooker crock with cooking spray. Cook on low 4 to 5 hours.

Homemade Bread Cubes: Cut 1½ pounds whole-wheat bread into ½-inch cubes. Spread out on 2 baking sheets and bake at 225° F for 1 hour, stirring after 30 minutes, until brittle, but not brown. Or cut the bread into cubes, spread on baking sheets and let dry at room temperature for 1 to 2 days, stirring occasionally.

CABBAGE ROLLS

The filling also tastes great in stuffed green peppers.

PREP:
30 MINUTES

BAKE:
1 HOUR

Yield:
12 CABBAGE
ROLLS

1 medium head savoy or other green cabbage, cored

1 medium onion, finely chopped (about 1 cup)

2 celery ribs, finely chopped (about 1 cup)

1 tablespoon olive oil

2 cups cooked brown rice

1 cup meatless burger

2 tablespoons chopped fresh parsley

½ teaspoon ground sage

½ teaspoon salt

2 (10¾-ounce) cans condensed tomato soup, undiluted

½ cup low fat cheese or nondairy cheese

Preheat the oven to 350°F. Cover the cabbage with cold water in a large bowl to loosen the leaves; set aside. In a large skillet, cook the onions and celery in olive oil until the vegetables are tender. Stir in the rice, meatless burger, parsley, sage, and salt. Remove 12 leaves from the cabbage, and cook them just until tender, about 6 to 8 minutes. Drain well.

Lay them flat and trim the spine off each leaf, to make it easier to roll. Place ⅓ cup rice mixture on each large cabbage leaf (less on smaller leaves), and fold in the sides. Starting at core end, carefully roll up each leaf, making sure the folded sides are snugly in each roll. (At this point the cabbage rolls may be frozen for up to 3 months.)

Spread 1 can tomato soup over the bottom of 11" x 13" baking dish. Place the cabbage rolls on top of the tomato soup, seam side down. Spoon 1 can tomato soup over the top of the cabbage rolls. Bake, covered, for 60 minutes, or until heated through and the cabbage is tender. During the last 5 minutes of baking time, sprinkle with cheese.

Nutrition Facts per Serving (1 cabbage roll): 120 calories, 3 g. total fat (0.5 g. saturated fat), 0 mg. cholesterol, 510 mg. sodium, 17 g. carbohydrate, 2 g. fiber, 5 g. sugars, 6 g. protein. **Daily Values:** 6% vitamin A, 60% vitamin C, 4% calcium, 10% iron. **Diabetic Exchanges:** 1 bread, ½ lean meat, ½ fat.

Serving Idea: Arrange the cabbage rolls on a platter and smother them with sautéed onions. Serve with squash and a green salad.

Bulgur Wheat: Replace the rice with 2 cups cooked bulgur wheat.

Cabbage Rolls With Mushrooms: Add one 4-ounce can chopped, drained mushrooms (or 4 ounces sliced fresh mushrooms) to vegetables while cooking.

Tomato Sauce: Replace tomato soup with 2½ cups of tomato sauce.

Unstuffed Cabbage: Slice the uncooked cabbage and stir-fry it until it becomes limp. Add the remaining ingredients; simmer, covered, until the cabbage is tender. Or bake it.

Microwave: Microwave the onions and celery in oil in a microwave-safe dish for 8 to 10 minutes on high, or until the vegetables are tender and translucent. Stir in the rice, meatless burger, and seasonings. Place 4 to 6 cabbage leaves in a large covered casserole, and microwave on high for 4 to 5 minutes, or until they become tender. Repeat, until all the cabbage leaves are cooked. Microwave the rolls in a covered casserole on high 10 to 12 minutes, rotating the dish ¼ turn and basting the rolls every 4 minutes. Let rest, covered, 5 minutes.

Stove Top: Simmer the cabbage rolls in a covered skillet for 20 to 30 minutes.

Slow Cooker: Cover, and cook on low for 6 to 7 hours. Top the rolls with cheese just before serving.

CREAM SAUCE MIX

PREP:
5 MINUTES

YIELD:
MINI MIX: ½ CUP
(MAKES 2 CUPS
CREAM SAUCE)
MEGA MIX:
4 CUPS (MAKES
16 CUPS CREAM
SAUCE)

¼ cup plus 2 tablespoons *(3 cups)* nonfat milk powder

1½ tablespoons *(¾ cup)* unbleached all-purpose flour

1½ tablespoons *(¾ cup)* cornstarch or modified cornstarch

¼ teaspoon *(2 teaspoons)* onion powder

¼ teaspoon *(2 teaspoons)* salt

⅛ teaspoon *(1 teaspoon)* garlic powder

Combine the ingredients, whisking until evenly distributed. Store in an airtight container in a cool, dry place for up to six months. Affix a label that includes the date, complete Cream Sauce ingredients (below), and cooking instructions. Stir mix to distribute seasonings before using. Use ½ cup mix with 2 cups water.

Nutrition Facts per Serving (½ cup): 170 calories, 0 g. total fat (0 g. saturated fat), 0 mg. cholesterol, 720 mg. sodium, 31 g. carbohydrate, 0 g. fiber, 13 g. sugars, 10 g. protein. **Daily Values:** 10% vitamin A, 2% vitamin C, 30% calcium, 2% iron. **Diabetic Exchanges:** 1 skim milk, 1 bread.

Nondairy Cream Sauce Mix: Replace nonfat milk powder with 1 tablespoon *(½ cup for mega mix)* tofu milk. (The amount of tofu milk needed may vary according to the brand that is used.) Use about 3 tablespoons of mix per recipe of Cream Sauce.

CREAM SAUCE

A basic white sauce ready to be transformed into stroganoff, à la king, or curry sauce. May also be used to replace condensed cream soups.

2 cups water

½ cup Cream Sauce Mix (p. 240)

1 tablespoon oil or margarine

Whisk ingredients in a saucepan. Heat over medium-high heat, stirring frequently until the mixture boils. Reduce heat, and simmer 1 minute, or until heated through and the mixture thickens.

PREP:
5 MINUTES

COOK:
5 MINUTES

YIELD:
2 CUPS

Nutrition Facts per Serving (¼ cup): 35 calories, 1.5 g. total fat (0 g. saturated fat), 0 mg. cholesterol, 90 mg. sodium, 4 g. carbohydrate, 0 g. fiber, 2 g. sugars, 1 g. protein. Daily Values: 2% vitamin A, 0% vitamin C, 4% calcium, 0% iron. Diabetic Exchanges: free.

Microwave: Microwave the ingredients on high for about 4 minutes, or until the mixture thickens and bubbles. After the first 2 minutes, stir every minute. Remove from microwave, and stir; let stand 1 minute, and stir again.

Other Seasonings: Garlic, bay leaf, basil, thyme, other herbs, vegetable broth powder, or seasoned salt.

Fat-free Sauce: Omit the oil or margarine.

Replacing (1 can) Condensed Soup: Reduce water to 1¼ cups and microwave 3 minutes on high, stirring every minute. (Stove top: simmer until mixture thickens.) Flavor as desired.

Cream of Celery Sauce: Stir and cook ½ cup diced celery (about 1 rib) in 1 tablespoon oil or margarine until tender. (Or microwave on high 5 to 7 minutes.) Stir in 2 cups water, ½ cup Cream Sauce Mix, and ½ teaspoon celery salt. Cook, as directed in step two.

Cream of Mushroom Sauce: Stir and cook 1 cup chopped fresh mushrooms (about 4 ounces) in 1 tablespoon oil or margarine until tender. (Or microwave on high 4 to 5 minutes.) Stir in 2 cups water, ½ cup Cream Sauce Mix, and ¼ teaspoon salt. Cook, as directed in step two. (Or drain and chop one 4-ounce can of sliced mushrooms, and add to the prepared sauce.)

Cream of Onion Sauce: Stir and cook 1 cup chopped onion in 1 tablespoon oil or margarine until tender. Stir in 2 cups water, ½ cup Cream Sauce Mix, ¼ teaspoon onion powder, and ¼ teaspoon salt. Cook, as directed in step 2.

Cheese Sauce: Stir into prepared Cream Sauce: 1 cup shredded reduced-fat cheddar cheese (or nondairy cheese) and ⅛ teaspoon salt.

À la King Sauce: To the Cream of Onion sauce, stir in one 15-ounce can drained and rinsed garbanzos or 1½ cups diced chicken-style Wheat Meat (p. 276) or vegetarian chicken alternative, ½ cup frozen peas, and 2 teaspoons vegetarian chicken-style seasoning. Heat until hot. Serve over brown rice or whole-grain toast triangles.

CURRIED TOFU WITH BROCCOLI

Colorful, flavorful—and quick.

2 tablespoons oil or margarine

1 medium onion, chopped

1 (14- to 16-ounce) package extra-firm tofu

2 cloves garlic, minced

OR

½ teaspoon garlic powder

3 teaspoons curry powder (or to taste)

3½ cups water

1 cup Cream Sauce Mix (p. 240)

1 tablespoon vegetarian chicken-style seasoning

2½ cups broccoli flowerets

PREP:
10 MINUTES

COOK:
10 MINUTES

YIELD:
8 SERVINGS

OR

1 (10-ounce) package frozen chopped broccoli, thawed

½ cup low fat sour cream (or nonfat plain yogurt,
   nondairy sour cream or yogurt)

cooked brown rice

Heat the oil in a nonstick skillet over medium-high heat. Add onions; stir and cook until tender. Cube the tofu into ¾-inch pieces. Stir in the tofu, garlic, and curry powder; cook for 2 minutes. Stir in the water, Cream Sauce Mix, and vegetarian chicken-style seasoning. Cook, stirring frequently until the mixture thickens. Steam the broccoli flowerets until tender. Just before serving, stir in the broccoli and sour cream. Simmer until heated through but not boiling. Taste, and adjust seasoning. Serve over brown rice.

Nutrition Facts per Serving (1 cup): 200 calories, 9 g. total fat (2 g. saturated fat), 5 mg. cholesterol, 420 mg. sodium, 17 g. carbohydrate, 3 g. fiber, 7 g. sugars, 13 g. protein. **Daily Values:** 20% vitamin A, 60% vitamin C, 45% calcium, 35% iron. **Diabetic Exchanges:** 1 protein, 1 skim milk, 1 vegetable, ½ fat.

Curried Tofu With Broccoli and Mushroom Soup: Replace water and Cream Sauce Mix with two 10¼-ounce cans condensed cream of mushroom soup plus 1 can water.

Curried Chicken-style With Broccoli: Replace tofu with 2 to 3 cups cubed chicken-style Wheat Meat (p. 276) or chicken-style alternative. Reduce chicken-style seasoning to 1 teaspoon.

PECAN PATTIES

Keep a stash of these versatile patties in the freezer for a quick entrée.

8 ounces whole-wheat bread (about 8 slices)

1 cup quick or rolled oats

1 cup pecans

1 cup onion, cut into chunks (1 small)

1 cup sliced celery (about 2 ribs)

½ cup water

¼ cup cholesterol-free egg product

OR

2 egg whites

OR

1 egg

½ teaspoon salt

½ teaspoon rubbed sage, oregano, basil, or savory

½ teaspoon paprika

1 clove garlic

OR

½ teaspoon garlic powder

1 teaspoon reduced-sodium soy sauce or soy sauce alternative

PREP:
20 MINUTES

COOK:
20 MINUTES

YIELD:
12 PATTIES

Using a food processor or blender, process the bread until finely ground. Measure 4 cups soft bread crumbs into a large mixing bowl and stir in oats. Using a food processor or blender, grind the pecans, and add them to the mixing bowl. Grind the remaining ingredients until finely ground, and add them to the dry ingredients, stirring until thoroughly mixed. To absorb the moisture, let the mixture stand 5 minutes (if using rolled oats, 10 to 15 minutes). Mixture should be thick, moist, and congealed.

Preheat the oven to 350°F. Coat a baking sheet with cooking spray. Using a ¼-cup measure or scoop, form into 3½-inch patties. Place patties on the prepared baking sheet, and bake for 15 minutes, or until the bottoms of the patties are lightly browned and firm. Turn the patties over and bake another 5 minutes. (Or using a non-stick skillet over medium-high heat, brown both sides of the patties, about 4 to 5 minutes on each side.) Store patties in an airtight container in the refrigerator for up to 5 days or in the freezer for up to 6 months.

Nutrition Facts per Serving (1 patty): 150 calories, 8 g. total fat (1 g. saturated fat), 0 mg. cholesterol, 220 mg. sodium, 17 g. carbohydrate, 3 g. fiber, 2 g. sugars, 4 g. protein. **Daily Values:** 2% vitamin A, 4% vitamin C, 2% calcium, 6% iron. **Diabetic Exchanges:** 1 bread, 1½ fats.

Other Nuts: Replace pecans with walnuts, sunflower seeds, almonds, or cashews.

Pecan Burgers: Serve in sandwiches with your favorite trimmings.

Eggless Patties: Omit egg.

Spaghetti and Nutballs: Replace sage with Italian seasonings. Form into 1-inch nutballs. Bake at 350°F for 15 minutes. Serve with marinara sauce and spaghetti.

Pecan Patties with Brown Gravy: Place patties, overlapped slightly, in a 9" x 13" casserole dish. Cover them with 4 cups Brown Gravy (p. 249) or 2 cans low-fat mushroom soup mixed with 1 can of water. Cover and bake at 350°F for 25 to 30 minutes, or until hot and the gravy bubbles (30 to 40 minutes for frozen patties).

> **Nutrition Facts per Serving (1 patty with ½ cup gravy):** 180 calories, 8 g. total fat (1 g. saturated fat), 0 mg. cholesterol, 550 mg. sodium, 23 g. carbohydrate, 3 g. fiber, 3 g. sugars, 5 g. protein. **Daily Values:** 2% vitamin A, 4% vitamin C, 4% calcium, 8% iron. **Diabetic Exchanges:** 1½ breads, 1½ fats.

Serving Idea: Serve with stuffed baked potatoes, peas, tossed salad, and strawberry shortcake.

Microwave: Place 6 patties, overlapped slightly, in a 2-quart microwave-safe casserole dish. Cover the patties with 2 cups gravy. Cover, and cook 6 to 8 minutes on high, rotating a half turn after 5 minutes. If the patties are frozen, cook them 12 to 15 minutes. Let stand 5 minutes.

BROWN GRAVY MIX

This tasty gravy combines the old-fashioned method of browning the flour with the working-ahead, timesaving strategy of making it into a mix.

PREP:
10 MINUTES

YIELD:
MINI MIX: 1½ CUPS (MAKES 8 CUPS GRAVY)
MEGA MIX:
3 CUPS MIX (MAKES 16 CUPS GRAVY)

1¼ cup *(2½ cups)* unbleached all-purpose flour

2 tablespoons plus 2 teaspoons *(⅓ cup)* vegetarian beef-style seasoning

2 teaspoons *(4 teaspoons)* onion powder

1 teaspoon *(2 teaspoons)* salt

Using a dry skillet over high heat, brown the flour, stirring constantly until it starts to brown. Reduce the heat to medium-high, and continue browning the flour until it becomes straw-colored, about 4 minutes. Transfer the flour to a mixing bowl, and whisk in remaining ingredients. When the mixture is cool, store it in an airtight container in a cool, dry place for up to 3 months. Affix a label that includes the date, complete ingredients for Brown Gravy (p. 249), and cooking instructions.

Oven Browning: Spread flour evenly on a baking pan and bake at 350° F for about 15 minutes, stirring every 5 minutes, until straw-colored.

BROWN GRAVY

Fast and fat-free!

4 cups water

⅔ cup Brown Gravy Mix (p. 248)

½ teaspoon browning sauce, optional

COOK:
5 MINUTES

—

YIELD:
4 CUPS

Before measuring, stir the mix to distribute seasonings. Combine the ingredients in a small saucepan over medium-high heat, whisking with a wire whip until the gravy is smooth. Heat, stirring frequently, until the gravy thickens and bubbles. Cook for 1 to 2 minutes.

Nutrition Facts per Serving (¼ cup): 20 calories, 0 g. total fat (0 g. saturated fat), 0 mg. cholesterol, 210 mg. sodium, 5 g. carbohydrate, 0 g. fiber, 0 g. sugars, 1 g. protein. **Daily Values:** 0% vitamin A, 0% vitamin C, 0% calcium, 2% iron. **Diabetic Exchanges:** free.

Creamy Brown Gravy: Substitute milk or nondairy milk for half the liquid.

Chipped Meatless Gravy: Add 2 cups chopped Wheat Meat (p. 276), or meatless beef or sausage to Creamy Gravy.

Mushroom Gravy: Add two 4-ounce cans sliced and drained mushrooms or 8 ounces (3¼ cups) fresh mushrooms, sliced and sautéed.

Microwave: Heat in a 2-quart microwave-safe dish for 4 to 5 minutes, or until hot and thickened, stirring every 2 minutes.

PIZZA BRAID

A tasty and attractive alternative to sandwiches for a picnic.

PREP:
30 MINUTES
PLUS DOUGH
PREPARATION

BAKE:
30 MINUTES

YIELD:
2 (15-INCH)
BRAIDED LOAVES
(12 SERVINGS)

1½ cups grated reduced-fat mozzarella cheese, or nondairy cheese

1 cup sliced ripe olives

1 (4-ounce) can sliced mushrooms, drained, or sliced fresh mushrooms

¼ cup sun-dried tomatoes, rinsed, drained, and chopped

½ cup chopped onions

½ cup spaghetti, marinara, or pizza sauce

2 large garlic cloves, pressed

1 teaspoon oregano leaves

½ teaspoon basil leaves

2¼ pounds Pizza Dough (p. 253)

OR

2 pounds frozen whole-wheat bread dough, thawed
Spaghetti, marinara, or pizza sauce for dipping,
optional

Lightly flour a work surface, and coat a baking sheet with cooking spray. Combine the cheese, olives, mushrooms, tomatoes, onions, spaghetti sauce, garlic, oregano, and basil; set aside. Divide the dough in half, and cover one of the dough halves with plastic wrap. Shape the remaining dough into a ball, and roll it out on the prepared surface into a 15" x 10" rectangle. Transfer the dough to the prepared baking sheet.

Spread half the filling (about 1½ cups) over the center length of the dough. Using a sharp knife, table knife, or baker's bench knife, make cuts, at 1-inch intervals, from the filling to the edges of the dough. Alternating sides, fold the strips at an angle across the filling, pinching the ends of the strips together. Coat the dough with cooking spray or brush it with olive oil. Repeat the process with the remaining dough.

Place the braid in the center of a cold oven. Set the oven temperature at 375°F, and bake the braid for 30 minutes or until it is golden brown and the filling bubbles. Transfer the braid to a wire rack and let it cool 10 minutes before cutting into 1¼-inch slices. Serve warm or at room temperature. Serve with spaghetti sauce for dipping, if desired. If making ahead, allow the braid to cool before storing it. Wrap the braid in plastic wrap and store it in an airtight container (a 2-gallon resealable bag works well) in the refrigerator for up to 1 week. For freezer storage, wrap the braid in 2 sheets of plastic wrap, and store it in an airtight container in the freezer for up to 3 months.

Herbed Pizza Braid: Use herbed pizza dough (see Pizza Dough variations, p. 254).

Spinach-Pesto Braid: Replace pizza filling with filling from Calzones (p. 335).

ABOUT PIZZA

- Hand-pressing the dough into shape is preferable to using a rolling pin, which removes air bubbles and makes a tougher crust.
- Use a pizza peel, a long-handled paddle, to transfer pizza to and from the oven. If you don't have one, use oven mitts and a flat baking sheet.
- A preheated pizza stone simulates brick-oven baking (even heat distribution, absorbs moisture) and produces a crisp, light crust. Or for a fraction of the price of a pizza stone, you can purchase ½-inch thick, unglazed stone tiles from a tile store and have them cut to fit your oven's rack.
- If you don't have a pizza stone or a tile-lined rack, use a pizza pan (preferably black) or a large flat baking sheet. You may need to increase the baking time by 2 to 3 minutes.
- •Prepare the toppings first and have them ready to place on the dough. Once the dough is on the pizza peel, quickly add the toppings before the gluten relaxes and the dough becomes hard to transfer to the baking stone.
- Adding the cheese near the end of baking allows it to stay

soft and requires less cheese.

▪ See About Whole-Grain Breads (p. 133).

PIZZA DOUGH

Use this whole-wheat dough for calzones and braided breads, too.

1½ cups plus 2 tablespoons warm water (13 ounces)

2 tablespoons olive oil

1½ teaspoons salt

2 tablespoons honey or other sweetener

2 cups plus 2 tablespoons whole-wheat bread flour

2 cups unbleached bread flour

2 tablespoons vital wheat gluten

1½ teaspoons instant yeast

OR

2¼ teaspoons active dry yeast

PREP:
5 MINUTES

DOUGH CYCLE:
1½–2 HOURS IN BREAD MACHINE

YIELD:
2¼ POUNDS DOUGH (MAKES 2 [14-INCH] THIN–CRUST PIZZAS)

Place the ingredients in the bread machine in the order listed or as recommended by the manufacturer. Select the dough cycle and press start. Check the dough after 5 minutes of kneading, and adjust the amount of water or flour as necessary to produce a soft ball. When the dough cycle ends, follow the recipe for whole-wheat Pizza (p. 255).

Nutrition Facts per Serving (1/16): 130 calories, 2.5 g. total fat (0 g. saturated fat), 0 mg. cholesterol, 220 mg. sodium, 24 g. carbohydrate, 2 g. fiber, 1 g. sugars, 4 g. protein. **Daily Values:** 0% vitamin A, 0% vitamin C, 0% calcium, 8% iron. **Diabetic Exchanges:** 1½ breads.

Hand-kneaded Method: Combine the ingredients in a mixing bowl. Coat your hands with cooking spray, and knead the dough on a lightly floured surface, adding as little flour as possible, until the dough is smooth and elastic, about 7 to 10 minutes. Preheat the oven to 200° F and turn it off. Place the dough in a large heat-proof bowl, and cover it with a damp towel. Place the dough in the warm oven until the dough doubles in size (about 1 hour; 1½ to 2 hours at room temperature).

Standing Mixer Method: Combine the ingredients in the bowl of a standing mixer. Set the mixer on low speed and, using the dough hook, knead the dough about 5 to 7 minutes, or until it becomes elastic. Follow the remaining Hand-kneaded Method directions.

Herbed Pizza Dough: Add 1 tablespoon Italian Seasoning Mix (p. 259), or 1 teaspoon dried chives, 1 teaspoon basil leaves, and 1 teaspoon oregano leaves.

Pizza Dough Mix: Except for the yeast, store the dry ingredients in an airtight container at room temperature for up to 1 month, or in the refrigerator or freezer for up to 3 months.

PIZZA

Better than take-out.

2¼ pounds Pizza Dough (p. 253)

OR

2 pounds frozen whole-wheat bread
dough, thawed

2 tablespoons stone-ground cornmeal

olive oil to brush on crust, optional

1⅓ cups pizza sauce

1⅓ cups sliced ripe olives

1 cup sliced mushrooms

3 cups shredded part-skim mozzarella
cheese or nondairy cheese

PREP:
20 MINUTES

BAKE:
9–15 MINUTES
PER PIZZA

YIELD:
2 (14-INCH)
THIN PIZZAS

About 30 minutes prior to baking, adjust the oven rack to the low position; place the pizza stone, baking tiles, pizza pan, or inverted baking sheet on the rack. Preheat the oven to 450° F, and lightly flour a work surface. Remove half the dough from the bread machine, and place it on the prepared surface. (Keep the remaining dough in the bread machine with the lid closed to prevent it from drying out.) Using your fingers, shape the dough into an 8-inch diameter disk; continue flattening the dough, from the center to the edges, until it is about 12 inches in diameter. Let the dough rest for several minutes to relax the gluten; resume stretching the dough until it is 14 inches in diameter.

Sprinkle 1 tablespoon cornmeal on the pizza peel, and transfer the dough to it. Brush the dough with olive oil, if desired. Spread ⅔ cup pizza sauce over the dough, leaving a 1-inch border around the edge. Working quickly, distribute ⅔ cup olives and ½ cup mushrooms over the dough. With a quick jerk of the hand, immediately slide the dough onto the heated pizza stone. Bake the pizza for 7 to 8 minutes (8 to 10 minutes, if using a pizza pan). Sprinkle 1½ cups cheese on the pizza, and bake it an additional 2 to 3 minutes (3 to 5 minutes, if using a pizza pan), or until the cheese melts, the toppings are hot, and the edge of the crust is lightly browned.

Remove the pizza from the oven and allow it to cool for 2 to 3 minutes. Using a pizza wheel, kitchen scissors, or a sharp knife, cut the pizza into 8 wedges. Serve hot. Repeat the process for the remaining dough, or select another option (below). To store, cool the pizza to room temperature, then place it in an airtight container in the refrigerator for up to 1 week or in the freezer for up to 3 months. Partially defrost the pizza, and reheat it at 350°F.

Nutrition Facts per Serving (⅛ pizza): 220 calories. 8 g. total fat (3 g. saturated fat), 10 mg. cholesterol, 510 mg. sodium, 28 g. carbohydrate, 3 g. fiber, 1 g. sugar, 11 g. protein. **Daily Values:** 10% vitamin A, 8 % vitamin C, 20% calcium, 10% iron. **Diabetic Exchanges:** 1½ breads, 1 lean meat, 1 fat.

Toppings: Try other toppings: artichoke hearts, sliced onions, bell peppers, zucchini, tomatoes, chopped fresh spinach, grated carrots, steamed broccoli or cauliflower flowerets, asparagus, sun-dried tomatoes, roasted vegetables, shredded basil leaves, or pineapple tidbits.

Pesto Pizza: Brush a circle of the dough with olive oil. Prick the crust with a fork to prevent bubbles from forming during baking.

Bake at 450°F for 10 to 12 minutes, or until the crust begins to brown. Remove the pizza from the oven and spread Pesto (p. 316) over it, leaving a ½-inch border around the edge. Serve immediately. Or spread ¼ to ⅓ cup (about 4 frozen cubes) Pesto on a prebaked crust. Bake for 6 to 8 minutes, or until hot.

Other Sizes: This dough may also be used to make two 12-inch medium-thick pizzas (bake 11 to 15 minutes), eight 6-inch medium-thick pizzas (bake 7 to 11 minutes), eight (8-inch) Calzones (p. 335), or two Pizza Braids (p. 250).

Prebaked Pizza Crust: Prick the flattened dough with a fork at 1-inch intervals. Preheat a baking stone to 450°F; bake the pizza crust on the baking stone for 5 minutes. Cool. Store the baked crust in an airtight container in the refrigerator for up to 6 days or in the freezer for up to 3 months. Thaw at room temperature before using. Cover the crust with sauce and toppings. Bake at 450°F in the middle of the oven for 6 to 8 minutes, or until the toppings are hot. Add cheese, and bake an additional 2 to 3 minutes, or until the cheese melts. For an extra crisp crust, place the crust directly on the oven rack.

Refrigerated Pizza Dough: Refrigerate the pizza dough in an airtight container for up to 2 days.

Frozen Pizza Dough: Divide the dough in half and shape it into a ball. Flatten each half into a disk, and place it in an airtight container (a quart freezer bag works well) for up to 3 months. Defrost the dough, loosely wrapped and at room temperature, for 4 to 9 hours; in the refrigerator, for 8 to 16 hours; overnight; or microwave it on low (10 percent), for 10 minutes. Turn the dough over and rotate it a quarter turn; let it rest 10 minutes. Repeat steps 1 or 2 times, until the dough is thawed. Thawing times vary. Check the dough frequently.

Personal Pita Pizza: Use whole-wheat pocket bread instead of pizza crust. Place on a baking pan. Spread with 1 to 2 tablespoons pizza sauce, and top with vegetables. Bake 4 to 5 minutes at 425°F. Add cheese, and bake 1 to 2 more minutes until the cheese melts.

English Muffin Pizza: Use toasted whole-wheat English muffins instead of pizza crust.

French Bread Pizza: Use whole-wheat French bread instead of pizza crust.

PIZZA SAUCE

So simple to make.

PREP:
5 MINUTES

YIELD:
1⅓ CUPS
(SAUCE FOR 2
[14-INCH]
PIZZAS)

1 (6-ounce) can tomato paste

¾ cup water (1 tomato paste can)

2 teaspoons extra-virgin olive oil

½ teaspoon salt

1 tablespoon Italian Seasoning Mix (p. 259)

Whisk ingredients except Italian Seasoning Mix together in a bowl. Crush the Italian Seasoning Mix between fingers to release flavors; stir into the sauce. Let stand 10 minutes. Spread sauce on pizza crust, using about ⅔ cup sauce for a 14-inch pizza. Freeze extra sauce for up to 6 months.

Nutrition Facts per Serving (4 teaspoons): 15 calories, 0.5 g. total fat (0 g. saturated fat), 0 mg. cholesterol, 85 mg. sodium, 2 g. carbohydrate, 0 g. fiber, 0 g. sugars, 0 g. protein. **Daily Values:** 6% vitamin A, 8% vitamin C, 0% calcium, 2% iron. **Diabetic Exchanges:** free.

Garlic: Add 1 minced garlic clove.

Basil: Add 1 tablespoon minced fresh basil.

Crushed Tomato Pizza Sauce: Replace tomato paste and water with one 28-ounce can crushed tomatoes. Double the amount of oil and Italian Seasoning Mix, but do not double the amount of salt. Makes 3 cups.

ITALIAN SEASONING MIX

A versatile "thyme-savor" that can be adjusted to suit your taste.

1 teaspoon *(¼ cup)* **dried oregano leaves**

1 teaspoon *(¼ cup)* **dried basil leaves**

½ teaspoon *(2 tablespoons)* **dried parsley**

½ teaspoon *(2 tablespoons)* **onion powder**

½ teaspoon *(2 tablespoons)* **garlic powder**

⅛ teaspoon *(1½ teaspoon)* **thyme**

PREP:
5 MINUTES

YIELD:
MINI MIX:
1 TABLESPOON
MEGA MIX:
¾ CUP

Combine seasonings, and store in an airtight container in a cool, dark place for up to 6 months. Before using, stir to distribute seasonings, and crush herbs between fingers to release the flavors.

Nutrition Facts per Serving (1 tablespoon): 0 calories, 0 g. total fat (0 g. saturated fat), 0 mg. cholesterol, 0 mg. sodium, 0 g. carbohydrate, 0 g. fiber, 0 g. sugars, 0 g. protein. **Daily Values:** 0% vitamin A, 0% vitamin C, 0% calcium, 0% iron. **Diabetic Exchanges:** free.

Serving Idea: Use to flavor pizza sauce, pizza crust, bread, pasta, spaghetti sauce, and salad dressing.

Additional Herbs: Add rosemary or marjoram.

 # SKILLET CHILI MACARONI

Great for camping or a quick one-dish entrée.

PREP:
10 MINUTES

COOK:
15-20 MINUTES

YIELD:
4½ CUPS
(6 SERVINGS)

1 cup water

¾ cup elbow macaroni, preferably whole-grain

½ cup beef-style textured soy protein (TSP) granules

3 tablespoons dried minced onions

1 tablespoon Mexican Seasoning Mix (p. 307)

1 teaspoon dried parsley flakes

1 teaspoon dried cilantro

¼ teaspoon salt

¼ **teaspoon garlic powder**

1 **(14½-ounce) can diced tomatoes**

1 **(15½-ounce) can red kidney beans, rinsed and drained**

1 **(8-ounce) can tomato sauce**

¼ **cup shredded reduced-fat cheese or nondairy cheese**

Combine all ingredients except cheese in a large skillet or medium saucepan. Bring to a boil over medium-high heat. Reduce the heat, cover, and simmer, stirring occasionally, for 10 to 15 minutes, or until the macaroni is tender. Add water as needed. Taste and adjust seasonings. Remove from heat and garnish with cheese. Serve hot. Store leftovers in an airtight container in the refrigerator for up to 1 week.

Nutrition Facts per Serving (¾ cup): 210 calories, 1.5 g. total fat (0 g. saturated fat), 0 mg. cholesterol, 630 mg. sodium, 36 g. carbohydrate, 10 g. fiber, 7 g. sugars, 14 g. protein. **Daily Values:** 15% vitamin A, 25% vitamin C, 4% calcium, 8% iron. **Diabetic Exchanges:** 2 breads, 1 lean meat.

Serving Idea: Serve with green beans, tossed salad, and fresh fruit.

Instead of Mexican Seasoning: Use 2 teaspoons chili powder and 1 teaspoon cumin.

Unflavored TSP: Add 1 teaspoon beef-style seasoning or ½ teaspoon salt.

Skillet Chili Macaroni Mix: Combine the dry ingredients and store them in an airtight container in a cool, dry place for up to 6 months. For added convenience, store the mix and the canned goods in a small paper bag. Fold over the top of the bag and staple. Or store in a resealable gallon bag, label, date, and include instructions or cookbook page number. Store in pantry.

STIR-FRY SEASONING MIX

A convenient way to season stir-fry vegetables.

PREP:
5 MINUTES

YIELD:
MINI MIX:
2 TABLESPOONS
MEGA MIX:
1½ CUPS

1 tablespoon *(½ cup)* cornstarch or modified cornstarch

2 teaspoons *(⅓ cup)* vegetarian chicken-style seasoning

1 teaspoon *(2 tablespoons plus 2 teaspoons)* onion powder

¼ teaspoon *(2 teaspoons)* garlic powder

Combine the ingredients and store them in an airtight container for up to 6 months.

Nutrition Facts per Serving (2 tablespoons): 15 calories, 0 g. total fat (0 g. saturated fat), 0 mg. cholesterol, 210 mg. sodium, 3 g. carbohydrate, 0 g. fiber, 1 g. sugars, 0 g. protein. **Daily Values:** 0% vitamin A, 0% vitamin C, 0% calcium, 0% iron. **Diabetic Exchanges:** free.

SPEEDY STIR-FRY VEGETABLES

An easy one-dish meal.

1 cup water

2 tablespoons Stir-fry Seasoning Mix
   (p. 262)

1 tablespoon reduced-sodium soy sauce or
   soy sauce alternative

2 cloves minced garlic

1 tablespoon oil

1 pound frozen stir-fry vegetables (about
   5 cups)

Hot cooked brown rice

PREP:
5 MINUTES

COOK:
5 MINUTES

YIELD:
4 SERVINGS

Combine the water, Stir-fry Seasoning Mix, soy sauce, and garlic; set aside. In a large skillet or wok, heat the oil over high heat. Add the vegetables and stir-fry for 1 minute. Stir the sauce mixture, and pour it into the skillet, stirring constantly. Bring the mixture to a boil and boil 1 minute or until crisp-tender. Serve over brown rice.

Nutrition Facts per Serving (1 cup without rice): 90 calories, 3.5 g. total fat (0 g. saturated fat), 0 mg. cholesterol, 430 mg. sodium, 12 g. carbohydrate, 3 g. fiber, 5 g. sugars, 2 g. protein. **Daily Values:** 100% vitamin A, 30% vitamin C, 4% calcium, 25% iron. **Diabetic Exchanges:** 2 vegetables, 1 fat.

Fresh Vegetables: Use 1 pound fresh vegetables instead of frozen. Increase the cooking time as needed.

Frozen Vegetable Blends: Replace stir-fry vegetables with frozen vegetable blends (such as broccoli, cauliflower, and carrots). After boiling for 1 minute, cover, reduce heat to medium-high and cook until crisp-tender.

Microwave: Place the vegetables in microwave-safe dish and cover. Microwave on high for 2 minutes. Stir in the sauce mixture, and microwave an additional 2 to 3 minutes, stirring every minute.

Stir-fry Vegetables With Sesame: Add a dash of sesame oil, and garnish with sesame seeds.

Stir-fry Vegetables With Ginger: Add grated gingerroot to taste.

Main Dish Stir-fry: Add 1½ to 2 cups cubed extra-firm tofu, Wheat Meat (p. 276), or meatless beef-style or chicken-style alternative with the sauce mixture.

STROGANOFF

A tasty alternative to boxed noodle dishes.

4 ounces (about 1½ cups) sliced fresh
mushrooms

OR

1 (4-ounce) can sliced mushrooms, drained
½ cup chopped onions
2 tablespoons oil or margarine
1 clove garlic, minced
2 cups diced beef-style Wheat Meat
(p. 276)

OR

2 cups vegetarian beef alternative

OR

2 cups frozen and thawed firm tofu cubes
3½ cups water
1 cup Cream Sauce Mix (p. 240)
2 teaspoons vegetarian beef-style seasoning
½ cup low-fat sour cream, or nonfat plain
yogurt or nondairy sour cream or yogurt
cooked noodles or brown rice

In a nonstick skillet over medium heat, stir and

PREP:
10 MINUTES

COOK:
10 MINUTES

YIELD:
6 SERVINGS
(6 CUPS)

cook mushrooms and onions in oil or margarine until tender. Stir in garlic and Wheat Meat or vegetarian beef alternative or tofu cubes and brown for 2 to 3 minutes. Stir in water, Cream Sauce Mix, and vegetarian beef-style seasoning. Cook, stirring frequently until thickened. Just before serving, stir in low-fat sour cream, nonfat plain yogurt, or nondairy sour cream or yogurt. Cook until hot, but not boiling. Taste and adjust seasoning. Serve over noodles or brown rice.

Nutrition Facts per Serving (1 cup without noodles or rice): 160 calories, 7 g. total fat (1.5 g. saturated fat), 10 mg. cholesterol, 620 mg. sodium, 17 g. carbohydrate, 0 g. fiber, 7 g. sugars, 7 g. protein. **Daily Values:** 6% vitamin A, 4% vitamin C, 15% calcium, 4% iron. **Diabetic Exchanges:** 1 lean meat, 1 bread.

Double Mushroom Stroganoff: Replace water and Cream Sauce Mix with two 10¼-ounce cans condensed cream of mushroom soup plus 1 can water.

SWEET-AND-SOUR TOFU AND VEGETABLES

Also delicious with pineapple chunks, green pepper strips, and onions.
If you replace the tofu with Wheat Meat, reduce the soy sauce by about half.

¾ cup pineapple juice

3 tablespoons tomato sauce

2 tablespoons Stir-fry Seasoning Mix
   (p. 262)

2 tablespoons reduced sodium soy sauce or
   soy sauce alternative

1 tablespoon lemon juice

1 tablespoon honey or other sweetener

2 cloves minced garlic

1 tablespoon oil

1 14- to 16-ounce package extra-firm tofu
   or frozen, thawed, and drained tofu, cut
   into ¾-inch cubes

1 pound frozen stir-fry vegetables (about 5
   cups)

Hot cooked brown rice

½ cup roasted cashews

PREP:
10 MINUTES

MARINATE:
10–15 MINUTES

COOK:
5 MINUTES

YIELD:
4 SERVINGS
(6 CUPS)

In a bowl, stir together pineapple juice, tomato sauce, Stir-fry Seasoning Mix, soy sauce, lemon juice, honey, and garlic. Stir tofu cubes into seasoning mixture. Marinate for 10 to 15 minutes. In a large skillet or wok, heat oil over high heat. Add vegetables and stir-fry 1 minute. Stir sauce mixture and pour into skillet. Stir constantly and bring to a boil. Boil 1 minute. Serve over brown rice. Garnish with roasted cashews.

Nutrition Facts per Serving (1½ cups without rice): 270 calories, 12 g. total fat (1.5 g. saturated fat), 0 mg. cholesterol, 440 mg. sodium, 25 g. carbohydrate, 3 g. fiber, 13 g. sugars, 18 g. protein. **Daily Values:** 110% vitamin A, 50% vitamin C, 70% calcium, 80% iron. **Diabetic Exchanges:** 2 lean meats, 2 vegetables, 1 fruit.

TACOS

Fun, fast, and flavorful—with less fat!

PREP:
15 MINUTES

COOK:
5 MINUTES

YIELD:
12 TACOS

1½ cups shredded lettuce

1 medium tomato, chopped

¾ cup shredded reduced-fat cheese or nondairy cheese

½ cup chopped onion

½ cup salsa

⅓ cup reduced fat sour cream or nondairy alternative

⅓ cup sliced olives

Chopped avocados or guacamole, optional

12 ounces vegetarian burger

¾ cup water

2½–3 tablespoons Mexican Seasoning Mix (p. 307), or to
taste

1 tablespoon chopped dried onion

1 teaspoon unbleached all-purpose flour

12 corn tortillas

Place the lettuce, tomato, cheese, onion, sour cream, olives, and avocados in separate bowls; cover bowls with plastic wrap. Combine the burger, water, Mexican Seasoning Mix, dried onion, and flour in a 2-quart microwave-safe dish. Cover, and microwave on high for about 6 minutes, or until hot, stirring after 3 minutes. Set aside. Coat a nonstick skillet with cooking spray; preheat the skillet over medium heat. Cover the tortillas with a moistened paper towel, and microwave them on high for 2 minutes, or until they are hot and limp. Place about 3 tablespoons taco filling in the center of each tortilla and fold in half. Heat the tacos in the skillet until they are lightly browned on both sides. Remove plastic wrap from bowls, and have each person assemble their own tacos.

Nutrition Facts per Serving (1 taco): 140 calories, 3.5 g. total fat (1.5 g. saturated fat), 5 mg. cholesterol, 300 mg. sodium, 18 g. carbohydrate, 3 g. fiber, 2 g. sugars, 10 g. protein. **Daily Values:** 15% vitamin A, 10% vitamin C, 15% calcium, 10% iron. **Diabetic Exchanges:** 1 lean meat, 1 bread.

Serving Idea: Serve with corn and fresh blueberries.

Refried Bean Filling: Fill tacos with 3 tablespoons refried beans instead of vegetarian burger.

Taco Seasoning Mix: Combine Mexican Seasoning Mix, dried onion, and flour. Store in an airtight container for up to 6 months.

ABOUT FREEZING TOFU

- Freezing changes the texture of tofu: it becomes chewier. Frozen and thawed tofu can be used to make Tofu Nuggets (p. 271) and added to such dishes as Speedy Stir-fry Vegetables (p. 263), Stroganoff (p. 265), Vegetable Stew (p. 273), or Curried Tofu With Broccoli (p. 243).
- Firm or extra-firm fresh tofu (not shelf-stable) works best.
- Freezing tofu cubes or slices is a good way to deal with leftover tofu odds and ends.
- To freeze: drain and remove tofu from a 1-pound package. Slice it into 1-inch cubes. Place the cubes in an airtight container and freeze them for at least 4 hours, or until they become firm. Use them within 3 months.
- Defrost frozen tofu in the refrigerator for 12 hours, or with the microwave defrost cycle, 8 to 10 minutes.
- After thawing the tofu, squeeze out the excess water before using it in a recipe.

TOFU NUGGETS

A fun and kid-friendly food.

1 pound frozen tofu cubes, thawed and
drained

2½ tablespoons Scrambled Tofu Seasoning
(p. 181)

½ cup Crispy Coating Mix (p. 272)
Reduced-fat tartar sauce or ketchup,
optional

PREP:
15 MINUTES

FREEZE:
4 OR MORE
HOURS

BAKE:
20–25 MINUTES

YIELD:
4 SERVINGS

Preheat the oven to 400° F. Combine Scrambled
Tofu Seasoning Mix and Crispy Coating Mix in a
shallow bowl or pie plate. Dip tofu cubes into the
coating mix, coating all sides. Place the cubes on a
nonstick baking sheet, and bake for 20 to 25 minutes,
or until they are lightly browned and crispy. If desired, serve with reduced-fat tartar sauce.

Nutrition Facts per Serving (½ cup): 180 calories, 9 g.
total fat (1.5 g. saturated fat), 0 mg. cholesterol, 840 mg. sodium,
12 g. carbohydrate, 4 g. fiber, 1 g. sugars, 18 g. protein. **Daily
Values:** 6% vitamin A, 4% vitamin C, 70% calcium, 70% iron.
Diabetic Exchanges: ¼ cup = 1 medium-fat meat.

Serving Idea: Serve with pasta salad, oatmeal-raisin
cookies, and grapes.

CRISPY COATING MIX

A basic make-ahead mix that's worth keeping on hand.

PREP:
10 MINUTES

YIELD:
4 CUPS

8-10 cups corn- or wheat-flake cereal, preferably whole-grain (about 11 ounces)

1 cup wheat germ

4 teaspoons dried parsley, crushed

4 teaspoons paprika

1 teaspoon onion powder

1 teaspoon celery salt or vegetable seasoning salt

½ teaspoon garlic powder

Process the cereal in a food processor or blender until finely crushed. (Or place the cereal in a plastic bag and crush it with a rolling pin.) Measure 3 cups of crumbs into a bowl. Stir in the remaining ingredients with a wire whisk until evenly distributed. Store the mix in an airtight container at room temperature for up to 1 month or in the refrigerator for up to 3 months.

Nutrition Facts per Serving (1 tablespoon): 20 calories, 0 g. total fat (0 g. saturated fat), 0 mg. cholesterol, 50 mg. sodium, 4 g. carbohydrate, 0 g. fiber, 0 g. sugars, 1 g. protein. **Daily Values:** 4% vitamin A, 4% vitamin C, 0% calcium, 6 % iron. **Diabetic Exchanges:** free.

Serving Idea: Use for a crispy coating on Tofu Nuggets or Cutlets, and Wheat Meat (p. 276).

Sesame Seeds: Add ½ cup sesame seeds.

VEGETABLE STEW

Colorful and flavorful.

1 tablespoon olive oil

1 medium onion, cut into ½-inch slices

2 celery ribs, sliced

2 cloves garlic, minced

5 medium red potatoes (about 1¼ pounds), cut into 1-inch pieces

3 cups water

2 cups peeled baby carrots

OR

2 medium carrots, cut into ½-inch slices

1 (15½-ounce) can dark red kidney beans, drained and rinsed

1 tablespoon tomato paste

OR

½ cup canned diced tomatoes

PREP:
25 MINUTES

COOK:
30 MINUTES

YIELD:
12 CUPS

1 tablespoon vegetarian beef-style seasoning

1 bay leaf

½–1 teaspoon dried thyme leaves

¼ teaspoon salt

2 cups frozen peas, thawed

¼ cup minced fresh parsley

OR

4 teaspoons dried parsley flakes

Heat the oil in a large saucepan over medium heat. Stir in the celery and onion; cook until the vegetables are tender, about 5 minutes. Stir in the garlic and cook 1 minute. Stir in the potatoes, water, carrots, kidney beans, tomato paste, beef-style seasoning, bay leaf, thyme, and salt. Bring the mixture to a boil, cover, and reduce heat; simmer until the vegetables are tender, about 20 minutes.

To thicken the stew using a blender or food processor, remove 1 cup of the potatoes and 1½ to 2 cups of liquid, and process until smooth. Return puree to the saucepan. (Or thicken the stew with 1 tablespoon cornstarch dissolved in 1 tablespoon water.)

Stir in the peas, and cook until they are heated through, about 5 minutes. Taste, and adjust seasonings; remove bay leaf. Garnish with parsley. Serve hot. Store in an airtight container in the refrigerator for up to 1 week.

Nutrition Facts per Serving (1 cup): 130 calories, 1.5 g. total fat (0 g. saturated fat), 0 mg. cholesterol, 380 mg. sodium, 24 g. carbohydrate, 5 g. fiber, 5 g. sugars, 5 g. protein. **Daily Values:** 90% vitamin A, 20% vitamin C, 4% calcium, 8% iron. **Diabetic Exchanges:** 1 bread, 1 vegetable.

Serving Idea: Serve with Whole-Wheat Biscuits (p. 149), coleslaw, and Fruit Crumble (p. 204).

Vegetable Stew With Wheat Meat: Add 2 cups beef-style Wheat Meat (p. 276) or meat substitute cut into bite-size pieces.

Vegetable Stew With Small Whole Onions: Replace onion slices with 1 cup frozen small whole onions. Omit sautéing.

Pressure Cooker Vegetable Stew: Cook onion, celery, and garlic in a large pressure cooker. Add the remaining ingredients except peas and parsley. Seal pressure cooker and bring to high pressure over medium-high heat. Pressure-cook for 2 to 3 minutes. Reduce the pressure quickly under cold running water. Proceed with recipe.

Slow Cooker Vegetable Stew: Combine all ingredients except peas and parsley in a 3½-quart slow cooker. Cover, and cook on low 8 to 9 hours, or on high 4 to 5 hours until the vegetables are tender. Thicken the stew as desired. Stir in the peas, cover, and cook on high about 15 minutes, or until the peas are heated through. Taste and adjust seasonings; remove the bay leaf. Garnish with parsley.

ABOUT WHEAT MEAT

- Also called gluten or seitan.
- Vital wheat gluten is concentrated wheat protein. Look for it at natural-food stores. Some supermarkets stock vital wheat gluten next to the flour, as it is often used in whole-grain breads.
- Results may vary with different brands of vital wheat gluten. If the dough is not stiff and cohesive, knead in vital wheat gluten, one tablespoon at a time.
- The wheat meat will nearly double in size while simmering.
- Freeze the broth with the wheat meat, or thicken it to use as gravy.

WHEAT MEAT AND BROTH

Wheat Meat, which uses vital wheat gluten (e.g., Do-pep),
is a versatile, high protein, low-fat meat substitute.

PREP:
20 MINUTES

STANDING:
60 MINUTES

COOK:
60 MINUTES

YIELD:
32 LARGE PIECES

2 cups plus 2 tablespoons vital wheat gluten

½ cup soy flour

½ cup quick oats

3 tablespoons vegetarian chicken-style seasoning

1½ tablespoons onion powder

1 teaspoon garlic powder

½ teaspoon salt

1⅔ cups water

Wheat Meat Broth:

10 cups water

½ cup reduced-sodium soy sauce or soy sauce alternative

3 cloves garlic, minced

3 bay leaves

¼ teaspoon salt

Wheat Meat: Combine the dry ingredients in a mixing bowl. Pour water into the mix all at once. Quickly stir until the mixture is evenly moistened and forms a ball (the mixture should be stiff and cohesive). Knead for 1 minute to assure thorough mixing. Shape the dough into a 16-inch-long roll. Wrap the roll in plastic wrap and let stand for 1 to 2 hours. Store the dough in an airtight container in the refrigerator for up to 3 days or in the freezer for up to 6 months.

Wheat Meat Broth: Bring the Wheat Meat Broth ingredients to a boil in a large saucepan. Unwrap the gluten roll on a cutting board and, using a serrated knife, cut the 16-inch log into 1/2-inch slices. Drop the Wheat Meat pieces into the boiling broth, keeping the broth boiling. Cover, reduce the heat to medium, and gently boil for 15 to 60 minutes. Remove the pan from heat, and allow the Wheat Meat and Broth to cool for 1 hour. Remove the bay leaves. Store the Wheat Meat and Broth in an airtight container in the refrigerator for up to 1 week or in the freezer for up to 6 months.

Nutrition Facts per Serving (2 pieces): 60 calories, 0 g. total fat (0 g. saturated fat), 0 mg. cholesterol, 550 mg. sodium, 7 g. carbohydrate, 0 g. fiber, 1 g. sugars, 6 g. protein. **Daily Values:** 0% vitamin A, 0% vitamin C, 2% calcium, 4% iron. **Diabetic Exchanges:** 1/2 lean meat, 1/2 bread.

Beef-style Wheat Meat: Replace the chicken-style seasoning with beef-style seasoning. Add 2 teaspoons browning sauce with the water.

Wheat Meat Mix: Store the dry ingredients in an airtight container at room temperature for up to 2 weeks, or in the refrigerator or freezer for up to 6 months.

Broth Additions: Add to the broth: 1 finely chopped medium onion, 2 finely chopped celery ribs, and/or 2 finely chopped medium carrots.

Pressure-cooked Wheat Meat: Pressure-cook Wheat Meat pieces for 20 to 30 minutes. For a firmer, sliceable texture, form the dough into two 6-inch logs. Pressure-cook for 15 minutes.

Chewy Wheat Meat: Decrease soy flour to 2 tablespoons, and decrease oats to 1 tablespoon.

Extra-chewy Wheat Meat: Omit soy flour and oats. Shape the dough into an oblong shape about 6 inches long; let rest for 5 minutes. Place dough in the boiling broth in pressure cooker. Seal, and pressure-cook for 15 minutes. Release pressure, and allow the Wheat Meat to cool in the broth for 1 hour. Thinly slice the Wheat Meat, cut it into cubes, or grind it.

Wheat Balls: Pinch off small pieces of dough (about 1½ inches in diameter) and drop them into the boiling broth. Cook according to recipe. Serving Idea: Stir the cooked wheat balls into spaghetti sauce. Heat on low in a slow cooker until hot, about 3 to 4 hours. Serve over spaghetti.

WHEAT MEAT CUTLETS

A simple and delicious way to serve Wheat Meat.

PREP:
5 MINUTES

COOK:
5 MINUTES

YIELD:
4 SERVINGS

1 tablespoon olive or vegetable oil

¾ cup Breading Meal (p. 279), seasoned bread crumbs, or Crispy Coating Mix (p. 272)

8 large Wheat Meat pieces

Heat the oil in a large nonstick skillet over medium heat. Pour the Breading Meal into a shallow bowl. Coat both sides of the Wheat Meat with the breading meal and place in the skillet. Fry until the

Wheat Meat pieces are lightly browned on both sides. Serve plain or with gravy or barbecue sauce.

Nutrition Facts per Serving (2 cutlets): 140 calories, 4 g. total fat (0 g. saturated fat), 0 mg. cholesterol, 620 mg. sodium, 17 g. carbohydrate, 3 g. fiber, 1 g. sugars, 9 g. protein. **Daily Values:** 0% vitamin A, 0% vitamin C, 2% calcium, 8% iron. **Diabetic Exchanges:** 1 lean meat, 1 bread.

BREADING MEAL

For coating Wheat Meat Cutlets, Tofu Cutlets, or meat alternatives.

¾ **cup whole-wheat flour**

¼ **cup nutritional yeast flakes**

1 **teaspoon onion powder**

½ **teaspoon garlic powder**

¼ **teaspoon salt**

PREP:
5 MINUTES

YIELD:
2 CUPS

Combine the ingredients in an airtight container and store in a cool place or in the refrigerator for up to 3 months.

Nutrition Facts per Serving (1 tablespoon): 25 calories, 0 g. total fat (0 g. saturated fat), 0 mg. cholesterol, 35 mg. sodium, 5 g. carbohydrate, 1 g. fiber, 0 g. sugars, 2 g. protein. **Daily Values:** 0% vitamin A, 0% vitamin C, 0% calcium, 2% iron. **Diabetic Exchanges:** free.

Additions: Add corn flour, potato flour, wheat germ, or celery seed.

WHEAT MEAT IN GRAVY

A slow cooker works great for heating
Wheat Meat for an after-church potluck.

Drain broth from the Wheat Meat, and add 2 tablespoons flour or 1 tablespoon cornstarch per cup of broth to thicken. Add sautéed onions and mushrooms, if desired. Cook over medium–high heat, stirring frequently until thickened.

Place the Wheat Meat in a slow cooker and cover with gravy. Heat on low for 3 to 4 hours. (Or place the Wheat Meat in a casserole dish, cover with gravy, and bake at 350°F for 30 minutes or until hot.)

Nutrition Facts per Serving (2 pieces): 80 calories, 0 g. total fat (0 g. saturated fat), 0 mg. cholesterol, 720 mg. sodium, 11 g. carbohydrate, 0 g. fiber, 1 g. sugars, 7 g. protein. **Daily Values:** 0% vitamin A, 0% vitamin C, 2% calcium, 4% iron. **Diabetic Exchanges:** 1 lean meat, ½ bread.

Sour Cream: Just before serving, stir in reduced–fat sour cream, nondairy sour cream, or nonfat plain yogurt.

OLD-FASHIONED WHEAT MEAT

Here's how to prepare Wheat Meat using inexpensive, common ingredients. Vary the flavor by substituting a different strongly flavored savory broth.

4 cups whole-wheat bread flour

4 cups unbleached all-purpose flour or unbleached bread flour

3½ cups water

PREP:
30–45 MINUTES

STANDING:
30–120
MINUTES

COOK:
45–60 MINUTES

YIELD:
32 SMALL PIECES

In a large bowl, stir together the flour and water. Transfer the dough to a work surface and knead it for 5 to 10 minutes by hand or with a dough hook until a smooth, elastic ball is formed. Return the dough to the bowl and cover it completely with cold water. Soak the dough for a minimum of 30 minutes, preferably 1 to 2 hours. Or soak the dough overnight in the refrigerator. (Soaking softens the starch, making it easier to wash out.) Place a colander in the sink, and drain off the water; knead the dough under running water to wash out the starch, alternating the water temperature between warm and cold water (warm water softens the gluten, and cold water firms the gluten). At first the rinse water will be quite milky. Continue rinsing the dough until the rinse water is nearly clear, about 10 to 30 minutes (leaving a little starch in the Wheat Meat makes it more tender). When the Wheat Meat is well washed, it will be reduced to about 2 cups; it will be in one (shiny) piece with a firm, elastic consistency. Shape the dough into a 16-inch-long roll and allow it to drain.

Prepare Wheat Meat Broth, reducing water to 6 cups. Using a serrated knife, slice roll into ¼-inch pieces. Keep the pieces separated to prevent sticking together. Drop the pieces into the boiling broth. Cover, reduce heat to medium, and boil gently for 1 hour. Remove pan from heat, and allow Wheat Meat and broth to cool for 1 hour. Remove the bay leaves. Store the Wheat Meat and broth in an air-tight container in the refrigerator for up to 1 week or in the freezer for up to 6 months.

Nutrition Facts per Serving (4 pieces): 70 calories, 0 g. total fat (0 g. saturated fat), 0 mg. cholesterol, 640 mg. sodium, 8 g. carbohydrate, 0 g. fiber, 0 g. sugars, 8 g. protein. **Daily Values:** 0% vitamin A, 0% vitamin C, 0% calcium, 4 % iron. **Diabetic Exchanges:** 1 lean meat, ½ bread.

BEANS

BEANS AND EMISSION CONTROL

The Digestion Question

"Beans once a day keep the doctor away." We know the benefits of beans: high in fiber, cholesterol-lowering, protein-rich, inexpensive, and versatile. But the negative reputation of beans as a gas-forming food leads many people to ask: What can be done for emission control?

According to gastroenterologists the intestines normally contain gas, which is expelled an average of 14 times a day. When big sugar molecules from beans and other foods reach the large intestine undigested, bacteria in the colon ferment these sugars and produce additional gas. While flatus cannot be banished from the body, simple bean soaking and cooking techniques can minimize it.

Unleaded Legumes

The problematic sugars in dry beans dissolve easily in water, and soaking and rinsing make the beans more digestible. The nutrient loss is negligible. Various soaking techniques are listed below. The American Dry Bean Board recommends the hot soak.

- *Hot-soak:* Sort and rinse one pound of beans and place in a large saucepan with 10 cups water (or water to cover beans by two to three inches). Heat water to boiling. Boil two to three minutes. Remove pan from heat, cover, and let stand at least four or more hours. Drain and rinse thoroughly. Add six cups water, two teaspoons salt, and one to two tablespoons olive oil or vegetable oil. Simmer until beans are tender.

- *Quick soak:* Same as hot soak, except soak beans one to two hours.

- *Long-soak:* Sort and rinse one pound of beans, and place in a large saucepan. Add 10 cups water (or water to cover beans by two to three inches). Soak beans overnight or 12 to 24 hours. Drain, rinse, add water, and cook.

Additional Processing

Some people find digestibility improved by freezing, pressure cooking, sprouting, or additional rinsing of beans.

- *Soak and freeze:* Rinse and drain soaked beans thoroughly. Freeze at least 12 hours. The water breaks down the starch molecules as it freezes. This method also decreases cooking time, especially helpful with longer-cooking garbanzos and soybeans.
- *Soak and pressure cook:* Pressure-cook soaked beans five to 25 minutes, depending on variety.
- *Sprout and cook:* Soak the beans using the long-soak method, then rinse and drain. Place beans in a sprouting tray, and sprout for one to two days, rinsing two to three times daily. (Sprouts may not be very visible.) Or place soaked beans in a single layer between sheets of damp paper towel on a baking sheet. Keep paper towels moist. Rinse in a colander two to three times daily. Sprouting eliminates most of the indigestible sugars.
- *Multiple rinse:* Cook soaked beans for 30 minutes. Replace water and cook 30 minutes. Drain, replace water, and continue cooking until tender.

Antigas Additives

Because digestive systems differ, a universal solution does not exist. Some people seem to have cast-iron stomachs like a Sherman tank, while others are like high-performance cars that require extra attention. But patient experimentation can help you find antigas additives that work for you.

- Sue adds summer savory to every pot of beans.
- Barb says papaya enzyme works best for her. She also finds her body digests beans better when not combined with grains at the same meal.
- Doug discovered that beans and fruit eaten together become a volatile combination for him.
- Rachel can eat beans again because Beano eliminates the painful cramping (and some of the gas).

286

▪ Amber noticed a considerable improvement after she started discarding the soak water.

Experiment with the following antigas additives to find what works best for your body. Some of the older remedies include the Appalachian tradition of cooking a carrot with beans, and the use of kombu in Japan.

Baking soda: Cook beans with one-fourth teaspoon baking soda. Destroys valuable nutrients and can make beans mushy.

Beano: A food enzyme that breaks down nondigestible sugars so they can be absorbed by the body. Take the drops or tablets with the first bite of beans (or other gas-producing foods). Beano is derived from food-grade fungus, *Aspergillus niger*. Consult with a doctor if you have mold allergies that cause breathing problems. For more information, call AkPharma, Inc., 1-800-257-8650. Available in supermarkets and pharmacies.

Carrot: Cook a small whole peeled carrot with the beans.

Charcoal: Take four large charcoal capsules before eating and four after eating. This also decreases absorption of minerals. Do not take within two hours of medications. Available at natural food stores.

Fennel: Soak beans with one teaspoon fennel. Adds a distinctive licorice taste.

Garlic: Cook beans with one to two teaspoons garlic powder or several cloves of minced garlic.

Ginger: Cook beans with fresh gingerroot or powdered ginger. Or after the last mouthful of beans, take one teaspoon grated ginger and one teaspoon lime juice.

Kombu: Soak and cook beans with a four- to six-inch strip of kombu, a Japanese seaweed related to kelp, instead of salt. Available at natural food stores.

Meat tenderizer: Cook beans without salt until almost tender, and add meat tenderizer containing papaya enzyme.

Papaya enzyme: Cook beans with six papaya tablets or two tablespoons papaya enzyme. Or chew one to two papaya enzyme tablets after a meal containing beans.

Summer savory: Cook beans with one-half teaspoon summer savory.

Emission Control

Additional helps for improving the digestibility of beans include:

- Cook beans thoroughly.
- Rinse canned beans to remove the dissolved sugars.
- Chew beans slowly and thoroughly to mix with digestive enzymes in the mouth.
- Avoid drinking beverages with meals. Fluids dilute digestive juices.
- Improve digestion by avoiding snacking, which allows the digestive system to rest between meals.
- Walk after meals to improve digestion.

Other Gas Producers

Other foods can produce gas. If you experience excessive flatulence, evaluate your diet for other troublesome foods such as broccoli, cabbage, corn, onions, apple juice, pears, raisins, fructose, sorbitol, and wheat germ. You may find it helpful to keep a food diary.

Excessive gas can also be a sign of lactose intolerance, the inability to digest milk sugar. To test for lactose intolerance, eliminate milk and milk products from the diet to see if it makes a difference. Some find relief with a wheat-free diet. Antibiotics can kill good bacteria in the colon and decrease the body's ability to deal with high-fiber foods such as beans. Swallowing extra air from drinking fountains, carbonated drinks, and chewing gum can also contribute to excessive flatulence.

The Bean Routine

Many people experience greater intestinal tolerance after three weeks of regularly eating beans. Some call it "bean stomach," because in cultures in which people eat beans regularly, flatulence is not usually a problem. For example, Mexicans typically slowly cook unsoaked beans in a covered pot, without stirring, until beans are tender (similar to using a slow cooker).

If beans or other high-fiber foods are new to your diet, start with small portions, and increase your intake gradually. Begin with the more easily digestible legumes, such as lentils and Anasazi beans. (The beans hardest to digest include limas, navy, split peas, soybeans, and black-eyed peas.) Drink at least six to eight glasses of water daily to help your body handle the increased dietary fiber. Then enjoy the high-fiber, cholesterol-lowering, protein-rich, great-tasting benefits of routine bean cuisine.

BEAN BURRITOS

Keep these make-ahead bean burritos in the freezer for grab-and-go lunches.

1 (30-ounce) can vegetarian refried beans

OR

3½ cups homemade refried beans

½ cup grated reduced-fat Monterey Jack, cheddar, or mozzarella cheese or nondairy cheese

Taco sauce or salsa, as desired

8 (10-inch) flour tortillas, preferably whole-wheat

PREP:
10 MINUTES

YIELD:
8 BURRITOS

Assemble the ingredients. Place the tortillas on a

plate between two moistened paper towels. Microwave on high for 1 minute, or until the tortillas are warm and softened. (Or wrap the tortillas in foil and warm them in a 275°F oven for 15 to 20 minutes.) Spread a heaping ⅓ cup of refried beans in the middle of each tortilla. Sprinkle 1 tablespoon cheese over the beans. Top the burrito with taco sauce, as desired. Fold in the sides of the tortilla, and roll it tightly from the bottom up; place it seam side down on work surface. Repeat the assembly process. Place each burrito inside a resealable sandwich bag. Store the bagged burritos in an airtight container in the refrigerator for up to 3 days or in the freezer for up to 3 months.

To heat 1 burrito:

- *Frozen:* Wrap burrito in a paper towel. Microwave on high about 1 minute; turn burrito over, microwave about 1 minute. Let stand 1 minute.
- *Thawed:* Wrap burrito in a paper towel. Microwave on high about 1 minute.
- *Room temperature:* Microwave burrito on high 30 to 40 seconds or until hot.

Nutrition Facts per Serving (1 burrito): 260 calories, 3.5 g. total fat (1 g. saturated fat), 0 mg. cholesterol, 790 mg. sodium, 44 g. carbohydrate, 5 g. fiber, 1 g. sugars, 11 g. protein. **Daily Values:** 0% vitamin A, 0% vitamin C, 6% calcium, 15% iron. **Diabetic Exchanges:** 2½ breads, 1 lean meat.

Additions: Sour cream or nondairy sour cream, chopped onions, green chiles, sliced olives, cooked black beans, meatless burger, or brown rice.

Flavored Tortillas: Replace flour tortillas with flavored tortillas, such as tomato, spinach, or pesto.

To Serve Burritos Immediately: Microwave the refried beans until they are hot (about 3 to 4 minutes). Heat the tortillas. Put out an assortment of toppings. People assemble their own burritos.

BEAN ENCHILADAS

These low-fat enchiladas hold their shape best in the microwave.
For milder enchilada sauce, prepare Enchilada Sauce (p. 294), or combine one
8-ounce can tomato sauce and one 10-ounce can mild enchilada sauce.

2½–3 cups mild Enchilada Sauce (p. 294)

½ cup chopped onions

2 cloves garlic, minced

1 teaspoon oil

1 (16-ounce) can vegetarian refried beans
(about 2 cups)

½ cup grated reduced-fat Monterey Jack
cheese, cheddar cheese, or nondairy cheese

½ cup sliced olives

2 tablespoons finely chopped fresh cilantro
or 2 teaspoons dried

12 corn tortillas

½ cup grated reduced-fat Monterey Jack
cheese, cheddar cheese, or nondairy cheese

olives, cilantro, sliced green onions, or
sour cream for garnish

PREP:
20 MINUTES

MICROWAVE:
4–5 MINUTES

STANDING:
3 MINUTES

YIELD:
12 ENCHILADAS
(4–6 SERVINGS)

Sauce:

- Coat two 9" x 9" microwave-safe pans with cooking spray.
- Pour ¾ cup enchilada sauce in the bottom of each pan.

Filling:

- Stir onions, garlic, and oil together in a microwave-safe dish.
- Cover, and microwave on high for 2 or 3 minutes, or until soft. (Or stir and cook in a nonstick skillet.)
- Stir in the refried beans, ½ cup cheese, olives, and cilantro.

Tortillas:

- Cover tortillas with a damp paper towel.
- Heat them in the microwave on high about 2 minutes, or until they are hot and pliable. (Or divide the tortillas into two stacks, and wrap each stack in aluminum foil. Bake at 350°F for 10 minutes, or until the tortillas are heated through and softened.)

Assembly:

- Place a warm tortilla in the sauce in the pan.
- Place 2 to 3 tablespoons of bean filling down the center of the tortilla (a No. 30 scoop works great for this).
- Roll the tortilla tightly in the sauce.
- Place tortilla seam side down, and move it to the side of the pan to allow room for assembling more enchiladas.
- Assemble the remaining 5 enchiladas, and fill the pan.
- Sprinkle ¼ cup cheese over the enchiladas.
- Assemble the second pan.
- Cover pan with plastic wrap. (May be refrigerated or frozen for up to 6 months at this point.)

Heating:

- Fold back one corner of the plastic wrap to allow steam to escape.
- Microwave on high 4 to 5 minutes, or until the enchiladas are hot and the cheese melts; rotate the dish once during cooking.
- Let stand 3 minutes.

- Or bake at 350° F for 15 to 20 minutes, or until the enchiladas are heated through (20 to 25 minutes, if refrigerated).

Serving:

- Garnish, as desired, with olives, cilantro sprigs, sliced green onions, or sour cream (or nondairy sour cream).
- Heat the remaining enchilada sauce and serve on the side.

Nutrition Facts per Serving (per enchilada): 150 calories, 3.5 g. total fat (0.5 g. saturated fat), 0 mg. cholesterol, 480 mg. sodium, 25 g. carbohydrate, 4 g. fiber, 2 g. sugars, 6 g. protein. **Daily Values:** 8% vitamin A, 6% vitamin C, 10% calcium, 8% iron. **Diabetic Exchanges:** 2 breads.

Serving Idea: Serve with corn, green salad, and honeydew melon.

Bean Enchiladas With Brown Rice: Add 1 cup cooked brown rice to filling.

Bean Enchiladas With Meatless Burger: Add ½ cup meatless burger (or leftover taco filling) to the filling

Black Bean Enchiladas: Replace refried beans with refried black beans.

Bean Enchiladas With Green Chiles: Add one 4-ounce can chopped green chiles to the filling.

Veggie Enchiladas: Add 1 cup cooked zucchini, broccoli, carrots, or corn.

Spicy Enchiladas: Add, to taste: chopped jalapeño pepper, red-pepper flakes, or cayenne pepper.

9" x 13" Pan: Double the amount of sauce and place the enchiladas side by side in 2 rows.

Enchilada Casserole: Have 3 cups enchilada sauce ready. Coat a 9" x 13" pan with cooking spray. Stack the tortillas, cut them 4

times, and form 8 stacks of small triangles. Spread ¾ cup enchilada sauce on the bottom of the pan. Layer with 3 stacks of tortilla triangles. Spread with one third of the filling. Repeat layers two more times. Top with remaining enchilada sauce, and sprinkle with cheese. (Place the casserole in an airtight container and store in the freezer for up to 6 months.) Bake at 350° F for about 30 minutes or until the enchiladas are heated through.

Slow Cooker Enchilada Casserole: Following Enchilada Casserole directions, layer the ingredients in a slow cooker. Cook on low for 4 to 5 hours. Sprinkle with cheese just before serving.

ENCHILADA SAUCE

Surprisingly easy to make; plus, you control the spiciness.
This recipe makes a mild sauce. Adjust it to suit your taste buds.

PREP:
5 MINUTES

COOK:
10–15 MINUTES

YIELD:
2½ CUPS

1½ cups water

1 (8-ounce) can tomato sauce

1 tablespoon olive oil

2 tablespoons unbleached all-purpose flour

2-3 teaspoons mild chili powder

1 teaspoon onion powder

1 teaspoon garlic powder

1 teaspoon paprika

1 teaspoon salt

1 teaspoon lemon juice

½ teaspoon oregano leaves

Bring the sauce ingredients to a boil over medium-high heat, stirring frequently. While assembling the enchilada filling, reduce the heat, and simmer at least 10 minutes.

Nutrition Facts per Serving (¼ cup): 35 calories, 1.5 g. total fat (0 g. saturated fat), 0 mg. cholesterol, 200 mg. sodium, 5 g. carbohydrate, 0 g. fiber, 1g. sugars, 1 g. protein. **Daily Values:** 6% vitamin A, 6% vitamin C, 2% calcium, 2% iron. **Diabetic Exchanges:** 1 vegetable.

Microwave: Combine the ingredients in a 1-quart microwave-safe casserole. Microwave on high for 5 minutes, stirring half way through cooking, or until the mixture thickens slightly. Let stand 5 minutes.

Additions: Add sautéed onion or minced garlic.

Enchilada Sauce Seasoning Mix: Combine the dry ingredients, and store in an airtight container for up to 6 months.

BLACK BEAN TAQUITOS

Fun foods don't have to be fat-filled foods! Great to pack in lunches.

6 corn tortillas

¾ cup refried black beans or mashed black beans mixed with ¼ cup salsa

¼ cup reduced-fat Monterey Jack cheese or cheddar cheese

1 tablespoon diced green chiles, optional

Salsa or guacamole, optional

PREP:
5 MINUTES

COOK:
5 MINUTES

YIELD:
6 TAQUITOS

Place the tortillas on a microwave-safe plate, and cover them with a damp paper towel. Microwave on high for 30 seconds. Flip the tortillas over, and microwave them another 30 seconds. (Or wrap the tortillas in foil, and heat them in a 350°F oven for 10 to 15 minutes, or until they are softened.)

Spread 2 tablespoons beans, 2 teaspoons cheese, and ½ teaspoon diced green chiles down the center of each tortilla. Roll up tightly into a flute shape, and place them seam side down in a nonstick skillet over medium heat. Heat the taquitos until the bottoms are crispy and remain rolled, about 2 to 3 minutes. Turn the taquitos over and heat them an additional 2 to 3 minutes. (Or bake at 350°F for 6 to 8 minutes, turn them over, and bake another 6 to 8 minutes, or until they are heated through and slightly crispy.) Serve hot with salsa or guacamole, if desired. Store taquitos in the refrigerator for up to 1 week or in the freezer for up to 3 months.

Nutrition Facts per Serving (1 taquito): 100 calories, 2 g. total fat (0.5 g. saturated fat), 5 mg. cholesterol, 160 mg. sodium, 17 g. carbohydrate, 3 g. fiber, 1 g. sugars, 5 g. protein. **Daily Values:** 0% vitamin A, 4% vitamin C, 10% calcium, 6% iron. **Diabetic Exchanges:** 1 bread, ½ lean meat.

Heating Frozen Taquitos:

- *Microwave:* Heat 2 at a time on high for 1 minute.
- *Oven:* Place taquitos on a baking sheet; bake at 425°F for 15 to 20 minutes, or until they are heated through and light brown.
- *Stove Top:* Heat on a nonstick skillet over medium heat for about 5 minutes; turn them over, and heat another 5 minutes, or until they are heated through.

Taco Filling: Replace refried beans with Taco Filling (p. 268).

BLACK BEANS WITH CILANTRO AND LIME

A wonderful combination of flavors.

6 cups water

2½ cups black beans, sorted and rinsed (1 pound)

1 cup chopped bell pepper (about 1 medium)

OR

¼ cup dried bell pepper

1 cup chopped onion (about 1 medium)

OR

¼ cup dried minced onion

6 cloves garlic, minced

OR

1½ teaspoons garlic powder

1 tablespoon olive oil

2 teaspoons salt

2 bay leaves

2 teaspoons dried oregano leaves

1½ teaspoons ground cumin

¼ cup minced fresh cilantro (about ½ bunch)

OR

4 teaspoons dried cilantro

1 tablespoon lime or lemon juice

PREP:
10 MINUTES

SLOW COOK:
LOW: 6–10 HOURS
HIGH: 4–5 HOURS

YIELD:
16 (½-CUP) SERVINGS

Combine the water, beans, bell pepper, onion, garlic, oil, salt, and bay leaves in a 3½-quart slow cooker. Cover, and cook until the beans are tender (low, for 6 to 10 hours; high, for 4 to 5 hours). Remove the bay leaves. To thicken, transfer 2 cups of the beans to a bowl and mash with a potato masher. Add the mixture to the slow cooker. Stir in the oregano, cumin, cilantro, and lime juice.

Nutrition Facts per Serving (½ cup): 110 calories, 1.5 g. total fat (0 g. saturated fat), 0 mg. cholesterol, 300 mg. sodium, 19 g. carbohydrate, 7 g. fiber, 2 g. sugars, 7 g. protein. **Daily Values:** 2% vitamin A, 15% vitamin C, 4% calcium, 10% iron. **Diabetic Exchanges:** 1 bread, ½ lean meat.

Serving Idea: Serve over brown rice, with winter squash and a green salad.

Stove Top Method: Soak the beans (overnight, for best color retention); drain and rinse. Bring beans to boil with 4 cups water, bell pepper, onion, garlic, oil, salt, and bay leaves. Reduce heat and simmer until beans are tender, about 1½ hours. Proceed with remainder of recipe.

Canned Beans: In a skillet or microwave, stir and cook the onions, bell pepper, and garlic in olive oil until the vegetables are tender. Add four 15-ounce cans black beans (drain 2 cans), oregano, cumin, and bay leaves. Add water if desired. Simmer 5 to 10 minutes. Proceed with remainder of recipe.

Black Bean Mix: Combine dried bell pepper, dried onion, garlic powder, and salt in one seasoning packet. Combine oregano, cumin, and dried cilantro in another seasoning packet. Store both packets with black beans. To cook: Add water, olive oil, and lime juice.

Pressure Cooker Method: Soak beans; drain and rinse. Combine beans with 4 cups water, bell pepper, onion, garlic, salt, and bay leaves in a pressure cooker. Seal lid. Bring to high pressure over high heat. Pressure-cook 12 to 14 minutes. Release pressure. Test beans for doneness; simmer longer, if needed. Proceed with remainder of recipe.

LENTIL LOAF

*Delicious smothered with brown gravy. Bread crumbs vary in their
ability to absorb moisture, and the moisture content of cooked lentils
varies, too. Start with the minimum amount of bread crumbs
and add more as needed to form a thick, cohesive mixture.*

1 medium onion, finely chopped (¾ cup)

1 tablespoon olive oil

2 cups cooked lentils (p. 302)

¼ cup chopped walnuts, pecans, or
sunflower seeds

2 tablespoons tomato paste

1 teaspoon vegetarian beef-style seasoning

1 clove garlic, minced

½ teaspoon savory or sage

½-¾ cup fine dried seasoned bread crumbs

PREP:
15 MINUTES

BAKE:
45 MINUTES

YIELD:
5 (½-CUP)
SERVINGS

Preheat the oven to 375°F (350°F for a glass
pan). Coat a loaf pan with cooking spray. Microwave
onions and oil in a microwave-safe dish on high for
4 to 5 minutes, until tender (or stir and cook in a skillet). In a mixing bowl, combine the cooked onions
with the remaining ingredients. The mixture should
be thick and cohesive; if not, stir in additional bread
crumbs. Transfer the mixture to the prepared pan.
Bake for 45 minutes. Serve with brown gravy. Store
the loaf in an airtight container in the refrigerator for
up to 1 week or in the freezer for up to 6 months.

Nutrition Facts per Serving (½ cup): 210 calories, 7 g. total fat (0.5 g. saturated fat), 0 mg. cholesterol, 400 mg. sodium, 29 g. carbohydrate, 8 g. fiber, 3 g. sugars, 11 g. protein. **Daily Values:** 4% vitamin A, 8% vitamin C, 4% calcium, 20% iron. **Diabetic Exchanges:** 2 bread, ½ lean meat, ½ fat.

Lentil Loaf With Carrots: Add ½ cup grated carrots.

Lentil Patties: Use ¾ cup bread crumbs and add ¼ cup quick oats. Using a ¼-cup measure or a No. 16 scoop, form mixture into patties. Brown patties on both sides in a small amount of oil or bake at 350° F for 15 to 20 minutes; turn patties and bake an additional 5 to 10 minutes.

Lentil Patty Mix: ½ cup bread crumbs, ¼ cup quick oats, ¼ cup chopped walnuts, 3 tablespoons minced dried onion, 1 teaspoon beef-style seasoning, ½ teaspoon garlic powder, ½ teaspoon savory. To prepare complete recipe: add 2 cups cooked lentils, and 2 tablespoons tomato paste. Store in an airtight container or resealable plastic bag for up to 6 months.

SAVORY BEANS

*So simple to prepare in the slow cooker. Use this recipe
as a guide, then try other types of beans and different
seasonings to create your own slow cooked beans.*

2½ cups pinto beans (1 pound)

5-6 cups water

1 medium onion, diced

2 celery ribs, diced

1 small green pepper, seeded and diced

2 cloves garlic, minced

1 tablespoon olive oil

1¾-2 teaspoons salt

½ teaspoon oregano leaves

½ teaspoon thyme

PREP:
10 MINUTES·

SLOW COOKER:
LOW: 8-10
HOURS
HIGH: 4-5
HOURS

YIELD:
16 (½-CUP)
SERVINGS

Sort and rinse the beans. If desired, presoak beans
and rinse. In a 3½-quart slow cooker, combine all ingredients. (Use 5 cups water when cooking on low,
and 6 cups when cooking on high.) Cover and cook
on low for 8 to 10 hours, or on high for 4 to 5 hours,
or until the beans are tender. Serve hot. Store the
beans in an airtight container in the refrigerator for
up to 1 week or in the freezer for up to 6 months.

Stove Top Method: Soak the beans, drain, and rinse. Add the remaining ingredients and bring the mixture to a boil. Reduce heat, cover, and simmer about 1½ hours or until tender.

Pressure Cooker Method: Soak the beans, drain, and rinse. Combine the ingredients in pressure cooker. Seal and bring to pressure. Pressure-cook 4 to 6 minutes. (Refer to pressure cooker manual or cookbook for times for other beans.) Release pressure.

Lentils: Omit soaking. Cook on stove top 30 to 45 minutes, or pressure-cook 6 to 8 minutes.

SEVEN-LAYER FIESTA DIP

*Beware—this dip is habit-forming! Makes a refreshing
main dish on a hot summer day.*

PREP:
20 MINUTES

YIELD:
6 CUPS

1 (16-ounce) can vegetarian refried beans
(about 2 cups)

½ cup mild salsa

1 (12.3-ounce) box firm silken tofu,
drained (about 1½ cups)

4 teaspoons Mexican Seasoning Mix (p. 307)

2 teaspoons lemon juice

¾ teaspoon salt

2 green onions, thinly sliced (about ½ cup)

1 large tomato, finely chopped

½ cup finely chopped fresh cilantro (about ½ bunch)

½ cup sliced black olives

½ cup shredded reduced-fat Monterey Jack or cheddar cheese

Tortilla chips, pita chips, or fresh vegetables

Combine the refried beans and salsa. Spread the mixture on the bottom of a shallow baking dish. Using a blender or food processor, process the tofu, Mexican seasoning, lemon juice, and salt until smooth. Spread the tofu mixture over the beans and salsa layer. Layer the onions, tomato, cilantro, olives, and cheese. Serve, or refrigerate for up to 4 hours. Serve with tortilla chips, pita chips, or fresh vegetables. Store leftover dip in an airtight container for up to 1 day.

Nutrition Facts per Serving (about 1 cup without chips): 160 calories, 5 g. total fat (1.5 g. saturated fat), 5 mg. cholesterol, 870 mg. sodium, 16 g. carbohydrate, 5 g. fiber, 4 g. sugars, 11 g. protein. **Daily Values:** 15% vitamin A, 20% vitamin C, 15% calcium, 15% iron. **Diabetic Exchanges:** 1 lean meat, 1 bread, ½ fat.

Serving Ideas: Serve for a Saturday night social with popcorn and fruit salad. As a main dish, serve with tossed salad and smoothies.

Seven-layer Fiesta Dip with Sour Cream: Replace the tofu with 1 cup nonfat sour cream and ¼ cup low-fat mayonnaise. Omit salt. No need to blend.

Creamy Tex-Mex Dip: Process the tofu, Mexican Seasoning, lemon juice and salt in a blender or food processor until smooth. Makes 1½ cups. Store in an airtight container in the refrigerator for up to 5 days.

Fiesta Dip: Prepare Creamy Tex-Mex Dip. Stir in refried beans, salsa, and ¼ cup chopped fresh cilantro. Garnish with a fresh cilantro sprig. Serve with tortilla chips. Makes 3½ cups. Store in an airtight container in the refrigerator for up to 5 days.

VEGETARIAN CHILI

Five minutes in the morning to put the ingredients in the
slow cooker . . . and the chili will be ready for dinner! Palate pleasing,
versatile and mild enough for tender taste buds, this is a great
make-ahead recipe—and it tastes even better the next day!

PREP:
5 MINUTES

SLOW COOKER:
HIGH: 8–10
HOURS
LOW: 14–16
HOURS

YIELD:
8 (1–CUP)
SERVINGS

2½ cups dried pinto, red, pink, kidney, or
    black beans (1 pound)

5 cups water

1 cup chopped onions

OR

¼ cup dried onion plus ¼ cup water

2½-3 tablespoons Mexican Seasoning Mix
    (p. 307)

2 teaspoons salt

1½ teaspoons olive oil

2 garlic cloves, minced

OR

½ teaspoon garlic powder

1 (8-ounce) can tomato sauce (about ¾
    cup)

Sort and rinse the beans. If desired, soak the beans, drain, rinse, and reduce water to 3½ cups. In a 3½-quart slow cooker, combine the ingredients. Cover and cook on high for 8 to 10 hours or on low for 14 to 16 hours, or until the beans are tender. Store the chili in an airtight container in the refrigerator for up to 1 week or in the freezer for up to 6 months.

Nutrition Facts per Serving (1 cup): 230 calories, 2 g. total fat (0 g. saturated fat), 0 mg. cholesterol, 760 mg. sodium, 42 g. carbohydrate, 13 g. fiber, 5 g. sugars, 13 g. protein. **Daily Values:** 15% vitamin A, 15% vitamin C, 8% calcium, 25% iron. **Diabetic Exchanges:** 1 lean meat, 2 bread.

Serving Ideas: Top with chopped onion, chopped fresh cilantro, and grated cheese or nondairy cheese. Serve with cornbread and a green salad. Or serve with rice or a baked potato, vegetable, and salad.

Substitutions: Replace the tomato sauce with ⅓ cup tomato paste and ½ cup water, or one 15-ounce can diced tomatoes. Add Mexican Seasoning Mix to taste.

Stove Top Vegetarian Chili: Soak the beans, drain, rinse, and replace water. Stir in onions, garlic, salt, and oil. Simmer until soft, about 1½ hours, adding more water if needed. Stir in the Mexican Seasoning Mix and tomatoes, and simmer at least 30 minutes, preferably 1 to 2 hours.

Pressure-cooked Vegetarian Chili: Soak the beans, drain, rinse, and add water to cover the beans by ½ inch, about 3 cups. Add onions and salt, and pressure-cook for 4 to 6 minutes. Release pressure. Add remaining ingredients and pressure-cook an additional 4 to 6 minutes. Or combine all ingredients and pressure-cook for 15 minutes.

Black Bean Chili With Canned Beans: Cook 1 medium chopped onion and 2 minced garlic cloves in 1 teaspoon oil until soft, adding water as needed. Stir in 2½ to 3 tablespoons Mexican Seasoning Mix and cook for 1 minute. Stir in three 15-ounce cans drained and rinsed black beans, one 14½-ounce can Mexican stewed tomatoes, and one 8-ounce can tomato sauce. Simmer for 10 minutes, adding water as needed for desired consistency. (For improved flavor, pressure-cook for 1 minute.) Makes about 5 cups.

Five-Bean Chili Mix: Use ½ cup each pinto beans, small red beans, pink beans, kidney beans, and black beans. In a separate small bag, combine ¼ cup chopped dried onions, 2 tablespoons Mexican Seasoning Mix, 2 teaspoons salt, and ½ teaspoon garlic powder. To prepare chili: add oil, tomato sauce, and water.

Chunky Chili: Add 2 cups coarsely chopped green pepper, one 28-ounce can diced tomatoes (4 cups), and an additional 1 cup coarsely chopped onions. Just before serving, stir in 2 cups meatless burger. Makes 12 cups.

Refried Beans: Cook as directed but omit the tomato sauce and decrease the water by ½ cup. Drain the cooked beans, reserving the liquid. Place beans in a mixing bowl and beat with an electric mixer until about ¾ of the beans are mashed. Gradually add a small amount of bean liquid to desired consistency. Or using a food processor or a potato masher, process the beans. Makes 4 cups.

MEXICAN SEASONING MIX

Delightfully seasons Vegetarian Chili, Vegetarian Tacos, Sloppy Joes, and Seven-Layer Dip. You'll wonder how you did without this versatile seasoning mix! The recipe is mild; adjust it to your taste.

1 tablespoon *(½ cup)* mild chili powder

1 tablespoon *(½ cup)* onion powder

2 teaspoons *(⅓ cup)* ground cumin

2 teaspoons *(⅓ cup)* paprika

1½ teaspoons *(3 tablespoons)* garlic powder

1½ teaspoons *(3 tablespoons)* dried oregano leaves

1 teaspoon *(2½ tablespoons)* dried cilantro or parsley flakes

½ teaspoon *(4 teaspoons)* ground coriander, optional

PREP:
10 MINUTES

YIELD:
MINI MIX:
¼ CUP
MEGA MIX:
2 CUPS

Combine the ingredients and stir to distribute evenly. Transfer ingredients to an airtight container; label and date. Store in a cool, dry place. Use within 6 months. Stir contents before each use.

Nutrition Facts per Serving (1 teaspoon): 10 calories, 0 g. total fat (0 g. saturated fat), 0 mg. cholesterol, 10 mg. sodium, 2 g. carbohydrate, 0 g. fiber, 0 g. sugars, 0 g. protein. **Daily Values:** 10% vitamin A, 2% vitamin C, 2% calcium, 2% iron. **Diabetic Exchanges:** free.

Extra Mild: Omit the chili powder and increase cumin (1 tablespoon, mini mix; ½ cup, mega mix); increase paprika (1½ tablespoons, mini mix; ⅔ cup mega mix); increase cilantro (2 teaspoons, mini mix; 3 tablespoons, mega mix).

Spicy: Add cayenne or crushed red-pepper flakes to taste.

GRAINS AND
PASTA

ABOUT BROWN RICE

- For fluffier rice, lightly toast the uncooked rice in a dry skillet before cooking. Heat over high heat, stirring frequently, until the rice kernels start to pop open. Reduce heat to medium and continue to stir and cook until lightly browned, about 2 to 3 minutes.

- I like to start the rice in a rice cooker before I leave for church. The rice cooker keeps the rice warm after cooking is completed. Then all I need to do is stir in the seasonings just before serving.

- The amount of water depends on the rice, cooking method, and personal preference. Use less water if you prefer firm, separate grains. Use more water for softer, stickier rice.

HERBED RICE PILAF

A flavorful side dish.

PREP:
10 MINUTES

COOK:
40–50 MINUTES

YIELD:
6 (½-CUP)
SERVINGS

1 tablespoon olive oil or margarine

2 cloves garlic, minced

1 cup basmati brown rice or long-grain
    brown rice

2–2¼ cups water

½ teaspoon salt

¼ cup thinly sliced green onion tops or
    2 teaspoons dried chopped chives

2 tablespoons slivered almonds or pine
    nuts, optional

4 teaspoons minced fresh basil or 1¼
    teaspoons dried basil leaves

2 teaspoons minced fresh thyme or ½
    teaspoon dried thyme leaves

1 tablespoon grated fresh Parmesan (or
    nondairy Parmesan)

In a saucepan, heat the oil or margarine over
medium heat. Stir in the garlic, and cook 1 minute.
Add the rice, stir, and cook 1 minute. Stir in the water
and salt, and bring to a boil. Cover, reduce heat, and
simmer 40 to 50 minutes, or until the liquid is ab-

sorbed and the rice is tender. Stir in green onions, almonds, basil, and thyme. Sprinkle with Parmesan cheese.

Nutrition Facts per Serving (½ cup): 140 calories, 5 g. total fat (0.5 g. saturated fat), 0 mg. cholesterol, 220 mg. sodium, 23 g. carbohydrate, 2 g. fiber, 0 g. sugars, 3 g. protein. **Daily Values:** 2% vitamin A, 2% vitamin C, 4% calcium, 4% iron. **Diabetic Exchanges:** 1½ breads, 1 fat.

Rice Cooker Pilaf: After cooking rice in oil, transfer to a rice cooker. Stir in 1½ cups water and salt. Cover and cook. Just before serving, stir in the seasonings.

Baked Herbed Rice Pilaf: Toast the rice in a dry skillet before beginning with recipe. After cooking rice in oil, transfer to a casserole dish. Increase the water to 2¼ cups. Cover and bake at 350° F 50 to 60 minutes, or until water is absorbed and rice is tender. Just before serving, stir in seasonings.

Instant Brown Rice Pilaf: Cook instant brown rice according to package directions for six servings, adding 1 tablespoon olive oil or margarine and ½ teaspoon salt. Stir in seasonings just before serving.

Triple Rice Pilaf: Use ⅓ cup each of basmati brown rice, long-grain brown rice, and wild rice. Increase water to 2½ cups.

Other Herbs: Add parsley, tarragon, marjoram, rosemary, or dill.

Herbed Rice Pilaf Mix: Combine ½ teaspoon each garlic powder, salt, dried chives, dried basil, and dried thyme. Store in an airtight container for up to 6 months in a cool dark place. To use, stir the mix into three cups hot cooked rice. Sprinkle with Parmesan cheese and nuts, if desired.

Pressure Cooker Pilaf: Pressure-cook 20 minutes. Allow pressure to release naturally, about 10 minutes. Proceed with remainder of recipe.

PASTA WITH BASIL AND GARLIC

Think of this scrumptious side dish as presto pesto pasta.
Keep mixes in the pantry for a quick pasta dish or a last-minute gift.

PREP:
5 MINUTES

COOK:
15 MINUTES

YIELD:
8 (½–CUP)
SERVINGS

8 cups water

½ teaspoon salt

4 teaspoons dried basil leaves

2 teaspoons vegetarian chicken-style seasoning

2 teaspoons dried parsley flakes

1½ teaspoons unbleached all-purpose flour

½ teaspoon garlic powder

¼ teaspoon salt

¼ cup water

1 tablespoon olive oil

8 ounces rotini pasta (corkscrew-shaped), preferably whole-grain (about 3 cups)

1 tablespoon Parmesan cheese or nondairy Parmesan

In a medium saucepan, bring the 8 cups water and salt to a boil. Pour the basil leaves, chicken-style seasoning, parsley flakes, flour, garlic powder, and salt into a small bowl; to release the herb flavors, crush the leaves between your fingers.

Stir in ¼ cup water and oil, and set aside for at

least 5 minutes. Cook the pasta in boiling water according to package directions. Drain pasta and toss with seasoning mixture. Sprinkle with Parmesan cheese and serve.

Nutrition Facts per Serving (½ cup): 110 calories, 2.5 g. total fat (0 g. saturated fat), 0 mg. cholesterol, 230 mg. sodium, 19 g. carbohydrate, 2 g. fiber, 1 g. sugars, 4 g. protein. **Daily Values:** 2% vitamin A, 0% vitamin C, 4% calcium, 8% iron. **Diabetic Exchanges:** 1 bread, ½ fat.

Serving Idea: Serve with Wheat Meat Cutlets (p. 278), asparagus spears, and a green salad.

Other Pasta Shapes: Measure pastas by weight as the volume varies.

Pasta Seasoning Mix With Basil and Garlic: Combine the dry seasonings in an airtight container or resealable plastic bag and store at room temperature for up to 6 months.

Pasta Salad: Omit olive oil. Add one 6½-ounce jar marinated artichoke hearts (quartered), ½ cup sliced ripe olives, 1 cup halved cherry tomatoes. Cover and refrigerate for 2 hours before serving.

ABOUT PESTO

- Frozen cubes of this reduced-fat pesto thaw quickly for a quick pasta meal.
- It's easy and economical to grow your own basil.
- Freeze a double or quadruple recipe in ice cube trays (a double batch will fill an ice cube tray). Designate separate ice cube trays to avoid garlicky ice. After the pesto is frozen, transfer the cubes to a freezer container.
- If the pesto seems dry, add 1 to 3 teaspoons of water or vegetable broth.
- A little of this potent sauce goes a long way: 1 to 2 tablespoons per serving.

PESTO

This herb sauce is delicious on pasta and pizza,
or in bread, calzones, and pasta salad.

PREP:
15 MINUTES

YIELD:
9 TABLESPOONS

¼ cup walnuts or pine nuts

1 cup packed basil leaves (about 1 ounce)

½ cup flat-leaf or curly parsley

2 tablespoons olive oil

1-2 cloves garlic, peeled and crushed

1 teaspoon lemon juice

½ teaspoon salt

¼ cup grated fresh Parmesan cheese or nondairy Parmesan cheese

Place the walnuts in a microwave-safe dish and microwave on high for 2 to 4 minutes, stirring every minute (microwave pine nuts on high for 1 minute, stirring after 30 seconds). (Or toast nuts in a dry skillet over medium heat, stirring frequently for 5 to 7 minutes; or toast the nuts in a preheated oven at 400° F for 4 to 5 minutes [2 to 3 minutes for pine nuts]. Watch carefully to prevent burning.)

Using a food processor or blender, process the nuts until finely chopped. Add the basil, parsley, olive oil, garlic, lemon juice, and salt, and process until finely chopped, stopping and scraping down the sides with a spatula as needed. Add the Parmesan cheese and process until mixed.

Transfer the mixture to an airtight container or heavy resealable bag and store in the refrigerator for up to 1 week or in the freezer for up to 1 year. Thaw pesto cubes overnight in the refrigerator or in the microwave at 50 percent power for about 1 minute for 4 cubes.

Nutrition Facts per Serving (1 tablespoon): 60 calories, 6 g. total fat (1 g. saturated fat), 0 mg. cholesterol, 180 mg. sodium, 1 g. carbohydrate, 0 g. fiber, 0 g. sugars, 2 g. protein. **Daily Values:** 8% vitamin A, 10% vitamin C, 6% calcium, 4% iron. **Diabetic Exchanges:** 1 fat, ¼ protein.

Serving Idea: Thin room-temperature pesto with a small amount of hot pasta cooking water. Toss with hot angel hair pasta. Serve with cooked carrots, tossed salad, and garlic bread.

Pesto With Extra Basil: Replace parsley with additional basil.

Pesto With Dried Basil: Replace fresh basil with parsley and add 1½ teaspoons dried basil.

Vegan Pesto: Omit Parmesan cheese.

SOUTHWEST COUSCOUS

A quick mix to fix.

PREP:
5 MINUTES

STANDING:
5 MINUTES

YIELD:
6 (½–CUP)
SERVINGS

1 cup water

1 tablespoon olive oil

1 tablespoon dried minced onion

1 tablespoon dried finely chopped tomato

1½ teaspoons Mexican Seasoning Mix or to taste

2 teaspoons dried minced bell pepper

1 teaspoon dried cilantro or parsley

½ teaspoon salt

½ teaspoon garlic powder

1 cup whole-wheat couscous

In a medium saucepan over medium heat, boil the water, olive oil, and seasonings. Remove saucepan from heat, and stir in the couscous. Cover and let stand 5 minutes. Fluff with a fork and serve.

Nutrition Facts per Serving (½ cup): 170 calories, 3 g. total fat (0 g. saturated fat), 0 mg. cholesterol, 200 mg. sodium, 31 g. carbohydrate, 5 g. fiber, 0 g. sugars, 6 g. protein. **Daily Values:** 4% vitamin A, 10% vitamin C, 2% calcium, 8% iron. **Diabetic Exchanges:** 2 breads, 1/2 fat.

Serving Idea: Serve with tacos, enchiladas, or mix with refried beans for a burrito filling.

Microwave: Combine all ingredients except couscous in a 2-quart microwave-safe container. Microwave on high until boiling, about 3 minutes. Stir in couscous. Cover and let stand 5 minutes. Fluff with a fork and serve.

Dried Corn: Add 2 tablespoons freeze-dried corn.

Southwest Couscous Mix: Combine the dry ingredients and transfer them to a small resealable plastic bag. Place the bag of couscous and seasoning mix in an airtight container or large resealable plastic bag, and store at room temperature for up to 6 months. Label the container with cooking directions.

SPINACH LASAGNA WITH TOFU

Goes together in a flash, and the noodles don't need to be cooked.

Prep:
15 minutes

Bake:
40-45 minutes

Standing:
10 minutes

Yield:
12 (3-inch-square)
servings

2 (12.3-ounce) packages firm or extra-firm silken tofu, drained

1 (10-ounce) package frozen chopped spinach, thawed and drained well or 4 cups chopped fresh spinach

1 tablespoon chopped fresh parsley

OR

1 teaspoon dried parsley flakes

1 tablespoon finely chopped fresh basil

OR

1 teaspoon dried basil leaves

½ teaspoon dried oregano

1 teaspoon salt

2 garlic cloves, minced

OR

½ teaspoon garlic powder

¼ cup grated Parmesan cheese or nondairy Parmesan

1 cup shredded reduced-fat mozzarella cheese or nondairy cheese

4½ cups spaghetti or marinara sauce (about 40 ounces)

9 uncooked lasagna noodles, preferably whole-grain (about 8 ounces)

½ cup shredded reduced-fat mozzarella cheese or nondairy cheese

Preheat the oven to 350° F. In a mixing bowl, combine the tofu, spinach, parsley, basil, oregano, salt, garlic, and cheeses. Pour 1½ cups spaghetti sauce into a 9" x 13" baking dish. Arrange 3 lasagna noodles over the sauce; avoid overlapping the noodles as they expand during cooking.

Spread half the tofu mixture over the noodles. Add another layer of noodles. Spread the remaining tofu mixture over noodles. Top with 1½ cups sauce. Arrange the remaining noodles in a layer. Top with remaining sauce. Cover the baking dish with foil. (At this point the lasagna may be stored in the refrigerator for up to 3 days or in the freezer for up to 3 months.)

Bake for 40 to 45 minutes or until the noodles are tender and the sauce bubbles. For refrigerated lasagna, bake an additional 15 minutes; if frozen, bake an additional 30 minutes. Five minutes before removing the lasagna from the oven, sprinkle ½ cup cheese over the casserole. Let stand 10 minutes before serving.

Nutrition Facts per Serving (½₂): 240 calories, 10 g. total fat (3 g. saturated fat), 10 mg. cholesterol, 990 mg. sodium, 28 g. carbohydrate, 5 g. fiber, 8 g. sugars, 14 g. protein. **Daily Values:** 70% vitamin A, 45% vitamin C, 20% calcium, 20% iron. **Diabetic Exchanges:** 1 protein, 1 bread, 2 vegetables, 1 fat.

Spinach Lasagna With Carrots: Add 1 cup shredded carrots.

Vegetable Lasagna: Replace the spinach with 2 cups (about 8 ounces) thawed and drained frozen chopped broccoli or mixed vegetables.

Zucchini Lasagna: Omit spinach. Layer 2 small thinly sliced zucchini on top of tofu.

Tofu Lasagna: Omit the spinach and cheeses. Add 1 tablespoon nutritional yeast and 1 teaspoon onion powder to tofu filling.

Lasagna With Italian-style Tomatoes: Reduce spaghetti or marinara sauce to 3 cups (one 26- to 28-ounce jar). Stir in one 14½-ounce can diced Italian-style tomatoes.

To Bake Immediately: Place the uncooked noodles in the 9" x 13" baking pan and cover with hot water and let soak while preparing the other ingredients. Drain water before using.

POTATOES

ABOUT GARLIC MASHED POTATOES

- Potatoes cooked with the skins on retain more nutrients and flavor. Hot potatoes are easier and quicker to peel than raw ones.

- Don't be alarmed by the amount of garlic. You can use a whole head of garlic, if you like; cooking mellows the flavor.

- A garlic peeler, a flexible plastic tube, is a quick way to peel garlic. Or you can press the cloves through a heavy-duty garlic press (no need to peel first).

- If you use a food mill, you don't have to peel the potatoes. It does an efficient job of mashing the potatoes, and only small flecks of the peel remain.

- An electric mixer also works for mashing potatoes; but avoid over mixing, which breaks down the starch cells and makes the potatoes gummy.

GARLIC MASHED POTATOES

A new twist on an old favorite.

PREP:
15 MINUTES

COOK:
20–25 MINUTES

YIELD:
8 (½-CUP)
SERVINGS

2 pounds (6–7 medium) russet baking potatoes, scrubbed

6–8 garlic cloves, peeled

OR

3–4 teaspoons ready-to-use minced garlic

Water

1 teaspoon salt

½–1 cup reserved potato water

2 tablespoons olive oil

Place the potatoes in a large saucepan with garlic and add enough water to just cover them. Bring to a boil, and boil the potatoes (covered) for 20 to 25 minutes or until tender. Drain, reserving potato water. Cool the potatoes slightly and, using a hot pad, peel while they are still hot. Using a potato masher, mash the potatoes. Stir in the salt, oil, and enough of the reserved potato water to the desired consistency. Beat the potatoes until fluffy. Taste and adjust seasoning. Store the potatoes in an airtight container in the refrigerator for up to 5 days.

Nutrition Facts per Serving (½ cup): 120 calories, 3.5 g. total fat (0 g. saturated fat), 0 mg. cholesterol, 300 mg. sodium, 21 g. carbohydrate, 2 g. fiber, 1 g. sugars, 2 g. protein. **Daily Values:** 0% vitamin A, 25% vitamin C, 0% calcium, 2% iron. **Diabetic Exchanges:** 1 bread, ½ fat.

Serving Idea: Serve with Lentil Loaf, Brown Gravy, peas, and spinach salad.

Pressure-cooked Garlic Mashed Potatoes: Place potatoes and garlic in a pressure cooker with 2 inches of water. Seal pressure cooker. Bring to high pressure over medium heat. Reduce heat slightly and pressure-cook for 15 minutes. Cool to release pressure. (Or slice potatoes into ½-inch slices and pressure-cook 5 minutes.)

Food Mill Method: Process the hot unpeeled potatoes in a food mill, one or two at a time. Proceed with recipe.

OVEN FRIES

A low-fat alternative to French fries.

PREP:
10 MINUTES

COOK:
40 MINUTES

YIELD:
4 (6-WEDGE)
SERVINGS

3 medium russet potatoes (about 2 pounds), scrubbed

1 tablespoon olive oil

¼ teaspoon salt

½ teaspoon paprika

Preheat the oven to 425° F. Coat a baking sheet with cooking spray and set aside. Cut each scrubbed potato lengthwise, forming 8 large wedges. In a large bowl, combine the oil, salt, and paprika. Add the potatoes, stirring until thoroughly coated. Spread the potatoes over the prepared baking sheet in a single layer. Bake 20 minutes. Using a spatula, turn the potatoes, and bake 15 to 20 minutes more, or until they are tender. If desired, sprinkle with salt. Serve hot with ketchup.

Nutrition Facts per Serving (6 wedges): 230 calories, 3.5 g. total fat (0.5 g. saturated fat), 0 mg. cholesterol, 160 mg. sodium, 46 g. carbohydrate, 4 g. fiber, 3 g. sugars, 4 g. protein. **Daily Values:** 4% vitamin A, 40% vitamin C, 2% calcium, 15% iron. **Diabetic Exchanges:** 2 wedges = 1 bread.

Serving Idea: Serve with veggie burgers with all the trimmings and cantaloupe.

Mexi Oven Fries: Season with Mexican Seasoning Mix (p. 307).

Other Flavorings: Add onion powder, garlic powder, or seasoned salt.

Crinkle-Cut Oven Fries: Using a ripple-edged cutter, cut the potatoes into ¼-inch slices. To make fries, cut slices crosswise. The potatoes may also be cut into ¼-inch thick strips for quicker baking.

SLOW-COOKED POTATOES

1½ pounds (about 10-12) small red potatoes, scrubbed

¼ cup water

Place scrubbed potatoes in the slow cooker with water. Cover and cook on high for 2½ to 3 hours (3 to 3½ hours for larger potatoes) or until tender when pierced with a fork.

PREP:
10 MINUTES

SLOW COOKER:
2½–3 HOURS
ON HIGH

YIELD:
6 (½-CUP)
SERVINGS

Nutrition Facts per Serving (½ cup): 70 calories, 0 g. total fat (0 g. saturated fat), 0 mg. cholesterol, 0 mg. sodium, 17 g. carbohydrate, 2 g. fiber, 1 g. sugars, 2 g. protein. **Daily Values:** 0% vitamin A, 20% vitamin C, 0% calcium, 2% iron. **Diabetic Exchanges:** 1 bread.

Stove Top Potatoes: Boil potatoes for 20 to 25 minutes or until tender.

Pressure-cooked Potatoes: Place potatoes in 1 to 2 inches of water. Pressure-cook 5 to 6 minutes.

STUFFED POTATOES

This recipe doubles easily, so while you're at it, make extra to freeze. For an attractive presentation, alternate stuffed potatoes and Broccoli-Stuffed Potatoes.

6 medium baking potatoes, scrubbed

½ cup boiling water

½ teaspoon salt

2 tablespoons margarine

2 tablespoons nonfat dry milk powder or nondairy milk powder

½ cup reduced-fat cheddar cheese or nondairy cheese, divided

2 green onions, finely chopped

OR

2 tablespoons minced chives

1 garlic clove, minced

Paprika and chopped chives for garnish

PREP:
30 MINUTES

BAKE:
45-50 MINUTES

YIELD:
12 (½-POTATO) SERVINGS

Preheat the oven to 400° F. Place the scrubbed potatoes on a baking sheet. Bake for 45 to 50 minutes or until the potatoes are tender when squeezed or pierced with a fork. Cool the potatoes for 10 minutes. Cut the potatoes in half lengthwise. Holding the hot potatoes with an oven mitt and using a spoon, scoop the insides of the potatoes into a mixing bowl, leaving about ⅛-inch of the potato skin.

Reset oven to 350° F. Using a potato masher, a food mill, or an electric mixer, mash the potatoes until they are smooth. Add the boiling water, salt, margarine, and milk powder, and stir until the potatoes are fluffy. Stir in ¼ cup of the cheese, green onions, and garlic. Taste and adjust seasoning. Mound filling into the potato skins, topping them with the remaining cheese. Garnish with paprika and chives if using. Bake uncovered 15 to 20 minutes or until heated through and the cheese melts. Or cover and microwave on high for 6 to 8 minutes, rotating ¼ turn after 5 minutes. Serve hot. Store in an airtight container in the refrigerator for up to 5 days or in the freezer for up to 3 months.

Nutrition Facts per Serving (½ stuffed potato): 100 calories, 2.5 g. total fat (0 g. saturated fat), 0 mg. cholesterol, 160 mg. sodium, 16 g. carbohydrate, 2 g. fiber, 2 g. sugars, 3 g. protein. **Daily Values:** 4% vitamin A, 15% vitamin C, 4% calcium, 6% iron. **Diabetic Exchanges:** 1 bread, ½ fat.

Serving Idea: Serve with Lentil Loaf (p. 299), green beans, and Waldorf Salad (p. 362).

Broccoli-stuffed Potatoes: Thaw, drain, and squeeze out the excess moisture from one 10-ounce package frozen chopped broccoli. Mix into mashed potatoes.

Microwave: Prick scrubbed raw potatoes with a fork and microwave on high for 18 minutes or until tender. Let stand 3 to 5 minutes. Proceed with recipe.

SANDWICHES

CALZONES WITH SPINACH, PESTO, AND TOFU

*These popular, portable pockets are perfect
to make ahead for picnics and lunches.*

1 medium onion, chopped

2 cloves garlic, minced

1 tablespoon olive oil

1 (12- to 14-ounce) package firm tofu

1 (10-ounce) package frozen chopped
spinach, thawed and squeezed dry

1½ cups shredded reduced-fat mozzarella
cheese or nondairy cheese

½ cup pesto

½ teaspoon salt

2¼ pounds (1 recipe) Pizza Dough (p. 253)

OR

2 pounds frozen whole-wheat bread
dough, thawed

Olive oil or cooking spray

Spaghetti or marinara sauce for dipping

PREP:
20 MINUTES
PLUS DOUGH
PREPARATION

BAKE:
15 MINUTES

YIELD:
16 (½-LARGE
CALZONE)
SERVINGS

Adjust oven racks to the low and upper-middle
positions. Preheat the oven to 450° F. Microwave
the onion, garlic, and oil on high for 5 minutes or
until soft (or stir and cook in a skillet). Stir in the
tofu, spinach, cheese, pesto, and salt.

Divide the dough into eight equal pieces, and

cover with a damp cloth. Working with one piece at a time, stretch the dough into an 8-inch circle. Place about ½ cup filling on the lower half of the circle, leaving a ½-inch border. Fold the top half of the dough over the filling. Turn the border over and press with your fingers to seal, or crimp it with a fork. Place four calzones on each large baking sheet. Spray the calzones with cooking spray. Bake for 20 to 25 minutes, until crisp and golden brown, rotating the baking sheets halfway through baking.

Serve warm with spaghetti or marinara sauce for dipping. Store the calzones in an airtight container for up to 1 week in the refrigerator, or double wrap them and store them in the freezer for up to 3 months.

Nutrition Facts per Serving (½ calzone): 230 calories, 9 g. total fat (2.5 g. saturated fat), 5 mg. cholesterol, 450 mg. sodium, 27 g. carbohydrate, 3 g. fiber, 1 g. sugars, 13 g. protein. **Daily Values:** 25% vitamin A, 8% vitamin C, 30% calcium, 25% iron. **Diabetic Exchanges:** 1 lean meat, 1 bread, 2 vegetables, 1 fat.

Serving Idea: Serve with a green salad and fresh fruit.

Pizza Calzones: Use filling from Pizza Braid recipe (p. 250).

Large Calzone: Form dough into 1 large calzone.

Quick Calzones: Place ¼ cup filling inside each whole-wheat pocket bread half. Wrap in foil and bake at 450° F for 12 to 15 minutes or until hot and the cheese melts.

French Roll Calzones: Cut a thin slice from the tops of individual French rolls (preferably whole-wheat). Hollow out the bottom of the rolls, leaving a ½-inch border around the edges. Spoon in the filling, and replace the tops of the rolls. Wrap the calzones individually in foil, and store them in an airtight container in the refrigerator for one day or in the freezer for up to 3 months. Bake at 375° F for 40 minutes if refrigerated; 60 minutes, if frozen.

CHICKEN-STYLE SALAD

Delicious in whole-wheat pocket bread.

1 (12.5-ounce) can **Worthington Low Fat Fri-Chik, drained and grated**

½ **cup diced celery**

1 **green onion, minced**

OR

1 **tablespoon dried minced onion**

2 **tablespoons reduced-fat mayonnaise**

1 **tablespoon minced parsley**

OR

1 **teaspoon dried parsley**

1 **teaspoon lemon juice**

PREP:
10 MINUTES

YIELD:
4 (½–CUP)
SERVINGS

Combine all the ingredients in a mixing bowl. Store in an airtight container in the refrigerator for up to 1 week.

Nutrition Facts per Serving (½ cup): 110 calories, 6 g. total fat (1 g. saturated fat), 0 mg. cholesterol, 490 mg. sodium, 4 g. carbohydrate, 2 g. fiber, 1 g. sugars, 11 g. protein. **Daily Values:** 2% vitamin A, 6% vitamin C, 2% calcium, 6% iron. **Diabetic Exchanges:** 2 lean meats.

Chives: Replace the green onion with 1 tablespoon minced chives or 1 teaspoon dried chives.

Cheese: Add ¼ cup grated reduced-fat cheese or nondairy cheese.

SANDWICH IDEAS

Curing the lunch-box blues.

- **Avocado:** Sliced avocado with alfalfa sprouts and roasted sunflower seeds.
- **Bean Burritos:** Vegetarian refried beans, grated cheese, sliced olives, taco sauce, or salsa rolled up in a flour tortilla. Do an assembly line and make a large quantity to freeze.
- **Beanwiches:** Vegetarian baked beans, finely chopped onion, and ketchup.
- **Calzones:** An endless variety of fillings stuffed inside bread dough.
- **Cream Cheese (or Tofu Cream Cheese) and . . .** chopped walnuts, pecans, toasted almonds, sunflower seeds, grated carrot, diced cucumber, green and/or red pepper, celery, diced orange, apple, raisins, chopped dates.
- **Cucumber:** Peeled and grated cucumber, grated onion, sour cream, salt, and dillweed.
- **Fruit and Nut:** Cottage cheese (or mashed tofu), lemon juice, chopped pecans or walnuts, raisins, and chopped dates.
- **Garbanzo Spread:** Drained and mashed canned garbanzos, chopped pickle, chopped celery, lemon juice, garlic salt, and mayonnaise.
- **Garden Deli:** Pocket bread with cream cheese, cucumber slices, tomato slices, and alfalfa sprouts. Add cheese if desired.
- **Greek:** Feta cheese and sliced cucumbers.
- **Hawaiian Delight:** Cream cheese, drained crushed pineapple, and finely chopped macadamia nuts.

- **Make-Ahead Hot Dogs:** Grate 6 meatless hot dogs; add 6 tablespoons ketchup and 2 tablespoons chopped pickles. Freeze in an ice-cube tray. When ready to use place two cubes in a sandwich bag. Spread the bread with mayonnaise and place in another bag. At lunchtime, spread the thawed filling on the bread.

- **Orange Peanut Butter:** ¼ cup peanut butter, 2 tablespoons orange juice concentrate. Good with raisins too.

- **Peanut Butter and . . .** crushed pineapple, banana, raisins, diced apple, applesauce, grated carrot.

- **Pocket Pizza:** Spread the inside of pocket bread with pizza or spaghetti sauce; fill with mozzarella cheese, sliced olives, and mushrooms.

- **Refried Beans:** Canned or homemade refried beans and mayonnaise.

- **Sloppy Joes:** Make with meatless burger. Can be frozen in individual portions.

- **Stir-fry:** Stir-fried vegetables in pocket bread with cream cheese or mayonnaise.

- **Submarine:** Meatless lunch-meat slices, sliced cheese, lettuce, pickle, tomatoes, alfalfa sprouts, sliced onion, mayonnaise, and Italian dressing on a whole-wheat roll.

- **Tofu Burgers:** Serve with mayonnaise, ketchup, lettuce, tomato, pickle, and onion on a whole-wheat bun.

- **Tofu Salad:** Mix tofu, grated onion, chopped celery, mayonnaise, and vegetarian chicken-style seasoning. Serve in whole-wheat pocket bread.

- **Tortilla Roll-ups:** Cover the tortilla with a spreadable ingredient, such as cream cheese, peanut butter, or beans. Roll up tightly and cut into 1-inch slices.

- **Vegetable Cottage Cheese:** Cottage cheese, lemon juice, chopped green onion, chopped carrot, and chopped celery.

- **Waldorf:** Whipped cream cheese (or tofu cream cheese), diced red apple, diced celery, and chopped walnuts.

SLOPPY JOES

*A favorite homemade fast food. Leftovers can be
frozen in individual portions for lunches or added to chili.*

PREP:
10 MINUTES

COOK:
10 MINUTES

YIELD:
8 (⅓-CUP)
SERVINGS

1 tablespoon olive or vegetable oil

1 small onion, chopped (about 1 cup)

1 small bell pepper, chopped

2 cloves garlic, minced

12 ounces vegetarian burger

¾-1 cup water

1 (8-ounce) can tomato sauce

1 (6-ounce) can tomato paste

1 tablespoon Mexican Seasoning Mix
   (p. 307) or to taste

1 teaspoon cornstarch

OR

2 tablespoons quick oats

1 teaspoon brown sugar or other sweetener

½ teaspoon salt

4 whole-wheat hamburger buns

   Chopped onions or sliced green onions,
   optional

Heat the oil in a nonstick skillet over medium-high heat. Stir and cook the onion, bell pepper, celery, and garlic until tender. (Or microwave on high in a covered microwave-safe dish for 5 to 6 minutes.) Add the vegetarian burger, stirring until it is brown, about 2 minutes. Stir in the water, tomato sauce, tomato paste, Mexican Seasoning, cornstarch, brown sugar, and salt, whisking until thoroughly mixed. Cook for 5 minutes over medium heat, stirring frequently, until the mixture is hot and thickens. Taste and adjust seasoning. Toast the hamburger buns. Spoon ⅓ cup mixture onto the bottom half of each bun. Top with onions, if desired. Cover with the bun tops or serve open-face. Store the mixture in an airtight container in the refrigerator for up to 1 week or in the freezer for up to 6 months.

Nutrition Facts per Serving (⅓ cup mixture plus ½ bun): 150 calories, 3 g. total fat (0 g. saturated fat), 0 mg. cholesterol, 650 mg. sodium, 22 g. carbohydrate, 4 g. fiber, 5 g. sugars, 10 g. protein. **Daily Values:** 20% vitamin A, 45% vitamin C, 4% calcium, 15% iron. **Diabetic Exchanges:** 1 lean meat, 1 bread, 1 vegetable.

Serving Idea: Serve with green beans, coleslaw, and blueberry crumble.

Instead of Mexican Seasoning Mix: Use ½ teaspoon chili powder and 1 teaspoon paprika.

Microwave: Combine the first 4 ingredients in a 1-quart microwave-safe dish. Cover and cook on high 6 to 8 minutes, stirring halfway through cooking. Stir in burger, and microwave 2 to 3 minutes. Stir in next 7 ingredients. Microwave 3 to 4 minutes until heated through and thickened. Let stand 3 minutes.

Slow Cooker Sloppy Joes: Cook on low for 3 to 4 hours.

Sloppy Joes With Celery: Stir and cook 1 to 2 diced celery ribs with onions and peppers.

Sloppy Joe Seasoning Mix: Using a blender or seed/coffee grinder, grind ¼ cup dried onion and ¼ cup dried bell pepper flakes until the pieces are smaller. Stir in ½ teaspoon garlic powder, Mexican Seasoning Mix, cornstarch, brown sugar, and salt. Store in a small airtight container or resealable plastic bag for up to 6 months.

TEX-MEX SALAD WRAPS

This flavorful fiesta for the taste buds makes a great portable meal or an easy no-cook main dish.

PREP:
15 MINUTES

YIELD:
ABOUT 5 CUPS

1 (15-ounce) can black beans, drained and rinsed (about 1½ cups)

1 (15-ounce) can corn, drained

OR

1½ cups frozen or cooked fresh corn

¾ cup finely chopped jicama

1 small roma tomato, chopped

½ cup chopped green onion or sweet onion

1 (4-ounce) can diced green chiles, drained

¼ cup chopped fresh cilantro

1 tablespoon lime juice

6 (10-inch) flour tortillas, preferably whole-wheat

Salsa, optional

Combine the ingredients in a bowl. Spoon about ¾ cup salad mixture on each tortilla. Roll up tightly.

If desired, serve with salsa. Store the extra salad mixture in an airtight container in the refrigerator for up to 3 days.

Nutrition Facts per Serving (1 wrap): 240 calories, 3.5 g. total fat (0.5 g. saturated fat), 0 mg. cholesterol, 710 mg. sodium, 48 g. carbohydrate, 5 g. fiber, 3 g. sugars, 9 g. protein. **Daily Values:** 6% vitamin A, 45% vitamin C, 4% calcium, 20% iron. **Diabetic Exchanges:** 2½ breads, 1 vegetable.

Serving Idea: Serve with Southwest Couscous, pudding, and fresh raspberries.

Bell Pepper: Replace tomatoes with chopped red or yellow bell pepper.

Olives: Add sliced ripe olives.

Avocado: Add chopped avocado.

Shredded Cheese: Add shredded reduced-fat cheddar cheese or nondairy cheese.

Shredded Lettuce: Add 3 cups shredded lettuce.

Broccoli Slaw: Replace the jicama with broccoli slaw or peeled, chopped broccoli stems.

Spanish Rice: Use a combination of Spanish Rice and Tex-Mex Salad for filling wraps.

Flavored Tortillas: Use flavored tortillas.

TOFU SANDWICH FILLING

Try this fast filling in pocket bread. Also good as a dip.

PREP:
10 MINUTES

REFRIGERATE:
1 HOUR

YIELD:
2 CUPS
(4 SERVINGS)

1 (12.3-ounce) package extra firm silken
   tofu, drained
2 tablespoons Scrambled Tofu Seasoning
   Mix (p. 181)
2 tablespoons reduced-fat mayonnaise
2 tablespoons finely chopped celery, optional
1½ tablespoons pickle relish
1 tablespoon minced dried onion
4 pita pockets, preferably whole-wheat
   Chopped lettuce
   Salsa, optional

Pat tofu dry with a paper towel. Mash the tofu with a fork in a bowl. Stir in the Scrambled Tofu Seasoning Mix, mayonnaise, celery, pickle relish, and dried onion. Refrigerate for 1 hour. Cut the pocket bread in half to form semicircles. Place ¼ cup sandwich filling in each pocket and top with chopped lettuce. (To prevent the moist filling from making the bread soggy, line the pocket bread with a lettuce leaf before filling, or pack the mixture and the bread in separate sandwich bags. At lunchtime fill the bread with the filling.) If desired, serve with salsa. Store the filling in an airtight container in the refrigerator for up to 1 week.

Nutrition Facts per Serving (1 sandwich): 140 calories, 3 g. total fat (0.5 g. saturated fat), 0 mg. cholesterol, 570 mg. sodium, 21 g. carbohydrate, 3 g. fiber, 2 g. sugars, 7 g. protein. **Daily Values:** 4% vitamin A, 4% vitamin C, 2% calcium, 10% iron. **Diabetic Exchanges:** 1 lean meat, 1 bread.

Dill: Add 1 tablespoon fresh minced dill or 1 teaspoon dillweed.

Basil: Omit pickle relish. Add 1 tablespoon fresh minced basil leaves or 1 teaspoon dried basil.

Vegan: Use vegan mayonnaise.

VEGGIE BURGERS

Serve with oven fries for a tasty low-fat meal.
Double or quadruple the recipe and freeze the burgers.

12 ounces vegetarian burger

½ cup dried seasoned fine bread crumbs

2 tablespoons dried onion

OR

½ teaspoon onion powder

2 tablespoons minced fresh parsley

OR

2 teaspoons dried parsley flakes

2 tablespoons quick oats

1 tablespoon water

2 teaspoons reduced-sodium soy sauce

PREP: 15 MINUTES

COOK: 10 MINUTES

YIELD: 6 (3½-INCH) BURGERS

2 cloves garlic, minced

OR

½ teaspoon garlic powder

½ teaspoon paprika

¼ cup cholesterol-free egg product

OR

2 egg whites

OR

1 egg

Combine the burger, bread crumbs, onion, parsley, oats, water, soy sauce, garlic, and paprika in a mixing bowl. Taste and adjust the seasoning. Stir in the egg. Adjust the consistency by adding more water or bread crumbs, 1 tablespoon at a time; the mixture should be fairly stiff and retain its shape when formed into burgers.

Using a ⅓ cup measure, shape the mixture into 3½-inch burgers. In a large nonstick skillet, cook over medium heat until browned, about 4 to 5 minutes. Turn burgers over and brown the other side. Serve hot. Store the cooked burgers in an airtight container in the refrigerator for up to 5 days or in the freezer for up to 6 months.

Nutrition Facts per Serving (1 burger): 130 calories, 3 g. total fat (0 g. saturated fat), 0 mg. cholesterol, 690 mg. sodium, 14 g. carbohydrate, 2 g. fiber, 2 g. sugars, 12 g. protein. **Daily Values:** 6% vitamin A, 6% vitamin C, 4% calcium, 15% iron. **Diabetic Exchanges:** 1 lean meat, 1 bread.

Serving Idea: Serve on whole-wheat hamburger buns with mayonnaise, ketchup, lettuce, tomatoes, pickles, and onions. Serve with oven fries, fresh vegetables, and dip.

Additions: ¼ cup shredded carrots, finely chopped celery, bell peppers, onions, green onion, or mushrooms.

Southwest Veggie Burgers: Replace water and soy sauce with ¼ cup salsa.

Zesty Veggie Burgers: Replace water and soy sauce with 2 tablespoons ketchup and 2 tablespoons barbecue sauce.

Beef-flavored TSP Granules: Microwave 1¼ to 1⅓ cups water for 3 minutes (or heat to nearly boiling) and pour over 1⅔ cups textured vegetable protein (TSP) granules. Stir and let stand 10 minutes or until the moisture is absorbed.

Unflavored TSP Granules: Follow the directions for beef-flavored TSP. Add with hot water: 1 tablespoon Braggs Liquid Aminos or reduced-sodium soy sauce, and 2 teaspoons vegetarian beef-style seasoning. For a darker color, add 1 to 2 teaspoons browning sauce.

Eggless Veggie Burgers: Omit the egg and add 3 tablespoons potato flour, or 1 tablespoon egg-replacement powder, plus 2 tablespoons water.

Veggie Burger Mix: Combine the dry ingredients; label and date the package, and include the directions. Store the package in an airtight container at room temperature for up to 6 months.

Veggie Burgers Using 1 (19-ounce) Can Meatless Burger: Increase the other ingredients to these amounts: ¾ cup bread crumbs; 3 tablespoons dried onion or ¾ teaspoon onion powder; 3 tablespoons fresh parsley or 1 tablespoon dried; 3 tablespoons quick oats; 1½ tablespoons water; 1 tablespoon soy sauce; 3 cloves garlic or ¾ teaspoon garlic powder; ¾ teaspoons paprika; and ⅓ cup cholesterol-free egg product, 3 egg whites, or 1 egg plus 1 egg white.

SALADS

BROCCOLI SUPREME SALAD

This make-ahead salad offers a surprisingly tasty fusion of flavors and textures.

⅓ cup reduced-fat mayonnaise

⅓ cup plain nonfat yogurt or sour cream

2 tablespoons honey or other sweetener

1 tablespoon lemon juice

½ teaspoon salt

6 cups broccoli flowerets, cut into bite-size pieces (about 1 pound)

½ cup chopped red or sweet onion

½ cup raisins or currants

¼ cup roasted sunflower seeds

Onion rings for garnish

PREP:
10 MINUTES

CHILL:
4 HOURS

YIELD:
6 CUPS

In a large bowl, combine the mayonnaise, yogurt, honey, lemon juice, and salt. Stir in the broccoli, onion, raisins, and sunflower seeds. If desired, garnish with onion rings. Cover and refrigerate at least 4 hours to blend the flavors. Store the salad in an airtight container in the refrigerator for up to 3 days.

Nutrition Facts per Serving (½ cup): 80 calories, 3.5 g. total fat (0.5 g. saturated fat), 0 mg. cholesterol, 160 mg. sodium, 12 g. carbohydrate, 2 g. fiber, 8 g. sugars, 2 g. protein. **Daily Values:** 20% vitamin A, 60% vitamin C, 4% calcium, 4% iron. **Diabetic Exchanges:** 1 vegetable, ½ fruit, ½ fat.

Pecans and Golden Raisins: Replace the sunflower seeds and raisins with pecans and golden raisins.

Cauliflower: Replace part of the broccoli with small cauliflower flowerets.

Vegetarian Bacon-flavored Bits: Garnish with vegetarian bacon-flavored bits.

Substitutions: Replace the yogurt with ⅓ cup sour cream, nondairy sour cream, or mayonnaise.

Vegan: Use vegan mayonnaise, vegan yogurt or sour cream, and replace honey with another sweetener.

CAESAR SALAD

A popular salad at potlucks. Great for entertaining.

PREP:
10 MINUTES

YIELD:
10 (1-CUP) SERVINGS

2 large romaine hearts, washed, dried, and torn into 1½-inch pieces

½ cup Caesar Salad Dressing (p. 353)

¼ cup Parmesan cheese, freshly grated, or nondairy Parmesan

1½ cups Garlic Croutons (p. 354)

Cover and refrigerate the prepared romaine (a salad spinner can speed up the process) until serving time. In a large bowl, add the Caesar Salad Dressing, tossing to coat well. Sprinkle with Parmesan cheese and croutons. Toss to mix. Serve immediately.

Nutrition Facts per Serving (1 cup): 100 calories, 6 g. total fat (1.5 g. saturated fat), 5 mg. cholesterol, 220 mg. sodium, 8 g. carbohydrate, 2 g. fiber, 1 g. sugars, 4 g. protein. **Daily Values:** 30% vitamin A, 25% vitamin C, 8% calcium, 6% iron. **Diabetic Exchanges:** ½ bread, 1 fat.

CAESAR SALAD DRESSING

At last—an anchovy- and egg-free Caesar salad dressing.

1 (12.3-ounce) package silken firm tofu

¼ cup plus 1 tablespoon lemon juice

¼ cup extra-virgin olive oil

¾ teaspoon salt

3-4 cloves garlic, peeled

2 teaspoons reduced-sodium soy sauce or Braggs Liquid Aminos

3 kalamata olives, pitted

PREP:
5 MINUTES

CHILL:
1 HOUR

YIELD:
2 CUPS

Using a blender, process the ingredients until smooth. Refrigerate at least 1 hour before serving. Store the dressing in an airtight container in the refrigerator for up to 2 weeks.

Nutrition Facts per Serving (1 tablespoon): 25 calories, 2 g. total fat (0 g. saturated fat), 0 mg. cholesterol, 75 mg. sodium, 1 g. carbohydrate, 0 g. fiber, 0 g. sugars, 1 g. protein. **Daily Values:** 0% vitamin A, 2% vitamin C, 0% calcium, 0% iron. **Diabetic Exchanges:** ½ fat.

GARLIC CROUTONS

Also delicious on tomato soup.

PREP:
10 MINUTES

MARINATE:
20–30 MINUTES

BAKE:
12–20 MINUTES

YIELD:
6 CUPS

½ cup extra-virgin olive oil

6 large garlic cloves, pressed through a
garlic press

½ teaspoon salt

About 1 pound whole-wheat bread

Combine the olive oil, garlic, and salt in a measuring cup, and set aside for 20 to 30 minutes. (If you don't have a garlic press, mince the garlic with knife. Sprinkle it with the salt and continue mincing until nearly pureed.)

Preheat the oven to 350°F (325°F for dark pans). Cut the bread into ½-inch cubes to make 8 cups. Spread the bread cubes out on a single layer on two jelly-roll pans. Drizzle the garlic oil through a fine-mesh strainer onto the bread cubes. Toss the cubes to coat evenly. Bake 12 to 20 minutes (depending on the moisture content of the bread), or until golden and dry, stirring and rotating pans two to three times during baking. Cool the cubes to room temperature. Store the croutons in an airtight container for up to 2 weeks.

Nutrition Facts per Serving (2 tablespoons): 50 calories, 3 g. total fat (0 g. saturated fat), 0 mg. cholesterol, 80 mg. sodium, 5 g. carbohydrate, 0 g. fiber, 0 g. sugars, 1 g. protein. **Daily Values:** 0% vitamin A, 0% vitamin C, 0% calcium, 2% iron. **Diabetic Exchanges:** ½ fat.

Quick Low-fat Croutons: Toast bread slices. Rub both sides with a cut garlic clove and spray with olive oil. Cut the toast into cubes and bake in oven. (Small quantities can easily be made in a toaster oven.)

CRANBERRY SALAD MOLD

Beautiful on the Thanksgiving table.
Keep cranberries in the freezer so you can enjoy this any time of year.

1 (12-ounce) package fresh or frozen cranberries, rinsed and drained

1 (12-ounce) can frozen apple juice concentrate (1½ cups)

¼ cup unflavored vegetarian gelatin

¼ cup granulated sugar or other sweetener

1 (12-ounce) can frozen apple juice concentrate (1½ cups)

1 cup diced celery (2 medium ribs)

1 cup diced apple (1 medium)

½ cup chopped walnuts or pecans

PREP:
20 MINUTES

CHILL:
4 HOURS

YIELD:
16 (½-CUP)
SERVINGS

Using a food processor, blender, or food grinder, grind the cranberries. Transfer the cranberries to a mixing bowl. Combine the apple juice concentrate, gelatin, and sugar in a microwave-safe bowl, and microwave on high for 5 minutes, stirring halfway through cooking, until the mixture is hot and the gelatin is dissolved (or heat the mixture in a saucepan).

Pour the hot mixture over the cranberries. Stir in the remaining ingredients. Pour the mixture into an 8-cup mold and refrigerate for 4 hours, or until firm. To unmold the salad: dip the mold in warm water just to the line of the gelatin for 10 seconds. Shake the mold slightly. Place a platter over the mold, and invert it onto a lettuce-lined platter.

Nutrition Facts per Serving (½ cup): 150 calories, 2.5 g. total fat (0 g. saturated fat), 0 mg. cholesterol, 25 mg. sodium, 29 g. carbohydrate, 2 g. fiber, 27 g. sugars, 3 g. protein. **Daily Values:** 0% vitamin A, 8% vitamin C, 2% calcium, 4% iron. **Diabetic Exchanges:** 2 fruits, ½ fat.

Strawberry-Cranberry Mold: Using a blender, process 1 bag cranberries, 2 cups fresh or thawed frozen strawberries, and 1 can apple juice concentrate until smooth. (If necessary, process ½ recipe at a time.) Stir in the hot juice and gelatin and pour into a 6-cup mold. Refrigerate for 4 hours or until firm.

LAYERED TACO SALAD

Our family's favorite Friday dinner.

3 cups Vegetarian Chili (p. 304)

4 cups reduced-fat tortilla chips, slightly crushed

¾ cup mild salsa

¾ cup grated reduced-fat cheese or nondairy cheese

1 green onion, sliced

3 cups chopped lettuce

1 large tomato, chopped

⅓ cup sliced olives

¼ cup reduced fat sour cream or nondairy sour cream

PREP:
20 MINUTES

YIELD:
6 (2-CUP) MAIN-DISH SERVINGS OR 12 (1-CUP) SALAD SERVINGS

Heat the chili in a 2-quart saucepan over medium heat, stirring occasionally. Place the chips in a 9" x 13" baking dish and crush them slightly. Just before serving, top the tortilla chips with beans. Layer the remaining ingredients in the order listed above. Serve immediately.

Nutrition Facts per Serving (2 cups): 270 calories, 7 g. total fat (2.5 g. saturated fat), 10 mg. cholesterol, 780 mg. sodium, 42 g. carbohydrate, 10 g. fiber, 5 g. sugars, 14 g. protein. **Daily Values:** 35% vitamin A, 35% vitamin C, 25% calcium, 20% iron. **Diabetic Exchanges:** 2 breads, 2 vegetables, 1 protein, 1 fat

Serving Idea: Serve with strawberry sorbet for dessert.

Microwave: Place the beans in a 2-quart microwave-safe casserole. Cover and microwave on high for 10 to 12 minutes or until hot, stirring after 5 minutes.

Slow Cooker: Heat the beans on high for 3 to 4 hours, or on low for 4 to 5 hours.

Additions: Add ½ cup chopped avocado or ¼ cup guacamole.

Creamy Herb Dressing: Replace the sour cream with Creamy Herb Dressing (p. 367) or reduced-fat ranch dressing.

Tossed Taco Salad: Combine the ingredients and serve in a large salad bowl.

Haystacks: Serve the ingredients separately, and each person assembles their own haystack.

Rice: Replace the tortilla chips with cooked brown rice.

PASTA SALAD WITH ASPARAGUS AND TOFU

The tofu resembles feta cheese in this springtime favorite.
Fresh basil makes a flavorful difference.

½ cup lemon juice

¼ cup grated Parmesan cheese or nondairy Parmesan

3 tablespoons minced fresh basil leaves

OR

1 tablespoon dried basil

3 tablespoons olive oil

2 cloves garlic, minced

¾ teaspoon salt

8 ounces firm or extra-firm tofu, drained

6 ounces penne pasta (about 2 cups)

1 pound fresh asparagus spears, washed and trimmed

PREP:
15 MINUTES

COOK:
10–15 MINUTES

CHILL:
2 HOURS

YIELD:
5 CUPS
(10 [½-CUP] SERVINGS)

To make the basil dressing, combine the lemon juice, Parmesan cheese, basil, olive oil, garlic, and salt in a medium bowl. Using your fingers, crumble the tofu into small pieces and stir in. Allow the dressing to marinate in the refrigerator while you assemble the remainder of the salad.

Cook the pasta according to the package directions (for best shape retention, undercook it slightly). Cut the washed and trimmed asparagus into 1½-inch pieces. Add asparagus during last 3 minutes of cooking. Rinse in cold water. Add to the marinated tofu, stirring to mix.

Cover the salad and refrigerate it for 2 hours before serving. Store the salad in an airtight container in the refrigerator for up to 5 days.

Nutrition Facts per Serving (½ cup): 150 calories, 7 g. total fat (1.5 g. saturated fat), 0 mg. cholesterol, 230 mg. sodium, 15 g. carbohydrate, 2 g. fiber, 1 g. sugars, 8 g. protein. **Daily Values:** 8% vitamin A, 20% vitamin C, 20% calcium, 20% iron. **Diabetic Exchanges:** 1 bread, ½ lean meat, 1 fat.

Rotini Pasta: Replace the penne pasta with 6 ounces rotini pasta (about 2½ cups).

Snow Peas: Replace the asparagus with raw snow peas, and add sliced ripe olives.

Broccoli: Replace the asparagus with 1 pound broccoli flowerets. Blanch about 2 minutes. Add chopped yellow and red bell peppers.

Zucchini and Cherry Tomatoes: Replace asparagus with 2 small zucchini cut lengthwise into quarters, then sliced. Add 1 cup cherry tomato halves.

POTATO SALAD

A colorful combination.

2 pounds (about 6 medium or 13 small) red potatoes, scrubbed

2 tablespoons lemon juice

1 celery rib, chopped

3 sliced green onions

½ cup chopped pickles

¼ cup minced fresh parsley

OR

4 teaspoons dried parsley

½ teaspoon salt

½ cup reduced-fat mayonnaise

PREP:
15 MINUTES

COOK:
25–30 MINUTES

CHILL:
2 HOURS

YIELD:
12 SERVINGS

Place the scrubbed potatoes in a large saucepan. Cover with water and bring to a boil. Cover the pan and reduce the heat. Cook the potatoes until they are tender, about 25 to 30 minutes for medium potatoes (15 to 20 minutes for new potatoes). Drain the potatoes and rinse with cold water. Cool the potatoes slightly and, using a serrated knife, cut them into ¾-inch cubes. Place the warm potatoes in a bowl and toss them with lemon juice. Add the remaining ingredients and stir to combine. Cover the salad and refrigerate it at least 2 hours. Store the salad in an airtight container in the refrigerator for up to 1 week.

Nutrition Facts per Serving (½ cup): 100 calories, 3.5 g. total fat (0.5 g. saturated fat), 0 mg. cholesterol, 250 mg. sodium, 17 g. carbohydrate, 2 g. fiber, 1 g. sugars, 2 g. protein. **Daily Values:** 2% vitamin A, 25% vitamin C, 2% calcium, 2% iron. **Diabetic Exchanges:** 1 bread, ½ fat.

Onion: Replace the green onion with ½ cup chopped sweet or red onion.

Dill: Add 1 tablespoon minced fresh dill or 1 teaspoon dried dill.

Additions: Add hard-boiled egg whites, thinly sliced radishes, shredded carrots, thinly sliced ripe olives, chopped cucumber, or chopped green bell pepper.

Vegan: Use vegan mayonnaise.

WALDORF SALAD

A cool and crunchy salad with a honey-yogurt dressing.

PREP:
10 MINUTES

YIELD:
2½ CUPS,
5 (½-CUP)
SERVINGS

2 tablespoons reduced-fat mayonnaise

2 tablespoons nonfat plain yogurt

1 teaspoon honey

½ teaspoon lemon juice

1 large red apple, cored and coarsely chopped (about 1½ cups)

1 celery rib, sliced (about ½ cup)

⅓ cup pitted dates or raisins, snipped

¼ **cup coarsely chopped walnuts or pecans, toasted if
desired**

Prepare the dressing in a medium bowl by combining the mayonnaise, yogurt, honey, and lemon juice, stirring until smooth. Add the apple, celery, dates, and nuts. Cover and refrigerate for up to 2 hours. Serve on a bed of lettuce.

> **Nutrition Facts per Serving (½ cup):** 120 calories, 6 g. total fat (0.5 g. saturated fat), 0 mg. cholesterol, 55 mg. sodium, 18 g. carbohydrate, 2 g. fiber, 14 g. sugars, 2 g. protein. **Daily Values:** 2% vitamin A, 6% vitamin C, 2% calcium, 2% iron. **Diabetic Exchanges:** 1½ fruit, 1 fat.

Vary the Dried Fruit: Replace the dates with 2 tablespoons dried cranberries or cherries.

Lemon Peel: Add ½ teaspoon finely chopped lemon peel.

Grapes: Add 1 cup green grape halves.

ABC Salad (Apples, Bananas, and Celery): Replace the dates with 1 small chopped banana.

Vegan Waldorf Salad: Replace the yogurt with eggless mayonnaise and increase the lemon juice to 1 teaspoon. Or replace the mayonnaise with eggless mayonnaise and replace the yogurt with nondairy yogurt or sour cream. Replace the honey with concentrated fruit sweetener or granulated sugar or other sweetener.

Main Dish Salad: Stir in 1 cup chopped chicken- or turkey-style soy protein product and ¼ cup chopped green onions. Stuff inside pocket bread.

SALAD
DRESSINGS
AND DIPS

CREAMY HERB DRESSING

A homemade version of the most popular salad dressing.

1 cup low-fat buttermilk

¾ cup reduced-fat mayonnaise

2 tablespoons minced fresh parsley

OR

2 teaspoons dried parsley flakes

1 teaspoon dried chopped onion or dried chives

½ teaspoon onion powder

1 garlic clove, minced

OR

½ teaspoon garlic powder

¼ teaspoon salt

¼ teaspoon celery salt or vegetable seasoning salt

PREP:
5 MINUTES

REFRIGERATE:
1 HOUR

YIELD:
1¾ CUPS

Combine the ingredients in a small pitcher, whisking until smooth. Refrigerate at least 1 hour. Store the dressing in an airtight container in the refrigerator for up to 2 weeks.

Nutrition Facts per Serving (1 tablespoon): 25 calories, 2 g. total fat (0 g. saturated fat), 0 mg. cholesterol, 90 mg. sodium, 1 g. carbohydrate, 0 g. fiber, 0 g. sugars, 0 g. protein. **Daily Values:** 0% vitamin A, 0% vitamin C, 2% calcium, 0% iron. **Diabetic Exchanges:** ½ fat.

Serving Idea: Serve over tossed salad, baked potatoes, or Layered Taco Salad (p. 357).

Creamy Dressing With Yogurt: Add ¼ cup plain nonfat yogurt. Or reduce mayonnaise to ⅓ cup and add ⅓ cup plain nonfat yogurt.

Creamy Basil Dressing: Add 1 tablespoon minced fresh basil or 1 teaspoon dried basil.

Creamy Dill Dressing: Add 1 tablespoon minced fresh dill or 1 teaspoon dried dill.

Additional Seasoning Ideas: 1 tablespoon minced fresh parsley, 2 tablespoons Parmesan or nondairy Parmesan cheese, 1 small minced garlic clove, 1 minced green onion.

Creamy Tofu-Herb Dressing: Using a blender, process one 12-ounce box soft silken tofu, 1 cup reduced-fat mayonnaise, and 1 teaspoon lemon juice until smooth. Transfer the mixture to another bowl. Stir in 1 tablespoon plus 1 teaspoon dried parsley flakes, 2 teaspoons dried chopped onion or dried chives, 1 teaspoon onion powder, 1 teaspoon garlic powder, ½ teaspoon salt, and ½ teaspoon celery salt or vegetable seasoning salt.

Creamy Herb Dressing Mix: Combine the dry ingredients and store them in an airtight container for up to 6 months.

DILL MIX

Makes a yummy dip, potato topping, spread, or flavoring for bread.

2 tablespoons *(1 cup)* dried dill

1 teaspoon *(2 tablespoons plus 2 teaspoons)* minced dried onion

½ teaspoon *(4 teaspoons)* celery seed

1 teaspoon *(2 tablespoons plus 2 teaspoons)* minced dried garlic

OR

½ teaspoon *(4 teaspoons)* garlic powder

PREP:
5 MINUTES

YIELD:
MINI MIX:
2 TABLESPOONS
(1 RECIPE)
MEGA MIX: 1 CUP
(8 RECIPES)

Combine the ingredients in a small bowl. Store the mix in an airtight container in a cool, dark location for up to 6 months.

Nutrition Facts per Serving (2 tablespoons): 35 calories, 0.5 g. total fat (0 g. saturated fat), 0 mg. cholesterol, 15 mg. sodium, 7 g. carbohydrate, 2 g. fiber, 1 g. sugars, 2 g. protein. **Daily Values:** 10% vitamin A, 10% vitamin C, 15% calcium, 15% iron. **Diabetic Exchanges:** 1 vegetable, ½ fat.

Dill Dip Mix With Sesame Seeds: Add 2 teaspoons *(⅓ cup)* sesame seeds to the mix.

Double Dill Dip Mix: Add ½ teaspoon *(4 teaspoons)* dill seed.

DILL DIP

PREP:
5 MINUTES

YIELD:
2 CUPS

1 cup reduced-fat mayonnaise or reduced-fat sour cream

1 cup reduced-fat sour cream or plain nonfat yogurt

2 tablespoons Dill Mix

½ teaspoon celery salt or vegetable seasoning salt

Combine the ingredients in a medium bowl until well mixed. Cover and refrigerate for at least 1 hour.

Nutrition Facts per Serving (1 tablespoon): 35 calories, 3 g. total fat (1 g. saturated fat), 5 mg. cholesterol, 85 mg. sodium, 1 g. carbohydrate, 0 g. fiber, 1 g. sugars, 1 g. protein. **Daily Values:** 2% vitamin A, 0% vitamin C, 2% calcium, 0% iron. **Diabetic Exchanges:** ½ fat.

Dill Potato Topping: Stir 2 tablespoons Dill Mix and ½ teaspoon celery salt or vegetable seasoning salt into 2 cups reduced-fat sour cream or nondairy sour cream and serve as a baked potato topping.

Dill Spread: Mix 1 tablespoon Dill Mix and ½ teaspoon celery salt or vegetable seasoning salt with 8 ounces reduced-fat cream cheese or nondairy cream cheese and serve as a spread for crackers, tortilla wraps, or stuffed celery.

Wheat Bread: Add 2 tablespoons with dry ingredients when making Wheat Bread (p. 146).

Tofu-Dill Dip: Omit the mayonnaise and sour cream. Using a blender or food processor, process one 12.3-ounce package firm silken-style tofu, 2 tablespoons fresh lemon juice, and 1 tablespoon light olive oil until smooth. Transfer the mixture to a bowl and stir in Dill Mix and 1 teaspoon celery salt or vegetable seasoning salt. Taste and adjust seasoning.

Vegan Dill Dip: Use vegan mayonnaise and sour cream or yogurt.

HONEY LEMON DRESSING

My children love this on their salads.

½ **cup lemon juice**

½ **cup water**

⅓ **cup olive oil**

¼ **cup honey**

2½ **tablespoons grated Parmesan cheese or**

nondairy Parmesan, optional

2 **tablespoons precooked cornstarch**

powder

OR

2-4 **tablespoons powdered fruit pectin**

1 **teaspoon salt**

PREP:
5 MINUTES

CHILL:
1 HOUR

YIELD:
1¾ CUPS

2-6 cloves garlic, peeled

5 medium fresh basil leaves

OR

½ teaspoon dried basil leaves

¼ teaspoon dried oregano leaves

Using a blender, process the ingredients until smooth. For easy pouring, store in a salad dressing bottle or a small pitcher. Refrigerate at least 1 hour. Store the dressing in the refrigerator for up to 1 month.

Nutrition Facts per Serving (1 tablespoon): 35 calories, 3 g. total fat (0 g. saturated fat), 0 mg. cholesterol, 110 mg. sodium, 3 g. carbohydrate, 0 g. fiber, 3 g. sugars, 0 g. protein. **Daily Values:** 0% vitamin A, 2% vitamin C, 0% calcium, 0% iron. **Diabetic Exchanges:** ½ fat, ¼ other carbohydrate.

SPINACH DIP

Especially attractive served in a hollowed-out bread round.

For beautiful presentation, I like to serve Spinach Dip accompanied by fresh vegetables arranged in a leaf lettuce-lined basket:

- Carrots cut on the diagonal—for better dipping—or baby carrots, celery, sliced cucumbers, broccoli flowerets, cherry tomatoes, and ripe olives.
- Garnish with turnip flowers: Thinly slice turnips horizontally, cut with a daisy-shaped cookie cutter. Cut flower centers from carrot tips, and stick them in the middle of the turnip flower atop a dab of dip or mayonnaise.

1 (10-ounce) package frozen chopped spinach, thawed, squeezed dry, and finely chopped

1 (16-ounce) container reduced-fat sour cream or nondairy sour cream

1 cup reduced-fat mayonnaise

1 (8-ounce) can sliced water chestnuts, drained and finely chopped

3 green onions, chopped

3 tablespoons dried onion

1 tablespoon vegetarian beef-style seasoning

1 teaspoon onion powder

½ teaspoon celery salt or vegetable seasoning salt

OR

¼ teaspoon salt

PREP:
15 MINUTES

CHILL:
2 HOURS

YIELD:
4 CUPS

In a bowl, combine the finely chopped spinach, sour cream, mayonnaise, water chestnuts, green onions, dried onion, beef-style seasoning, onion powder, and celery salt. Cover and refrigerate the dip for 2 hours to blend the flavors. Stir before serving.

Nutrition Facts per Serving (1 tablespoon): 25 calories, 2 g. total fat (0.5 g. saturated fat), 5 mg. cholesterol, 70 mg. sodium, 2 g. carbohydrate, 0 g. fiber, 1 g. sugars, 1 g. protein. **Daily Values:** 8% vitamin A, 2% vitamin C, 2% calcium, 6% iron. **Diabetic Exchanges:** free.

Yogurt-Spinach Dip: Replace the sour cream with one 16-ounce container low-fat plain yogurt.

Tofu-Spinach Dip: Using a blender or food processor, blend one 12.3-ounce package silken firm tofu until smooth. Use instead of sour cream.

Onion Seasoning Mix: Combine the dried onion, vegetarian beef-style seasoning, onion powder, and celery salt. Store in an airtight container for up to 6 months.

SOUPS

ITALIAN BEAN SOUP

Tasty and attractive.

2 cups navy or small white beans

6-7 cups water

1 medium onion, chopped

1 tablespoon olive oil

2 teaspoons salt

2 garlic cloves, minced

OR

½ teaspoon garlic powder

2 bay leaves

1 (15½-ounce) can diced or stewed tomatoes

1 cup elbow macaroni, preferably soy or whole-grain

1 teaspoon brown sugar or other sweetener

½ cup grated reduced-fat cheddar cheese or nondairy cheese, optional

PREP:	15 MINUTES
SOAK:	1-10 HOURS
COOK:	2-2½ HOURS
YIELD:	12 CUPS

Sort and rinse the beans. Place the beans in a large saucepan; add water to cover by 2 to 3 inches, and bring to a boil. Boil for 2 to 3 minutes. Turn off the heat. Cover and soak the beans for 1 to 4 hours (or overnight). Drain the beans, and add 6 to 7 cups water. Stir in the onion, olive oil, salt, garlic, and bay leaves. Simmer 1½ to 2 hours, or until the beans are tender. Stir in the tomatoes, macaroni, and sugar. Simmer 20 to 30 minutes, or until the macaroni is tender. Remove the bay leaves. Stir in the cheese, and simmer for 5 minutes, or until the cheese melts. Taste and adjust seasoning. Serve hot. Store the beans in an airtight container in the refrigerator for up to 1 week or in the freezer for up to 6 months. (The soup freezes best if it is made with a thicker pasta, such as small shells, or if it is frozen before adding the pasta.)

Nutrition Facts per Serving (1 cup): 130 calories, 2 g. total fat (0 g. saturated fat), 0 mg. cholesterol, 470 mg. sodium, 21 g. carbohydrate, 5 g. fiber, 3 g. sugars, 8 g. protein. **Daily Values:** 4% vitamin A, 10% vitamin C, 8% calcium, 10% iron. **Diabetic Exchanges:** 1 bread, ½ lean meat, 1 vegetable.

Slow Cooker: Place the beans, 9 cups water, onions, oil, salt, garlic, and bay leaves in a slow cooker. Cover and cook on low for 10 to 12 hours, or on high for 5 to 6 hours, or until the beans and onions are tender. Stir in tomatoes, macaroni, and sugar, and cook on high for about 30 minutes or until the macaroni is tender.

Canned Beans: Replace the cooked dry beans with 3 cans of beans, drained and rinsed. Add the onions, oil, ¾ teaspoon salt, garlic, and bay leaves. Simmer for 30 to 60 minutes, or until the onions are tender. Proceed with remainder of recipe.

For variety add other types of beans, such as small red beans, a combination of beans, or add Italian herbs.

LENTIL-BARLEY SOUP MIX

Alternate the lentil and barley layers in a clear jar to create an attractive gift.

1½ **cups lentils**

½ **cup pearl barley**

⅓ **cup dried chopped onion**

¼ **cup dried celery flakes**

2 **tablespoons dried parsley flakes**

2 **teaspoons salt**

½ **teaspoon oregano leaves**

¼ **teaspoon thyme leaves**

PREP:
5 MINUTES

YIELD:
ABOUT 3 CUPS
(1 MIX)

Sort the lentils and stir in the barley. Combine the dry seasonings and place them in a small bag. Store the seasoning mix with the lentils and barley in an airtight container for up to 6 months.

Carrots: Add ¼ cup dried diced carrots.

LENTIL-BARLEY SOUP

PREP:
5 MINUTES

SLOW COOKER:
Low: 12–14
HOURS
HIGH: 8–10
HOURS

YIELD:
10 CUPS

2¾ cups Lentil–Barley Soup Mix (1 recipe)

9 cups water

1 (14.5-ounce) can diced tomatoes

OR

2 cups chopped fresh tomatoes

2 tablespoons olive oil

Rinse and drain the lentils and barley, and place them in a 3½-quart slow cooker. Add the water, tomatoes, olive oil, and seasoning mix. Cover and cook on high for 8 to 10 hours, or on low for 12 to 14 hours, or until the lentils and barley are tender.

Nutrition Facts per Serving (1 cup): 160 calories, 3 g. total fat (0 g. saturated fat), 0 mg. cholesterol, 550 mg. sodium, 27 g. carbohydrate, 8 g. fiber, 4 g. sugars, 9 g. protein. **Daily Values:** 6% vitamin A, 15% vitamin C, 4% calcium, 20% iron. **Diabetic Exchanges:** 1 lean meat, 1 bread, 1 vegetable.

Stove Top: Increase the water to 10 cups. Bring to a boil. Reduce the heat, cover and simmer 1½ to 2 hours.

Pressure Cooker: Pressure-cook for 18 minutes.

Carrots: Add 1 large carrot, thinly sliced or shredded.

Spinach: Add one 10-ounce package of frozen chopped spinach or 4 cups chopped fresh spinach.

Fresh Celery: Omit dried celery from the mix and cook with 1 chopped celery rib.

NOODLE SOUP

A quick comfort food. The amount of chicken-style seasoning varies, depending on the brand you use and your taste.

8 cups water

6 ounces fine egg noodles (about 2 cups)

¼ cup vegetarian chicken-style seasoning

¼ cup minced fresh parsley

OR

4 teaspoons dried parsley

Bring the water to a boil in a saucepan. Stir in the egg noodles and chicken-style seasoning. Reduce the heat and cook the noodles according to the package directions. Stir in the parsley. Taste and adjust seasoning. Serve hot. Store in an airtight container in the refrigerator for up to 1 week.

PREP:
5 MINUTES

COOK:
10 MINUTES

YIELD:
8 CUPS

Nutrition Facts per Serving (1 cup): 80 calories, 1 g. total fat (0 g. saturated fat), 15 mg. cholesterol, 810 mg. sodium, 16 g. carbohydrate, 0 g. fiber, 2 g. sugars, 3 g. protein. **Daily Values:** 2% vitamin A, 4% vitamin C, 0% calcium, 6% iron. **Diabetic Exchanges:** 1 bread.

Noodle Soup With Vegetables: Add to the water: 2 sliced medium carrots, 2 sliced celery ribs, and 1 small chopped onion. Cover and simmer until the vegetables are nearly tender, about 15 minutes. Add the noodles, and proceed with the remainder of the recipe.

Noodle Soup With Peas: Add 2 cups frozen peas with the noodles.

Chicken-style Noodle Soup: Add 2 cups diced chicken-style Wheat Meat (p. 276) or vegetarian chicken alternative.

Egg-free Noodle Soup: Replace the egg noodles with ramen noodles or small-size pasta. Cook according to the package directions.

Rice Soup: Replace the noodles with 2 cups instant brown rice. Cook 5 minutes or until the rice is tender.

Noodle Soup Mix: Combine the noodles, chicken-style seasoning, and dried parsley in an airtight container or resealable bag. Label, date, and include the cooking directions. Store at room temperature for up to 6 months.

POTATO-BEAN SOUP WITH DILL

A flavorful way to enjoy vegetables.

2 teaspoons olive oil

2 medium carrots, shredded (about 1½ cups)

1 celery rib, chopped (about ¾ cup)

1 clove garlic, minced

4 cups water

2 pounds potatoes, peeled and cut into
¾-inch dice (about 4 cups)

2 tablespoons snipped fresh dill

OR

1 teaspoon dried dill

4 teaspoons vegetarian chicken-style
seasoning

½ teaspoon salt

1 tablespoon flour

½ cup reduced fat sour cream or nondairy
sour cream

1 (15-ounce) can small white beans, rinsed
and drained

PREP:
15 MINUTES

COOK:
45 MINUTES

YIELD:
8 CUPS

In a 3-quart saucepan, heat the oil over medium
heat. Stir in the carrots, celery, and garlic; cook for
about 10 minutes, or until tender. Add the water,

potatoes, dill, chicken-style seasoning, and salt, and bring to a boil over high heat. Cover, reduce the heat, and simmer for 20 to 25 minutes, or until the potatoes are tender. Remove 1½ cups of the potatoes, and place them in a blender. Add the flour and sour cream, and process until smooth (or mash with a fork or potato masher). Stir the beans into the soup, and heat until the mixture is hot, stirring occasionally. Taste and adjust the seasonings. Serve hot. Store the soup in an airtight container in the refrigerator for up to 1 week.

Nutrition Facts per Serving (1 cup): 150 calories, 2.5 g. total fat (1 g. saturated fat), 5 mg. cholesterol, 640 mg. sodium, 29 g. carbohydrate, 5 g. fiber, 4 g. sugars, 6 g. protein. **Daily Values:** 120% vitamin A, 15% vitamin C, 6% calcium, 6% iron. **Diabetic Exchanges:** 2 breads.

Serving Idea: Serve with a crusty whole-grain bread and a green salad.

Slow Cooker: Combine the olive oil, carrots, celery, garlic, water, potatoes, dill, chicken-style seasoning, and salt in a 3½-quart slow cooker. Cover and cook on low for 7½ to 8 hours, or on high for 3½ to 4½ hours, or until the potatoes are tender. Continue with remainder of recipe. If desired, add more dill before serving.

POTATO SOUP

On Christmas Eve we enjoy Potato Soup With Broccoli, served in
a tureen and garnished with chopped red pepper. I like serving
Spinach Dip in a hollowed-out bread round, accompanied by
a beautifully arranged platter of fresh vegetables.

4 cups water

4 pounds potatoes, peeled and cut into

　¾-inch dice (8 cups)

1 medium onion, chopped (about 1 cup)

4 teaspoons vegetarian chicken-style

　seasoning

1½ teaspoons salt

2 bay leaves

3 cups low-fat milk or nondairy milk

3 tablespoons unbleached all-purpose flour

3 tablespoons margarine or oil

2 tablespoons chopped fresh parsley or chives

OR

2 teaspoons dried parsley or chives

PREP:
30 MINUTES

COOK:
30 MINUTES

YIELD:
12 CUPS

　　In a large cooking pot, bring the water to a boil.
Stir in the potatoes, onion, chicken-style seasoning,
salt, and bay leaves; return to boiling. Reduce the
heat, cover, and simmer for 20 to 25 minutes, or
until the vegetables are tender. Transfer 2 cups of the
cooked potatoes to a blender. Add the milk, flour
and margarine, and process until smooth; return the
mixture to the pot. Cook over medium heat until

heated through and slightly thickened. Remove the bay leaves. Taste and adjust the seasonings. Garnish with parsley. Serve hot. Store the soup in an airtight container in the refrigerator for up to 1 week or in the freezer for up to 6 months.

> **Nutrition Facts per Serving (1 cup):** 160 calories, 3.5 g. total fat (1 g. saturated fat), 0 mg. cholesterol, 540 mg. sodium, 27 g. carbohydrate, 2 g. fiber, 5 g. sugars, 4 g. protein. **Daily Values:** 6% vitamin A, 15% vitamin C, 8% calcium, 2% iron. **Diabetic Exchanges:** 2 breads, ½ fat.

Serving Idea: Serve with whole-grain rolls, green salad, and oatmeal cookies.

Potato Soup With Broccoli: Steam 3 cups of bite-size broccoli flowerets until barely tender, about 2 to 3 minutes. Rinse the broccoli under cold water to stop the cooking. Stir the broccoli into the soup with the milk mixture.

Pureed Potato Soup: Omit the flour. Using a blender or an immersion blender, process until the soup is smooth.

Additional Seasonings: Add 1 diced celery rib. Garnish with chopped chives.

Creamy Potato Soup: Replace the milk with two 12-ounce cans reduced-fat evaporated milk or 3 cups double-strength nondairy milk.

Slow Cooker: In a 4- to 5-quart slow cooker, stir in the water, potatoes, onion, and seasonings. Cover and cook on low for 8 to 10 hours, or on high for 4 to 5 hours, or until the vegetables are tender. Proceed with remainder of recipe, except return the blended mixture to the slow cooker. Cook on high for about 30 minutes, or until thickened. Garnish and serve.

Pressure Cooker: Using a large pressure cooker, pressure-cook the water, potatoes, onion, chicken-style seasoning, salt, and bay leaves for 5 minutes. Proceed with the remainder of the recipe.

Chunky Potato Soup: Use diced boiling potatoes.

SLOW COOKER LENTIL SOUP

*Using garden-fresh vegetables, my friend Michaelan Bowers cooks
large pots of this soup every summer. She freezes it in
meal-sized containers to enjoy all winter long.*

2 cups lentils, sorted and rinsed

8 cups water

1 (8-ounce) can tomato sauce

1 (14.5-ounce) can diced tomatoes

OR

2 large tomatoes, chopped

1 large onion, chopped (1½ cups)

1 (10-ounce) package frozen chopped
spinach

OR

4 cups fresh spinach, chopped

2 medium carrots, shredded

½ cup minced fresh parsley

OR

2 tablespoons dried parsley

2 tablespoon olive oil

2 teaspoon salt

¼ teaspoon dried oregano leaves

¼ teaspoon dried thyme leaves

PREP:
10 MINUTES

SLOW COOK:
LOW: 12–14
HOURS
HIGH: 8–10
HOURS

YIELD:
16 CUPS

Using a 5- to 6-quart slow cooker, combine the
ingredients, and cook on low for 12 to 14 hours. (If

using a 3- to 4-quart slow cooker, divide the recipe in half.) Cover and cook on low for 12 to 14 hours, or on high for 8 to 10 hours, or until the lentils and vegetables are tender.

Nutrition Facts per Serving (1 cup): 110 calories, 2 g. total fat (0 g. saturated fat), 0 mg. cholesterol, 440 mg. sodium, 18 g. carbohydrate, 6 g. fiber, 4 g. sugars, 7 g. protein. **Daily Values:** 50% vitamin A, 10% vitamin C, 6% calcium, 15% iron. **Diabetic Exchanges:** 1 bread, 1 vegetable.

Stove Top: Use a 6-quart pot, and increase the water to 9 cups. Bring to boil. Reduce the heat, cover, and simmer for 1½ to 2 hours, longer if possible.

Swiss Chard: Replace the spinach with chopped Swiss chard.

Pressure Cooker: Pressure-cook 15 minutes.

SPLIT PEA SOUP

*For ease of preparation, leave the vegetables in large chunks,
then let the blender disguise them just before serving.*

2 cups green split peas

8 cups water

1 medium onion, quartered

2 celery ribs, cut into large chunks

1 large carrot, cut into chunks

2 cloves garlic, minced

OR

½ teaspoon garlic powder

2 teaspoons salt

½ teaspoon liquid smoke seasoning

OR

1 teaspoon hickory smoke seasoning

1 bay leaf

¼ teaspoon thyme

¼ teaspoon marjoram

Croutons or meatless bacon-flavored bits
for garnish

Prep:
10 minutes

Cook:
1½–2 hours

Yield:
8 cups

Rinse the peas. In a large pot combine the peas,
water, onion, celery, carrot, garlic, salt, liquid smoke
seasoning, bay leaf, thyme, and marjoram. Bring the
mixture to a boil. Reduce the heat, cover, and simmer for 1½ to 2 hours, or until the peas are tender.

Remove the bay leaf. Using a blender or immersion blender and working in batches, puree the soup until it is smooth. Serve hot. Garnish with croutons or meatless bacon-flavored bits.

> **Nutrition Facts per Serving (1 cup):** 170 calories, 0.5 g. total fat (0 g. saturated fat), 0 mg. cholesterol, 630 mg. sodium, 31 g. carbohydrate, 12 g. fiber, 6 g. sugars, 11 g. protein. **Daily Values:** 100% vitamin A, 6% vitamin C, 4% calcium, 10% iron. **Diabetic Exchanges:** 2 breads, ½ lean meat.

Serving Idea: Serve with pumpkin muffins and a salad.

Slow Cooker: Using a 3½-quart slow cooker, decrease the water to 6 cups and combine with the peas, onion, celery, carrot, garlic, salt, liquid smoke seasoning, bay leaf, thyme, and marjoram. Cover and cook on low for 9 to 10 hours, or on high for 4 to 5 hours, or until the peas are tender.

Split Pea Soup With Barley: Increase the water by 1 to 2 cups and add ½ cup pearl barley. Or add 2 cups cooked barley after blending and heat thoroughly.

Chunky Split Pea Soup: Dice the vegetables. Do not puree the soup.

Curried Split Pea Soup: Add 1 teaspoon curry powder, or to taste.

Yellow Split Pea Soup: Use yellow split peas.

Split Pea Soup Mix: Place the dry seasonings plus ¼ cup dried onion, ¼ cup dried celery, and ¼ cup dried carrots in a resealable plastic bag, and store it with the split peas; label and date. Store the packages in a cool, dark place for up to 6 months. For gift giving, layer 1 cup green split peas and 1 cup yellow split peas in a bag or pint jar. Include 1 seasoning mix and the cooking instructions.

TOMATO SOUP

Delicious with garlic croutons.

1½ cups water

1 (6-ounce) can tomato paste

2 teaspoons unbleached all-purpose flour

1 teaspoon honey or granulated sugar or other sweetener

½ teaspoon salt

½ teaspoon celery salt or vegetable seasoning salt

½ teaspoon paprika

1½ cups low-fat milk or nondairy milk

PREP:
5 MINUTES

COOK:
10 MINUTES

YIELD:
3¾ CUPS

Combine the water, tomato paste, flour, sweetener, salt, celery salt, and paprika in a saucepan, and whisk until well mixed. Heat the mixture over medium heat until it boils, stirring often. Reduce the heat and simmer for 2 minutes. Add the milk and heat just to a simmer. Taste and adjust seasonings.

Nutrition Facts per Serving (1 cup): 90 calories, 1.5 g. total fat (0 g. saturated fat), 5 mg. cholesterol, 600 mg. sodium, 16 g. carbohydrate, 2 g. fiber, 7 g. sugars, 5 g. protein. **Daily Values:** 30 % vitamin A, 35% vitamin C, 25% calcium, 6% iron. **Diabetic Exchanges:** 1¼ cups = 1 milk, 1 vegetable.

Serving Idea: Serve with whole-wheat crackers, grilled cheese or nondairy cheese sandwiches, and crunchy raw vegetables. (For low-fat grilled cheese sandwiches, coat the bread with cooking spray instead of margarine and use a nonstick skillet.)

Chunky Tomato Soup: Add one 14.5-ounce can diced tomatoes and 1 tablespoon minced fresh basil. Taste and adjust seasonings.

ABC Soup: Add ¾ cup water. When boiling, add ¼ cup alphabet pasta (preferably whole-grain). Reduce heat and cook 10 minutes, or until pasta is done. Taste and adjust seasonings.

Tomato-Rice Soup: Add ½ cup cooked brown rice.

Creamier Soup: Replace the water with additional milk or nondairy milk.

Vary the Seasonings: Add sautéed onion and garlic, fresh or dried basil, parsley, or dill. Or replace the tomato paste with one 6-ounce can seasoned tomato paste and omit the sweetener and salt.

Microwave: Microwave 6 to 8 minutes on high in a covered 2-quart casserole until hot, stirring halfway through cooking.

VEGETABLE-BARLEY SOUP

Simply soup-erb. And minimal chopping—thanks to frozen vegetables.

10 cups water

1 (14½-ounce) can diced tomatoes or
   stewed tomatoes

OR

1 large diced tomato

1 cup pearl barley

1 medium onion, chopped (about 1 cup)

OR

1 cup frozen small whole onions

1 celery rib, diced

3 cloves garlic, minced

3 bay leaves

2 tablespoons minced fresh parsley

OR

2 teaspoons dried parsley

2 teaspoons vegetarian beef-style seasoning

1 teaspoon celery salt, vegetable seasoning
   salt, or seasoned salt

½ teaspoon oregano leaves

½ teaspoon basil leaves

½ teaspoon summer savory

½ teaspoon thyme leaves, optional

¾ teaspoon salt

PREP:
20 MINUTES

SLOW COOK:
LOW: 8–9
HOURS
HIGH: 4–5
HOURS

YIELD:
16 CUPS

1 (16-ounce) package frozen mixed vegetables (green
    beans, carrots, peas, and corn), about 4 cups

1 (15-ounce) can kidney, garbanzo, or white beans,
    drained and rinsed

2 tablespoons minced fresh parsley

OR

2 teaspoons dried parsley

In a large saucepan, combine the water, tomatoes, barley, chopped
or whole onions, celery, garlic, bay leaves, parsley, beef-style seasoning, celery salt, oregano, basil, summery savory, thyme, and salt, and
bring the mixture to boiling. Reduce the heat, cover, and simmer for
30 minutes. Stir in the mixed vegetables and beans, and simmer about
30 minutes, or until the vegetables and barley are tender. Remove the
bay leaves. Taste and adjust the seasonings. Garnish with parsley. Serve
hot. Store the soup in an airtight container in the refrigerator for up
to 1 week or in the freezer for up to 6 months.

Nutrition Facts per Serving (1 cup): 100 calories, 0 g. total fat (0 g. saturated
fat), 0 mg. cholesterol, 420 mg. sodium, 20 g. carbohydrate, 5 g. fiber, 3 g. sugars,
4 g. protein. **Daily Values:** 25% vitamin A, 8% vitamin C, 4% calcium, 8% iron.
Diabetic Exchanges: 1 bread, 1 vegetable.

Slow Cooker: Combine all ingredients except the parsley in a
5-quart slow cooker. (If using a 3½-quart slow cooker, divide the
recipe in half.) Cover and cook on low for 10 to 11 hours, or on
high for 5 to 6 hours, or until the barley and vegetables are tender.
Garnish with parsley.

Other Vegetables: Replace the frozen mixed vegetables with 4
cups fresh or frozen vegetables such as green beans, carrots, cabbage,
zucchini, baby limas, or spinach.

MISCELLANEOUS

HOT COCOA MIX

Great for gift giving.

¼ cup *(6 cups)* nonfat dry milk

2 tablespoons *(3 cups)* reduced-fat nondairy creamer powder

1 tablespoon *(1½ cups)* cocoa powder, preferably Dutch-process

2 teaspoons *(1 cup)* granulated sweetener such as evaporated cane juice

¼ teaspoon *(2 tablespoons)* vanilla powder

1 pinch *(¹⁄₁₆ teaspoon)* salt

PREP:
5 MINUTES

YIELD:
MINI MIX:
6 TABLESPOONS
(1 SERVING)
MEGA MIX:
9 CUPS
(24 SERVINGS)

Combine the ingredients in a mixing bowl, whisking until well mixed. Store the mix in an airtight container for up to 1 year. Stir the contents before using.

Hot Cocoa: Stir 6 tablespoons Hot Cocoa Mix into 1 cup hot water.

Nutrition Facts per Serving (6 tablespoons): 130 calories, 3.5 g. total fat (0 g. saturated fat), 0 mg. cholesterol, 55 mg. sodium, 27 g. carbohydrate, 1 g. fiber, 12 g. sugars, 6 g. protein. **Daily Values:** 2% vitamin A, 0% vitamin C, 8% calcium, 10% iron. **Diabetic Exchanges:** 1 low-fat milk, ½ other carbohydrate.

Vanilla Extract: Omit vanilla powder. Add ¼ teaspoon vanilla extract just before serving.

Vanilla Bean: Omit vanilla powder. Add ¼ teaspoon vanilla extract with water. To add flavor, insert a vanilla bean in the center of the mix.

Cinnamon: Add a dash of cinnamon per serving. Or serve with a cinnamon stick.

Nutmeg: Add a dash of ground nutmeg per serving.

Peppermint: Add crushed peppermint candy, such as from a candy cane, to the mix.

Almond: Stir almond extract into the mix.

Slow Cooker Hot Cocoa: Combine the mix and water in a slow cooker. Heat on low for 3 to 4 hours until hot, stirring occasionally.

Nondairy Hot Cocoa Mix: Replace the nonfat dry milk with the amount of nondairy milk powder to make ¾ cup *(18 cups for mega mix)* milk. Amounts needed vary by brand, which affects the volume of the mix and the per-serving use.

To Use Noninstant Milk Powder: Use the amount of milk powder needed to make about ¾ cup *(18 cups)* of milk, about 2 tablespoons *(3 cups)* of powder. These measurements may vary by brand. Stir about ¼ cup mix into 1 cup water.

Hot Carob Drink Mix: Replace the cocoa powder with sifted carob powder.

ORANGE-PINEAPPLE PUNCH

A great way to use ripe bananas—fresh or frozen.

1 can (12 ounces) frozen orange juice concentrate

3 cans water (4½ cups), divided

2 bananas, peeled and cut in chunks

1 can (46 ounces) pineapple juice

PREP:
5 MINUTES

YIELD:
104 FLUID OUNCES
(13 CUPS)

Using a blender, process the orange juice concentrate, 1 can water, and bananas until smooth. Pour the juice into a gallon pitcher and stir in the remaining water and pineapple juice. Store in an airtight pitcher or container in the refrigerator for up to 1 week or in the freezer for up to 6 months.

Nutrition Facts per Serving (1 cup): 130 calories, 0 g. total fat (0 g. saturated fat), 0 mg. cholesterol, 0 mg. sodium, 32 g. carbohydrate, 1 g. fiber, 31 g. sugars, 1 g. protein. **Daily Values:** 2% vitamin A, 100% vitamin C, 4% calcium, 2% iron. **Diabetic Exchanges:** 2 fruits.

Strawberries: Add 2 cups fresh or frozen strawberries.

Coconut: Add ½ teaspoon coconut extract.

Orange-Pineapple Slushy: Freeze the orange-pineapple punch at least one day. Remove from the freezer 4 hours before serving and allow it to partially thaw. Using a table knife or a potato masher, break the punch into chunks until it becomes slushy. Or microwave it on the defrost cycle for 4 to 5 minutes. Transfer the punch to a large microwave-safe container and defrost it for an additional 4 to 5 minutes. Ladle the punch into glasses to serve.

PLAY CLAY SURPRISE MIX

An easy, inexpensive craft gift for children. Choose any flavor Kool-Aid except lemon, which requires additional coloring.

PREP:
5 MINUTES

YIELD:
1¾ CUPS MIX

1¼ cups all-purpose flour

½ cup salt

1 (0.13-0.17-ounce) package unsweetened soft drink mix

1½ teaspoons glitter

1 teaspoon cream of tartar

Combine the ingredients in a mixing bowl. Store the mix in an airtight container for up to 1 year. Include the directions in gift packages.

PLAY CLAY SURPRISE

Add water and oil to this play clay surprise,
then watch it change before your eyes!

1¼ cups Play Clay Surprise Mix (1 recipe)

1 tablespoon oil

1 cup boiling water

PREP:
5 MINUTES

YIELD:
2 CUPS

Combine the ingredients in a microwave-safe dish. Microwave on high for 1 minute. Remove the mix from the bowl and knead it on a flat surface until a smooth ball forms. Store the "clay" in an airtight container at room temperature for up to 3 months or in the refrigerator for longer storage.

Unscented: Omit the drink mix. Use ⅟₁₆ teaspoon paste food coloring (available where cake decorating supplies are sold) or ½ teaspoon liquid food coloring.

Peppermint: Add ½ teaspoon peppermint extract to the unscented dough.

Stove Top Method: Heat water to boiling in a 2-quart saucepan. Stir in the remaining ingredients. Cook over medium heat, stirring constantly until the mixture thickens.

POPCORN SNACK MIX

Coated with a honey-lemon glaze.

PREP:
10 MINUTES

BAKE:
30 MINUTES

YIELD:
16 CUPS

12 **cups plain air-popped popcorn**

4 **cups bite-sized wheat or multi-grain square cereal**

2 **cups pecan or walnut halves**

½ **cup honey**

⅓ **cup oil**

1 **tablespoon minced lemon peel**

¼ **teaspoon salt**

Preheat the oven to 300° F. Combine the popcorn, cereal, and nuts in a large bowl. Stir in the remaining ingredients in a microwave-safe measuring cup. Microwave on high about 2 minutes, or until the mixture bubbles for about 30 seconds; watch carefully to prevent the mixture from boiling over. Pour the hot liquid over the popcorn mixture, stirring to coat it evenly. Transfer the popcorn mixture to 2 baking pans. Bake for 30 minutes or until the mixture is crispy, stirring the mixture and rotating the pans every 10 minutes. Remove the pans from the oven. Stir the mixture occasionally as it cools. Store the popcorn mix in an airtight container for up to 1 month.

Nutrition Facts per Serving (½ cup): 110 calories, 7 g. total fat (0.5 g. saturated fat), 0 mg. cholesterol, 55 mg. sodium, 13 g. carbohydrate, 2 g. fiber, 5 g. sugars, 1 g. protein. **Daily Values:** 0% vitamin A, 0% vitamin C, 6% calcium, 10% iron. **Diabetic Exchanges:** 1 bread, 1 fat.

Stove Top Method: In a small saucepan bring honey, oil, and lemon peel to a boil over medium heat. Boil for 1 minute.

Vary the Nuts: Use whole or slivered almonds, cashews, or peanuts, or use a combination of nuts.

RASPBERRY ICED TEA CONCENTRATE

A versatile, low-calorie beverage base.

4 cups water

12 raspberry herbal tea bags

Bring the water to a boil. Add tea bags, paper tags removed. Reduce the heat, cover, and simmer for 5 minutes. Remove the saucepan from the heat, and remove the tea bags. Refrigerate the concentrate until it is cold, about 3 hours. Store the concentrate in an airtight container in the refrigerator for up to 1 week, or freeze it in covered ice-cube trays for up to 3 months. (The average ice-cube tray holds about 2 cups. One ice cube equals about 2 tablespoons.)

Serving Idea: Use the concentrate to make iced tea

PREP:
10 MINUTES

CHILL:
3 HOURS

YIELD:
4 CUPS
CONCENTRATE
(12 SERVINGS
TEA)

or to flavor smoothies or fruit gelatin. Add frozen tea concentrate cubes to freshly brewed tea to make a quick glass of iced tea.

Bulk Tea: Replace the tea bags with ¼ cup bulk herbal tea. After simmering, strain the tea through a fine-mesh strainer.

Vary the Flavors: Replace the raspberry tea with other flavors of fruit-flavored herbal tea such as cranberry, peach, or apple, pairing them with the same or a complementary flavor of juice.

RASPBERRY ICED TEA

Flavorful and refreshing. Use 1 part Iced Tea Concentrate to 2 parts water or juice.

PREP:
5 MINUTES

YIELD:
6 CUPS

2 cups chilled raspberry juice

2 cups club soda or water or raspberry juice

2 cups chilled Raspberry Iced Tea Concentrate

Pour the ingredients into a pitcher, and stir. Sweeten if desired. Pour the tea into ice-filled glasses and serve.

Nutrition Facts per Serving (1 cup): 45 calories, 0 g. total fat (0 g. saturated fat), 0 mg. cholesterol, 15 mg. sodium, 12 g. carbohydrate, 0 g. fiber, 10 g. sugars, 0 g. protein. **Daily Values:** 0% vitamin A, 35% vitamin C, 0% calcium, 0% iron. **Diabetic Exchanges:** 1½ cups = 1 fruit.

Single Serving: Place ice in a glass. Pour in ⅓ cup raspberry juice, 1/3 cup club soda or water, and ⅓ cup Iced Tea Concentrate; stir. Sweeten if desired.

Single Serving With Frozen Tea Concentrate: Pour ¾ cup water or juice over 3 frozen tea concentrate cubes. Let stand 5 to 10 minutes. Stir. Sweeten if desired.

SALSA

A fresh, flavorful fiesta for the taste buds. This recipe makes an extra-mild salsa. Increase the hotness as desired.

2 (14½-ounce) cans or 1 (28-ounce) can diced tomatoes

1 (15-ounce) can tomato sauce

1 large sweet onion, chopped (about 2 cups)

1 bell pepper, chopped

1 bunch cilantro, finely chopped

1 (7-ounce) can chopped green chiles

1-4 cloves garlic, minced

¼ cup lime juice from one large lime (or lemon juice)

1½ teaspoons salt

PREP:
25 MINUTES

CHILL:
4 HOURS

YIELD:
8 CUPS

Using a pastry blender or potato masher, chop the tomatoes into smaller pieces. Combine the ingredients in a large bowl. Cover the bowl and refrigerate for 4 hours or longer to allow the flavors to blend. Store the salsa in an airtight container in the refrigerator for up to 5 days or in the freezer for up to 3 months.

Nutrition Facts per Serving (½ cup): 15 calories, 0 g. total fat (0 g. saturated fat), 0 mg. cholesterol, 260 mg. sodium, 4 g. carbohydrate, 0 g. fiber, 2 g. sugars, 1 g. protein. **Daily Values:** 8% vitamin A, 20% vitamin C, 2% calcium, 2% iron. **Diabetic Exchanges:** free.

Serving Idea: Serve with tortilla chips, haystacks, tacos, burritos, or baked potatoes.

Fresh Tomato Salsa: Replace the canned tomatoes with 4 cups chopped fresh tomatoes. Increase the salt to 2 teaspoons.

Southwest Salsa: Add one 15-ounce can black beans, drained and rinsed, and 1 can corn, drained. Taste and adjust seasonings.

Hotter Salsa: Add chopped jalapeño pepper, cayenne, or red pepper flakes to taste.

BIBLIOGRAPHY

Breads

Ballard, Diana. *Whole Wheat Breadmaking: Secrets of the Masters Made Easy*. Springville, Utah: Cedar Fort, Inc., 1993.
> Provides step-by-step methods for hand-kneaded, bread machine, and dough hook whole-wheat breads.

Brody, Lora, and Millie Apter. *Bread Machine Baking: Perfect Every Time*. New York: William Morrow and Company, revised 1996.
> Seventy-five foolproof recipes custom-created for 23 of the most popular bread machines. Includes troubleshooting guide.

The Editors of *Cook's Illustrated*. *How to Make Pizza: An Illustrated Step-by-Step Guide to Thin-Crust, Deep-Dish, and Grilled Pizza*. Brookline, Mass.: Boston Common Press, 1997.
> Includes 38 ultimate recipes and 39 illustrations.

German, Donna Rathmell. *The Bread Machine Cookbook IV: Whole Grains and Natural Sugars*. San Leandro, Calif.: Bristol Publishing Enterprises, Inc., 1992.
> Contains 130 recipes for breads made with whole grains and natural sweeteners—no refried flours or sugars and low in fat.

———. *The Best Pizza Is Made at Home*. San Leandro, Calif.: Bristol Publishing Enterprises, Inc., 1994.
> Includes several whole-grain pizza dough recipes and a multitude of creative topping and sauce ideas.

Gregg, Sue. *Yeast Breads*. Riverside, Calif.: Eating Better Cookbooks, 1993.
> Focuses on making whole-grain breads with a standing mixer equipped with a dough hook, such as a Bosch or KitchenAid. Includes hand-kneading instructions.

Lambert Marjie. *The Bread Machine Book*. Edison, New Jersey: Chartwell Books, 1996.
> More than 100 recipes plus helpful ingredient and troubleshooting information.

Nightingale, Susan. *Electric Bread*. Anchorage, Alaska: Innovative Cooking Enterprises, I.C.E., Inc., 1998.

This book is set apart from the others by the thorough recipe testing (over 25,000 loaves in more than 200 bread machines). Packed with advice on ingredients, troubleshooting, and full-page photographs of each of the 50 recipes. Includes toll-free recipe support phone number.

Rehberg, Linda, and Lois Conway, *The Bread Machine Book of Helpful Hints: Dozens of Problem-solving and Troubleshooting Techniques for Getting the Most Out of Your Bread Machine.* New York: St. Martin's Press, 1995.
Extensive discussion of ingredients and factors for success with bread machine baking.

Robertson, Laurel, with Carol Flinders and Bronwen Godfrey. *Laurel's Kitchen Bread Book: A Guide to Whole-Grain Bread Making.* New York: Random House, 1984.
A helpful resource for learning whole-grain bread-making techniques. Includes dough hook, food processor, and hand-made methods.

Food Science

Corriher, Shirley. *Cookwise.* New York: William Morrow and Company, 1997.
Explains the science behind cooking and baking techniques in a readable way. Accompanied by recipes to illustrate the concepts.

McGee, Harold. *On Food and Cooking: The Science and Lore of the Kitchen.* New York: Collier Books, 1997.
Easy to understand scientific explanations about food science. Includes historical information.

Freeze-Ahead Foods

Bond, Jill. *Dinner's in the Freezer: More Mary and Less Martha.* Lake Hamilton, Fla.: Reed Bond Books, 1995.
A discussion of freeze-ahead methods and other home management topics. Includes about 50 recipes. Few vegetarian entrées. No index.

Gregg, Sue. *Meals in Minutes for Busy People: Freezer to Table.* Riverside, Calif.: Eating Better Cookbooks, 1997. Available from Eating Better Cookbooks, 8830 Glencoe Drive, Riverside, Calif. 92503. Orders: 1-800-998-2783.
Healthy recipes are grouped for preparing five freeze-ahead casseroles in one afternoon. About one quarter of the 26 casseroles are vegetarian. A

complete series of cookbooks featuring healthy eating is also available.

Hilton, Joni. *The Once-a-Week Cooking Plan: The Incredible Cooking Program That Will Save You 10 to 20 Hours a Week (and Have Your Family Begging for More!).* Rocklin, Calif.: Prima Publishing, 1999.
> A foolproof system of bulk preparation, freezing, organizing, and ways of getting kids involved.

Lagorborg, Mary Beth, and Mimi Wilson. *Once-a-Month Cooking.* Nashville: Broadman and Holman Publishers, 1999, revised.
> The newly revised classic for making entrées ahead and storing them in the freezer. A proven system for spending less time in the kitchen and enjoying delicious, homemade meals everyday.

Machel, Kelly. *Month of Meals: One Day to a Freezerful of Entrées.* Renton, Wash.: KRM de la KRM Publishing, 1997.
> Divides the process of cooking a month of meals in one day into nine steps. Few vegetarian entrées.

Martinez, Susie, Bonnie Garcia, and Vanda Howell. *Don't Panic . . . It's in the Freezer!* Lakewood, Colo.: MarshMello Graphics, 1997.
> Describes how to have healthy, gourmet-style food available to use in a moment's notice. About 90 make-ahead recipes that include amounts for larger quantities. Few vegetarian entrées or low-fat recipes.

Sanders, Sharon. *Prevention's Freezer Cookbook: Quick Dishes for and From the Freezer,* Emmaus, Pa.: Rodale Press, Inc., 1998.
> Rely on your freezer for quick, tasty, economical, and nutritious meals using this simple two-pronged strategy. Make *for* the freezer dishes to have on hand as effortless low-fat heat-and-eat meals. Turn to *from* the freezer dishes—made with healthful freezer staples—when you have only minutes to throw together a meal. Cost included for each recipe. Includes vegetarian main dishes.

Taylor-Hough, Deborah. *Frozen Assets: How to Cook for a Day and Eat for a Month,* Beverly Hills, Calif.: Champion Press, Ltd., 1999.
> A step-by-step plan to simplify and revolutionize the way you cook. Includes a 30-day meal plan, a two-week meal plan, and a 10-day holiday meal plan. Few vegetarian entrées.

Food Storage

Bailey, Janet. *Keeping Food Fresh.* New York: HarperCollins, 1989, revised.
     A handy reference on how to choose and store all types of food.

Cooperative Extension. Washington State University, King County, and U.S. Department of Agriculture. 506 Second Avenue, Suite 612, Seattle, WA 98104-2394, (206) 296-3900.
     Provides helpful information related to food preservation, safety, and storage.

National Food Safety Data Base, The. www.foodsafety.org.
     An excellent Internet resource operated by the United States Department of Agriculture.

Stevens, James Talmage. *Making the Best of Basics: Family Preparedness Handbook.* Seattle: Gold Leaf Press, 1997.
     A comprehensive book on in-home food storage that outlines step-by-step preparedness strategies. Contains charts to determine food quantities to store for up to one year, and details how to store and use grains and sprouts.

Walton Feed. Inc., 135 North 10th, P.O. Box 307, Montpelier, ID 83254, 1-800-269-8563. www.waltonfeed.com.
     Supplier of food storage products. "Insurance you can eat; better nutrition through natural foods." Web page contains helpful information about using food storage products, and includes nutritional values.

General Cooking

Anderson, Pam. *The Perfect Recipe: Getting It Right Every Time— Making Our Favorite Dishes the Absolute Best They Can Be.* New York: Houghton Mifflin, 1998.
     The executive editor of *Cook's Illustrated* magazine shares the methods and results of painstaking testing to arrive at the best recipe for each food selected. Includes step-by-step illustrations.

Barnes, Emily, and Sue Gregg. *The Fifteen-Minute Meal Planner.* Eugene, Oreg.: Harvest House Publishers, 1994.
     More than 50 quick-reading chapters provide a realistic approach to a healthy lifestyle. Includes a starter set of easy and tasty recipes using whole, natural ingredients. Includes many vegetarian recipes.

Conner, Sonja L., and William E. *The New American Diet.* New

York: Simon and Schuster, 1986.
> The lifetime family eating plan for good health. Low-fat, low-cholesterol, high-fiber recipes. Includes a section of vegetarian entrées.

Crocker, Betty. *Betty Crocker's New Cookbook*. New York: Macmillan, 1996.
> Contains more than 900 recipes, many with lighter calorie variations. Includes timesaving tips and nutritional analysis.

Cooking Light. P.O. Box 830549, Birmingham, Alabama 35283-0549.
> A magazine published 10 times a year that focuses on creative low-fat cooking. Includes a column called "The Inspired Vegetarian."

Cook's Illustrated. P.O. Box 7446, Red Oak, IA 51591-0446.
> A bimonthly magazine that conducts rigorous testing to find the ultimate recipe for a particular dish. Explains the process used to arrive at the master recipes and contains step-by-step illustrations. Includes taste tests of products, equipment reviews, cookbook reviews, and a section of quick tips.

Farrell-Kingsley, Kathy, and the editors of *Woman's Day*. *The Woman's Day Cookbook: Great Recipes, Bright Ideas, and Healthy Choices for Today's Cook*. New York: Viking, 1995.
> Contains more than 700 recipes, including low-fat substitutions. Features timesaving systems for meal planning, including "investment cooking" and "cook once—eat twice" dishes.

Foco, Zonya. *Lickety-Split Meals for Health Conscious People on the Go*. Walled Lake, Mich.: ZHI Publishing, 1998.
> Includes vegetarian entrées, slow-cooked meals, one-minute mini-meals, five-minute meals, 15-minute meals, 30-minute meals, and motivating health and fitness advice. Written by a registered dietitian.

Kerr, Graham. *Graham Kerr's Swiftly Seasoned*. New York: G. P. Putnam's Sons, 1996.
> Creative, quick, and low-fat cooking techniques, more than 120 recipes. Includes a chapter called, "Mainly Meatless and the MEV" (molded ethnic vegetables).

Kimball, Christopher. *The Cook's Bible: The Best of American Home Cooking*. New York: Little, Brown and Company, 1996.
> Features more than 400 recipes, reviews of kitchen equipment, and 200 step-by-step illustrations. Includes information about the thorough recipe testing for each master recipe. Written by the founder and editor of *Cook's Illustrated* magazine.

Molt, Mary, and Grace Severance Shugart. *Food for Fifty*. New York: Prentice-Hall, 1996, tenth edition.
> Designed specifically for institutional cookery, this is a classic reference book among food service professionals. Contains helpful charts for food equivalents and scoop sizes.

Rombauer, Irma S., Marion Rombauer Becker, and Ethan Becker. *Joy of Cooking,* New York: Scribner, 1997.
> Revised with more emphasis on healthy cooking. Contains reduced-fat recipes, ingredient descriptions, and cooking basics.

Taste of Home's Quick Cooking, P.O. Box 4003, Harlan, IA 51593-0176.
> A bimonthly magazine that focuses on quick-to-make recipes with homemade taste. Regular features include "Ten Minutes to the Table," "Fast, Delicious, and Nutritious," "Fast Fixes With Mixes," "Freezer Pleasers," "Handy Homemade Mixes," and "Slow-Cooked Specialties."

Witty, Helen, and Elizabeth Schneider Colchie. *Better Than Store-Bought*. New York: Harper and Row, 1979.
> Authoritative recipes for the foods that most people never knew they could make at home.

Gifts From the Kitchen

Phillips, Diane. *The Perfect Basket*. New York: Hearst Books, 1994.
> Gives numerous ideas, though not all food-related, for assembling gift baskets with themes.

Westland, Pamela. *Made for Giving: Gifts From the Kitchen*. Pleasantville, N.Y.: Reader's Digest, 1997.
> Step-by-step instructions for innovative and often elaborate packaging.

Young, Anne Van Wagner, editor. *Gifts of Good Taste*. Little Rock, Ark.: Leisure Arts, 1989.
> Contains many creative ideas for food gifts and packaging.

Hospitality

Mains, Karen Burton. *Open Heart, Open Home: The Hospitable Way to Make Others Feel Welcome and Wanted*. Wheaton, Ill.: Mainstay Church Resources, 1997, revised edition.
> An inspiring and encouraging classic on the topic of hospitality.

Stickle, Beverly Graham. *Hospitality on a Wing and a Prayer:*

Entertaining Without the Pressure to Be Perfect. Nampa, Idaho: Pacific Press Publishing Association, 1997.
> A heartfelt, humorous collection of hospitality disasters and successes, plus a wealth of practical ideas.

Van Pelt, Nancy. *Creative Hospitality: How to Turn Home Entertaining into a Real Ministry*. Hagerstown, Md.: Review and Herald Publishing Association, 1995.
> Full of creative ideas, shortcuts, and practical suggestions for making occasions special, including picnics and potlucks.

Mixes

Balmuth, Deborah L., editor. *Herb Mixtures and Spicy Blends*. Powonal, Vt.: Storey Communications, 1996.
> Homemade customized seasonings, instructions for drying and storing herbs, and suggestions for creating gift baskets.

Bean, Deanna and Lorna Shute. *Mix-A-Meal*. Elk Ridge, Utah: Mix-A-Meal, 1997.
> Mixes use dehydrated home storage products and are portioned to store in a No. 10 size can. Each recipe includes a mini mix for testing on a small scale.

Birnes, Nancy. *Cheaper and Better: Homemade Alternatives to Storebought Goods*. New York: Harper and Row, 1987.
> More than 300 homemade equivalents for name-brand products.

Eliason, Karine, Nevada Harward, and Madeline Westover. *Make-a-Mix*. Tucson, Ariz., Fisher Books, 1995.
> Revised, expanded version of a 1980 best-selling classic. Contains more than 60 easy do-it-yourself mixes with accompanying recipes.

Hartwig, Daphne Metaxas. *Make Your Own Groceries*. New York: Bobbs-Merrill Company, 1979.
> Also by the same author: *More Make Your Own Groceries* (1983).

Phillips, Diane. *The Perfect Mix*. New York: William Morrow and Company, 1993.
> Contains good ideas for mixes. Test recipes before giving as gifts.

Swedberg, Marnie. *Marnie's Kitchen Shortcuts*. New York: St. Martin's Griffin, 1996.

A proven system that helps save time, money, and fat grams while pulling off great-tasting meals that the whole family (and guests) will enjoy. Includes mixes and freeze-ahead recipes. Few vegetarian entrées.

Preserving

Alltrista Corporation. *Ball Blue Book: Guide to Home Canning, Freezing, and Dehydration*. Muncie, Ind.:, 1998.
Includes a troubleshooting guide, helpful charts, and recipes for low-sugar preserves.

Chadwick, Janet Bachand. *The Busy Person's Guide to Preserving Food*. Pownal, Vt.: Storey Communications, Inc., 1995.
Easy, step-by-step instructions for freezing, drying, and canning. Includes timesaving tips and shortcuts.

Greene, Janet, Ruth Hertzberg, and Beatrice Vaughan. *Putting Food By*. New York: Penguin USA, 1991, revised.
Includes information on preserving with less sugar and salt, canning and freezing convenience foods, and gift ideas.

Pressure Cooking

Keane, Maureen B., and Daneiella Chace. *Pressure Cooking the Meatless Way*. Rocklin, Calif.: Prima Publishing, 1996.
More than 125 recipes for making healthy fast food. Includes helpful charts and a glossary.

Sass, Lorna J. *Great Vegetarian Cooking Under Pressure*. New York: William Morrow, 1994.
Contains more than 150 recipes for "two hour taste in ten minutes" using the pressure cooker. Includes handy charts for cooking grains, vegetables, and dried beans.

Saving Money

Dacyczyn, Amy. *The Complete Tightwad Gazette*. New York: Villard Books, 1998.
The best from the newsletter by the same name. Well-researched, creative, and practical ideas such as the pantry principle and the price notebook.

McCoy, Jonni. *Miserly Moms: Living on One Income in a Two Income Economy*. Elkton, Md.: Full Quart Press, 1996.

Gives "Eleven Miserly Guidelines," including "keep track of food prices," "make your own whenever possible," and "institute a soup and bread night."

Sharing the Dividends

Partow, Donna. *No More Lone Ranger Moms*. Minneapolis: Bethany House Publishers, 1995.
Focuses on women helping women in practical ways and finding support networks, including shared meals, cookathons, and health food co-ops.

Robertson, Laurel. *Laurel's Kitchen Caring: Recipes for Everyday Home Caregiving*. Berkeley, Calif.: Ten Speed Press, 1997.
Features recipes for vegetarian comfort food, intended to benefit a body fighting to get well, whether it's the flu or a serious long-term illness.

Sheehan, Pauline J. *Hugs for Caregivers*. Mukilteo, Wash.: Winepress Publishing, 1998.
Encourages caregivers to take care of themselves and gives good advice on how to do it. Includes ideas for foods to share.

Slow Cookers

Haughton, Natalie. *The Best Slow Cooker Cookbook Ever*. New York: HarperCollins Publishers, 1995.
Includes helpful hints for using slow cookers and one chapter of meatless main courses.

Hoffman, Mable. *Healthy Crockery Cookery*. New York: HP Books, 1998.
By the bestselling author of several slow cooker books, it features guidelines for slow cooking and several chapters that include vegetarian recipes.

Mannes, Lisa L., editor. *Better Homes and Gardens Crockery Cookbook*. Des Moines: 1994.
Includes tips for using a slow cooker and one chapter featuring meatless dishes.

Vegetarian Cookbooks and Resources

Brackett, Neva. *Best Gourmet Recipes*. Seattle: Five Loaves Deli and Bakery, 1998, revised. 2719 E. Madison, Seattle, WA 98112l. 206-726-7989. www.tagnet.org/fiveloaves.
Innovative vegan recipes from the chefs of Five Loaves Deli and Bakery

in Seattle. Available at Adventist Book Centers (1-800-765-6955).

Brewer, Eileen, and Debbie Brewer. *The Best of Silver Hills: Delicious Vegetarian Cuisine.* Lumby, British Columbia, Canada: Silver Hills Publishing, 1996.
> A collection of the favorite and most frequently requested recipes from the Silver Hills Guest House in southern British Columbia.

Cummings, George. *Vegetarian Family Recipes.* Bakersfield, Calif.: Pacific Health Education Center, 1994. Available from: House of Manna, 5300 California Ave., Suite 1, Bakersfield, CA 93309. 1-800-540-5293.
> More than 300 low-fat, dairy-free recipes. Nutritional analysis included.

Davis, Gail. *So, Now What Do I Eat? The Complete Guide to Vegetarian Convenience Foods.* Corrales, N.M.: Blue Coyote Press, 1998.
> The cover describes this resource as "the ultimate no-cook vegetarian food book." Contains name-brand lists categorized by type of food, a glossary, and list of suppliers.

Hagler, Louise. *Tofu Cookery.* Summertown, Tenn.: The Book Publishing Company, 1991.
> Demonstrates the versatility of tofu with 200 dairy-free recipes for foods familiar to the American palate. Color photographs.

Lynch, Marcella. *Cooking by the Book.* Mountain View, Calif.: Marcella Lynch, 1994.
> Uses plant foods in tasty, attractive ways. A companion video of 13 cooking lessons is also available. Available from Adventist Book Centers (1-800-765-6955).

Melina, Vesanto, Brenda Davis, and Victoria Harrison. *Becoming Vegetarian.* Summertown, Tenn.: The Book Publishing Company, 1995.
> A reliable, comprehensive, and readable resource on vegetarian nutrition written by three registered dietitians. Includes user-friendly recipes with nutritional analysis.

Messina, Mark, and Virginia Messina. *The Simple Soybean and Your Health.* Garden City Park, N.Y.: Avery Publishing, 1994.
> How soy foods can lower risk of cancer and heart disease and enhance health. Fifty recipes.

————. *The Vegetarian Way: Total Health for You and Your Family.* New York: Crown Trade Paperbacks, 1996.
> A complete reference on all aspects of vegetarianism, including nutrient needs for all ages, meal plans, practical advice, and recipes.

Messina, Virgina, and Kate Schumann. *The Convenient Vegetarian: Quick and Easy Meatless Cooking.* New York: Macmillan, 1999.
> Includes homemade quick mixes, use of vegetarian convenience items, and planovers.

Peters, Cheryl Thomas. *More Choices for a Healthy Low-fat You.* Hagerstown, Md.: Review and Herald Pub. Assn., 1997.
> More than 120 recipes for tasty meals in 30 minutes or less. Recipes include nondairy and eggless alternatives. Available at Adventist Book Centers (1-800-765-6955).

Robertson, Laurel, Carol Flinders, and Brian Ruppenthal. *The New Laurel's Kitchen: A Handbook for Vegetarian Cookery and Nutrition,* Berkeley, Calif.: Ten Speed Press, 1986.
> A winning combination of sound nutritional advice and basic vegetarian recipes.

Vegetarian Journal. Vegetarian Resource Group. P.O. Box 1463, Baltimore, MD 21203. (410) 366-VEGE. www.vrg.org.
> A bimonthly magazine published by a nonprofit organization, featuring vegan nutrition and recipes. Excellent Web site for vegetarian and vegan nutrition. Free electronic newsletter.

Vegetarian Times. P.O. Box 446, Mount Morris, IL 61054-8081. 1-800-435-9610.
> A monthly magazine featuring vegetarian nutrition and cooking. Includes some dairy-free recipes.

Veggie Life. P.O. Box 412, Mount Morris, IL 61054-8163.
> A bimonthly magazine featuring vegetarian nutrition and cooking.

Vibrant Life. 55 West Oak Ridge Drive, Hagerstown, MD 21740. Or call the Adventist Book Center, 1-800-765-6955. www.vibrantlife.com.
> A bimonthly magazine featuring vegetarian recipes and articles promoting a healthy lifestyle. Also available: "Going Meatless," a 48-page special edition.

Wasserman, Debra. *Conveniently Vegan: Turn Packaged Foods into Delicious Vegetarian Dishes.* Baltimore, Md.: The Vegetarian Resource Group, 1997.
> One hundred fifty recipes using convenience foods along with fresh fruits and vegetables.

Women's Auxiliary to the Alumni Association. *An Apple a Day,* Volume 2. Loma Linda, Calif.: Loma Linda University School of Medicine, 1983.
> A lacto-ovovegetarian cookbook by doctors' wives with special sections on foods for 50 servings and microwave cooking.

Wheat Meat/Gluten

Boyd, Katheryn E. *Fun With Food Manual.* Bothell, Wash.: Washington Conference of Seventh-day Adventists, 1978.
> An out-of-print compilation of recipes used for teaching cooking classes. Includes detailed recipes for making gluten.

Burke, Abbot George. *Simply Heavenly: The Monastery Vegetarian Cookbook.* Geneva, Nebr.: Saint George Press, 1994.
> More than 1,400 favorite vegan recipes from the kitchen of Holy Protection Orthodox Monastery. Includes step-by-step information for making and flavoring gluten, including UnBeef, UnChicken, and UnBacon.

Jacobs, Barbara and Leonard Jacobs. *Cooking With Seitan: The Complete Vegetarian "Wheat-Meat" Cookbook.* Garden City Park, N.Y.: Avery Publishing Group, 1994.
> Explains step-by-step how to make and store seitan. Includes more than 250 recipes.

Moulton, LeArta. *The Amazing Wheat Book.* Provo, Utah: LM Publications, 1997.
> Fast, easy recipes for wheat meat, seasoning mixes, whole-wheat breads, crackers, and desserts.

Moulton, LeArta, and Rita Bingham. *Quick Wholesome Foods.* Provo, Utah: The Food Place, 1994.
> This 75-minute video covers five topics: gluten, whole-wheat bread using wheat and other grains, powdered milk, cheeses, and beans. Includes recipe booklet.

GLOSSARY

aluminum-free baking powder A double-acting baking powder made without aluminum sulfate, an ingredient thought to be potentially harmful. Rumford, the most common brand, is available in natural-food stores and some supermarkets.

apple wedger A small stainless-steel gadget that cores and slices fruits such as apples and pears into eight wedges. Useful for preparing apples for pie, apple crumble, and applesauce.

baker's bench knife A rectangular (3" x 6") piece of unsharpened stainless steel topped with a wooden or plastic handle; used to cut portions of dough, to clean wooden worktables and to lift or move food; also known as a bench scraper, dough scraper, or dough cutter. Available in kitchen specialty shops and restaurant supply stores.

barley flour Ground barley; a light-colored whole-grain flour replacement for all-purpose white flour; also used as a thickener for milk-based soups and sauces. Available in natural-food stores.

barley malt syrup A liquid sweetener made from sprouted barley. Contains enzymes that enhance the conversion of some of the starch in flour into yeast food for improved rising (interchangeable with diastatic malt). Use one half to one teaspoon per three cups of flour to replace one tablespoon of sweetener in yeast bread. Coating the measuring spoon with oil or cooking spray before measuring helps the sticky syrup slide out. Refrigerate after opening. Available at natural-food stores.

basmati brown rice An aromatic long-grain rice grown in the Himalayan foothills. Basmati means "queen of fragrance," an apt description of its distinctive sweet, nutty aroma and delicate flavor. Available in natural-food stores.

brown rice flour A gluten-free flour made from rice. Nutritionally superior to white rice flour.

browning sauce A dark-brown liquid seasoning containing

caramel coloring. Useful for enhancing the color of brown gravies. One brand, Kitchen Bouquet, is available in supermarkets.

Cha'i Pow Yu A ready-to-use canned braised gluten product made by Companion and exported from Taiwan. The bite-size pieces are packed in oil. Rinse the pieces with hot water and drain before adding them to recipes, such as Vegetable Stew (p. 273) or Stir-fry (p. 263). Available in Asian markets and Adventist Book Centers.

couscous A quick-cooking miniature pasta that is smaller than rice. Look for whole-wheat couscous in natural-food stores.

date pieces Small pieces of dates rolled in oat flour to prevent sticking. A convenient and economical form of cooking dates; available at natural-food stores. Discard any date stems, which are easier to spot after the dates are cooked. Date pieces, because of their oat-flour coating, often require more liquid than moist dates.

diastatic malt An all-natural, barley-based powder that improves the flavor, appearance, and shelf life of bread. This dry form can be used in bread mixes. See also "barley malt syrup." Available through King Arthur Flour (see Mail Order Sources, p. 428).

Dutch-processed cocoa Cocoa powder ground from beans treated with an alkali solution; the powder is milder, less acidic, and darker than untreated cocoa. Regular cocoa powder may be substituted, but the taste will be different.

Egg-replacement powder A powdered egg substitute containing leavening agents and stabilizers; manufactured by Ener-G Foods. Available at natural-food stores.

Egz-Actor A natural food binder for baking and cooking. Contains rice flour, modified starch, modified flax, arrowroot, and buckwheat flour. Produced by Spring Hill Foods, P.O. Box 323, Berrien Springs, MI 49103. Available at some Adventist Book Centers (1-800-765-6955).

food mill A tool used to strain and puree foods simultaneously (useful for applesauce and mashed potatoes); consists of a hopper with a hand-crank mechanism that forces the food through a perforated disk; most models have interchangeable disks with various-sized holes.

fruit pectin A white powder made from the pectin found in fruits; used as a thickener in foods such as jams and jellies; available in supermarkets.

gluten products The protein component of wheat that is concentrated, flavored, and cooked to make a high-protein alternative to meat. Can be homemade (Wheat Meat, p. 276) or canned (Cha'i Pow Yu).

Hickory Smoke Seasoning A meatless powdered seasoning made from dried torula (nutritional) yeast and sweet hickory smoke. Made by Bakon Yeast Incorporated, P.O. Box 651, Rhinelander, WI 54501. Available at natural-food stores and Adventist Book Centers (1-800-765-6955).

Honey Sweet A powdered honey useful for mixes. Individual packets are available in selected grocery stores. Contact Honey Sweet, 295 Forest Ave., Suite 976, P.O. Box 9715, Portland, ME 04104. Phone: 1-207-775-1616. www.honeysweet.com.

instant yeast Deactivated by drying at a much lower temperature than active dry yeast, producing more live cells. This process produces a faster and more vigorous response when flour and water are added; preferred for whole-grain breads. One of the most popular brands is SAF yeast, available at specialty stores, through *King Arthur Flour Baker's Catalogue, The Urban Homemaker,* and SAF 1-800-411-5149.

jicama (HEE-kah-mah): A legume that grows underground as a tuber; this large, bulbous root vegetable has a brown skin, white flesh, crisp, crunchy texture, and a sweet, nutty flavor; peeled, it is eaten raw or cooked; also known as a Mexican potato.

kalamata olives (kahl-uh-MAH-tuh) A medium-sized, purple-black Greek olive with a briny, almost smoky-sweet taste; available in most supermarkets. Can be used in Caesar salad dressing instead of anchovies.

lecithin A food additive used as a stabilizer, thickener, antioxidant, and/or emulsifer in processed foods such as candies, mayonnaise, margarine, and baked goods. Usually derived from soybeans, it delays staling of bread, produces a softer loaf, and improves rising. Replaces part or all of the oil in bread; useful in piecrusts. Available in granular and liquid forms at natural-food stores. The liquid form is more commonly available. The sticky consistency of liquid lecithin makes it harder to measure; measure oil first or coat the measuring spoon with cooking spray. Use the granular form in mixes.

Lora Brody's Bread Dough Enhancer Contains vital wheat gluten to improve rising, diastatic malt to enhance the growth of yeast, and ascorbic acid to strengthen gluten. Use one teaspoon per cup of flour in yeast breads. Available at specialty stores and through King Arthur Flour (see Mail Order Sources, p. 428).

meat substitutes A wide variety of refrigerated, frozen, and canned vegetable protein products designed to substitute for meat. Includes simulated beef-style and chicken-style products. See also "meatless burger" and "gluten products." Meat substitutes are available at natural-food stores, some supermarkets, Asian markets, and Adventist Book Centers (1-800-765-6955).

meatless burger A vegetarian alternative to hamburger, prepared from textured vegetable protein. It is available refrigerated, frozen, and canned at supermarkets, natural-food stores, and Adventist Book Centers (1-800-765-6955). See also "textured soy protein (TSP)."

modified cornstarch A food additive used as a stabilizer, thickener, and/or texturizer, commonly used in commercial food services such as restaurants and hospitals. It retains a smooth, pourable quality after being refrigerated, or frozen and thawed. Unlike regular cornstarch, it can withstand the extended heat of slow cooking or canning. Clear Jel is available in specialty stores, restaurant supply stores, and through mail order from The Urban Homemaker, Country Kitchen, or Sweet Celebrations.

mochiko rice flour An elastic thickener made from mochi, a short-grain, sweet, gelatinous rice with a high starch content; used in Japanese cuisine to make rice cakes and confections; freezes in soups and sauces without curdling; available in Asian food stores.

natural almond flavoring A nonalcoholic natural flavoring available at natural-food stores.

natural maple flavoring A nonalcoholic natural flavoring available at natural-food stores. This is an alternative to some supermarket brands of imitation maple flavoring that contain coffee extract and alcohol.

natural orange flavoring A nonalcoholic natural flavoring available at natural-food stores.

nutritional yeast Yellow, powdery flakes, rich in B vitamins and used as a flavor enhancer; also known as brewers' yeast, it is unrelated to baking yeast. The Red Star brand vegetarian nutritional yeast is fortified with vitamin B_{12}, often lacking in a vegan diet.

precooked cornstarch powder A precooked modified cornstarch derived from waxy corn; especially useful for making low-sugar freezer jams, fruit sauces, and glazes because it requires no cooking. To minimize lumping (the starch granules swell quickly), mix it with a granulated sweetener or process it in a blender. Instant Clear Jel is available in specialty stores and by mail order from King Arthur Flour and other companies.

powdered egg whites Cholesterol-free, fat-free egg substitutes that require no refrigeration, making them convenient for baking mixes and any time you need eggs in cooking. Available in the baking aisle of most supermarkets, and by mail order through King Arthur Flour (see Mail Order Sources, p. 428).

powdered fruit pectin Emulsifies the lemon juice and oil and gives body to Honey Lemon Dressing (p. 371). Sold with canning supplies at supermarkets.

salad spinner A tool used to remove moisture from the surface of salad greens; the produce is held in a perforated bowl sitting inside a container; the inner container is spun, displacing the water through centrifugal forces and through the perforations into the outer container. Use it to speed the washing of lettuce. Chop lettuce and place in the slotted inner bowl of the salad spinner, and immerse in cold water. Agitate to dislodge dirt, then drain. Repeat if needed, and spin dry. The spinner is the best container for refrigerating extra salad.

seitan (SAY-tan) Japanese for gluten that has been cooked in soy sauce. See "wheat meat" and "gluten products."

shelf-stable tofu Tofu that can be stored at room temperature for an extended period because of its packaging; has a silky texture and virtually no flavor, making it versatile; available in soft, firm, and extrafirm. Shelf-stable tofu is the best choice for uncooked recipes such as pudding or salad dressing. See also "tofu."

soy sauce alternative Unfermented, all-purpose liquid seasonings that contain less sodium and no preservatives. Braggs Liquid Aminos, which is made from vegetable protein, is available at natural-food stores.

soy flour A fine, light-beige high-protein flour made from hulled, cracked, and heat-treated soybeans. Although it does not have glutenin and gliadin, it is high in other proteins and is usually added to wheat flour for baking. To use as an egg replacement, use one tablespoon soy flour with two tablespoons water. Refrigerating or freezing prevents rancidity. Available in natural-food stores.

soy milk powder A powdered form of a high-protein milk alternative; available in natural-food stores.

stone-ground cornmeal Produced by grinding the corn between two slowly moving stones; the grain is crushed without separating the germ or generating excess heat; available in some supermarkets and in natural-food stores.

sweeteners Alternatives to granulated sugar and brown sugar are available at natural-food stores. Sucanat, a dark-brown granular sweetener, is made from evaporated cane juice. Because of minimal processing, Sucanat retains the vitamins and minerals found in the sugar cane plant. Other options: evaporated cane juice crystals; date sugar (ground dried dates); fructose (a white crystalline sugar, sweeter than granulated sugar, so less is needed). See also "Honey Sweet."

textured soy protein (TSP) A dry, granular, low-fat meat substitute made by compressing defatted soy flour until the protein fibers change structure; the generic term for textured vegetable protein (TVP). When reconstituted with boiling water, TVP resembles ground beef; available in unflavored granules and chunks in natural food. Flavored TSP is available at Adventist Book Centers and by mail order from the Urban Homemaker (see Mail Order Sources, p. 428).

tofu A versatile high-protein custard-like product made by co-agulating soy milk and pressing the curds into a block, similar to the way cheese is made from cow's milk. The more water that is pressed out of the tofu, the firmer it becomes. Refrigerated tofu is sold in produce cases of supermarkets, natural-food stores, and Asian markets. It is available in silken, soft, firm, and extrafirm in packages of 14 to 19 ounces. Cooking reduces the possibility of bacterial contamination; freezing develops a chewier texture. See also "shelf-stable tofu."

unbleached all-purpose flour A refined flour milled from wheat that has not been bleached with chlorine to make it whiter; bleaching also decreases the protein content. Bleached all-purpose flour may be substituted.

vegan (VEE-gun; VAY-gun) A vegetarian who eats a plant-based diet of grains, legumes, vegetables, fruits, nuts, and seeds. Animal products (milk, milk products, eggs, honey, and foods that involve animal processing, such as granulated sugar and vinegar) are excluded.

vegetable seasoning salt A seasoned salt containing vegetable flavorings, such as Vege-Sal, which contains no MSG; available at natural-food stores.

vegetarian burger A vegetable protein alternative to hamburger; available frozen, refrigerated, canned, and dried. Products vary in flavor and texture; experiment to find one that you like. Using a spoon, break up the canned or refrigerated burger before measuring; rehydrate the dry form (see "textured soy protein") first. Ground homemade Wheat Meat (p. 276) may also be substituted.

vegetarian chicken-style or beef-style seasoning A powdered meatless alternative to chicken or beef bouillon granules; vegetable broth powder may be substituted. A popular brand, McKay's Chicken-Style Instant Broth and Seasoning, manufactured by Dismat Corporation, is available in natural-food stores, Adventist Book Centers (1-800-765-6955), and some grocery stores.

vegetarian gelatin Made from carrageenan (derived from a red algae, also called Irish sea moss) rather than animal byproducts. Flavored varieties (e.g., Hain Dessert Mix, Emes Kosher Gel) and unflavored (e.g., Emes Kosher Gel) are available at natural-food stores.

vital wheat gluten A fine, powdery flour made from concentrated wheat protein that retains its elastic properties; useful in small amounts to strengthen structure and promote rising in whole-grain breads; available in natural-food stores and some supermarkets. Also used to make gluten steaks (see "wheat meat").

wheat meat A versatile meat substitute prepared from the protein (gluten) in wheat that has been concentrated by washing out the starch; it can also be made by adding water to vital wheat gluten. The raw gluten can be flavored and cooked in numerous ways; also called seitan.

white whole-wheat flour Flour milled from hard white winter wheat; lighter in color and milder in taste than red wheat. Available in natural-food stores, some supermarkets, and by mail order. King Arthur Flour is a leading producer (see Mail Order Sources, p. 428).

whole-wheat bread flour A whole-wheat flour designed especially for bread-making; contains a higher protein content, usually about five grams per quarter cup. Available in supermarkets and natural-food stores.

whole-wheat flour Milled from the entire wheat berry, including the bran and germ.

whole-wheat pastry flour Milled from soft white wheat, it is lighter in color and milder in flavor than pastry flour made from red wheat; contains less protein than whole-wheat flour; use in recipes calling for baking powder and baking soda, when tenderness is desired. Except for bread, replaces part or all of the all-purpose flour in many recipes. Available in natural-food stores and some supermarkets.

RESOURCES

Arrowhead Mills, 110 South Lawton, Hereford, TX 79045, 1-800-749-0730, (806) 364-0730.
> Carries whole grains and whole-grain mixes.

Baker's Catalogue, The; King Arthur Flour, P.O. Box 876, Norwich, VT 05055-0876, 1-800-827-6836, www.kingarthurflour.com.
> This catalog, with color photographs and recipes, provides inspiration for baking many varieties of breads (some need adapting for whole grains). A good source of 100 percent white whole-wheat flour, Saf yeast, and Instant Clear Jel.

Bob's Red Mill Natural Foods, Inc., 5209 S.E. International Way, Milwaukie, OR 97222, 1-800-553-2258, (503) 654-3215, www.bobsredmill.com.
> Specializes in nationwide distribution of whole-grain products. Extensive catalog.

Country Kitchen, 3225 Wells Street, Fort Wayne, IN 46808. (219) 482-4835. Orders: 1-800-497-3927. Fax: (219) 483-4091. www.countrykitchensa.com. cntryktchn@aol.com
> Supplier of baking supplies, cake-decorating, candy-making, and wedding supplies. Carries Clear Jel and Instant Clear Jel.

Gold Mine Natural Food Co., 1947 30th Street, San Diego, CA 92102, 1-800-475-FOOD (1-800-475-3663).
> Carries organic foods.

Mail Order Catalogue, The, P.O. Box 180, Summertown, TN 38483, 1-800-695-2241.
> Features TSP, nutritional yeast, and an extensive list of vegetarian books and cookbooks.

Mix-A-Meal, 588 E. Park Drive, Elk Ridge, UT 84651. E-mail: mixameal@itsnet.com. http://users.itsnet.com/~mixameal.
> Carries a full line of dehydrated products. Publisher of *Mix-A-Meal* cookbook.

Sweet Celebrations, P.O. Box 2137, Pocono Summit, PA 18846. (570) 543-2837. Orders: 1-800-55-BREAD. Fax: (570) 643-2837. www.urbanhomemaker.com. UrbanHome@aol.com.
> Features "old-fashioned skills for contemporary people." Offers kitchen supplies, equipment, food storage, and books for making healthy home-

made foods. Source for Clear Jel.

Walnut Acres Organic Farms, Penns Creek, PA 17862, 1-800-433-3998. www.walnutacres.com.

> Features "whole foods for healthy living, direct from America's original organic farm." Pancake and waffle mixes, bread mixes, vegetarian soup mixes, granolas, and more.

U.S./METRIC EQUIVALENCE INFORMATION

GENERAL FORMULA FOR METRIC CONVERSION

Ounces to grams	multiply ounces by 28.35
Grams to ounces	multiply grams by .035
Pounds to grams	multiply pounds by 453.5
Pounds to kilograms	multiply pounds by .45
Cups to liters	multiply cups by .24
Fahrenheit to centigrade	subtract 32 from Fahrenheit, multiply by 5, then divide by 9
Centigrade to Fahrenheit	multiply centigrade by 9, divide by 5, then add 32

GENERAL TABLE OF METRIC EQUIVALENTS

(Volume and Weight)

Volume

1 ounce	28.35
1 pound	453.59
1 gram	.035 ounces
1 kilogram	2.2 pounds

Weight

1 cup	16 tablespoons
	8 fluid ounces
	236.6 milliliters
1 tablespoon	3 teaspoons
1 liter	.5 fluid ounce
	14.8 milliliters
1 teaspoon	4.9 milliliters
	1000.0 milliliters
	1.06 quarts

1 bushel	4 pecks
1 peck	8 quarts
1 gallon	4 quarts
1 quart	2 pints
	4 cups
	473.2 milliliters

APPROXIMATE METRIC EQUIVALENTS

by Weight

U.S.	Metric
¼ ounce	7 grams
½ ounce	14 grams
1 ounce	28 grams
1¼ ounces	35 grams
1½ ounces	40 grams
1⅔ ounces	45 grams
2 ounces	55 grams
2½ ounces	70 grams
4 ounces	112 grams
5 ounces	140 grams
8 ounces	228 grams
10 ounces	280 grams
15 ounces	425 grams
16 ounces (1 pound)	454 grams

Metric	U.S.
1 gram	.035 ounce
50 grams	1.75 ounces
100 grams	3.5 ounces
250 grams	8.75 ounces
500 grams	1.1 pounds
1 kilogram	2.2 pounds

APPROXIMATE METRIC EQUIVALENTS
by Volume

U.S.	Metric
¼ cup	60 milliliters (0.56 deciliters)
⅓ cup	80 milliliters (0.75 deciliters)
½ cup	120 milliliters (1.13 deciliters)
⅔ cup	160 milliliters (1.5 deciliters)
1 cup	230 milliliters (2.27 deciliters)
1¼ cups	300 milliliters
1½ cups	360 milliliters
1⅔ cups	400 milliliters
2 cups	460 milliliters
2½ cups	600 milliliters
3 cups	700 milliliters (6.81 deciliters)
4 cups (1 quart)	.95 liter
1.06 quarts	1 liter
4 quarts (1 gallon)	3.8 liters

Metric	U.S.
50 milliliters	.21 cup
100 milliliters	.42 cup
150 milliliters	.63 cup
200 milliliters	.84 cup
250 milliliters	1.06 cups
1 liter	1.05 quarts

APPROXIMATE METRIC EQUIVALENTS
by Length

U.S.	Metric
⅛ inch	.3 centimeters
¼ inch	.6 centimeters
1 inch	2.5 centimeters
2 inches	5.08 centimeters
4 inches	10.16 centimeters
5 inches	13 centimeters
6 inches	15.24 centimeters
8 inches	20.32 centimeters
9 inches	22.86 centimeters
10 inches	25.4 centimeters
12 inches	30.48 centimeters
14 inches	35.56 centimeters
16 inches	40.64 centimeters
20 inches	50.8 centimeters

BRITISH AND U.S. FLUID VOLUME EQUIVALENTS

Imperial	U.S.
1 ounce	.96 ounce
1 pint	19.2 ounces
1 quart	38.4 ounces

U.S. MEASUREMENT EQUIVALENTS

Pinch or dash or few grains	Less than ⅛ teaspoon
1 teaspoon	60 drops; ⅓ tablespoon
3 teaspoons	1 tablespoon
1 tablespoon	1½ fluid ounce
2 tablespoons	⅛ cup
4 tablespoons	¼ cup
5⅓ tablespoons	⅓ cup
8 tablespoons	½ cup
½ cup	4 fluid ounces
10⅔ tablespoons	⅔ cup
12 tablespoons	¾ cup
16 tablespoons	1 cup
1 cup	8 fluid ounces
2 cups	1 pint
4 cups	1 quart
8 cups	2 quarts
1 pint	16 fluid ounces
2 pints	1 quart
1 quart	32 fluid ounces
4 quarts	1 gallon
8 quarts	1 peck
4 pecks	1 bushel

INDEX